Saving a fallen world

Saving a fallen world

Luke simply explained

by Michael Bentley

 EVANGELICAL PRESS

EVANGELICAL PRESS
12 Wooler Street, Darlington, Co. Durham, DL1 1RQ, England

© Evangelical Press 1992
First published 1992

British Library Cataloguing in Publication Data available

ISBN 0-85234-300-0

Other books by Michael Bentley in the Welwyn Commentary Series
Building for God's Glory
Living for Christ in a Pagan World

Printed and bound in Great Britain at the Bath Press, Avon

To all my dear brothers and sisters in Christ
in the Peloponnese area of Greece,
especially to my good friends
Sakis and Vasso Makris of Kalamata
and Nikos and Angeliki Bardoutsos of Corinth.

Contents

Preface

One evening some years ago a group of people from our church were sitting in the lounge of one of our elders discussing our forthcoming Bible study programme. One of them suddenly said, 'We never look at the Gospels.' This made me sit up with a start. I know that it was spoken in relation to the mid-week Bible Studies (which are not normally taken by myself), but I felt that God was calling me to do something about that. The problem was that I had just started preaching from Peter's first letter on Sunday mornings, and it seemed as though that would take rather a long time to complete.

However, almost two years later, I commenced preaching on Luke's Gospel. I remember the occasion well because we had just been forced to stop meeting in Great Hollands Community Centre, not because we were no longer welcome but because we were in imminent danger of breaking the fire regulations since so many more people were coming to our services. We then moved to the largest hall on our estate — Great Hollands Junior School.

For the next two years I preached on Luke. During that time, from 25 March 1990 until 15 March 1992, the Lord taught us many precious lessons. We also had the joy of seeing a number of people come to know the Lord as their Saviour and others were strengthened in their faith. The Lord graciously blessed us so that the congregation almost doubled again.

This book is the result of those years of ministry. It does not attempt to deal with difficult textual problems or complicated ideas; there are many excellent books written with those things in mind. A good number of our congregation had never attended an evangelical place of worship before they came to us so, of necessity, the words and concepts in these studies have had to be put in a simple, non-theological way.

At the heart of this Gospel we read that God has sent his Son to 'seek and to save what was lost' (19:10). Luke especially writes his Gospel account for Gentiles as well as for Jews; therefore it is truly a message for all kinds of people in this fallen world.

Because of the pressure of space, much has been omitted, but it is my prayer that the Lord will bless his own Word and that this book may, in some small way, help God's people to understand the Bible in a fuller and richer way.

Michael Bentley
Bracknell
November 1992

1.
The promise of a Saviour

Please read Luke 1

Introduction: Why Luke wrote his Gospel (1:1-4)

If we were asked the question, 'Which writer contributed the most to the New Testament?' we would probably say, 'Paul, because he wrote so many letters to various churches and individuals.' But the correct answer is Luke. Luke wrote two books: the Gospel that bears his name and the Acts of the Apostles (or the Acts of the Holy Spirit). Luke also has the distinction of being the only Gentile (non-Jewish) writer to contribute to the New Testament. He came from either Antioch (in Syria) or Philippi (in north-eastern Greece). When we read Luke's Gospel we discover that he either explains, or does not mention, particular Jewish customs which Gentiles would not have understood. In contrast to this Matthew (who wrote, in the first instance, for Jews) assumes that his readers understand the significance of many of the Jewish customs and rituals. Luke is also the longest of the four Gospels.

Other Gospels had already been written

Luke begins, **'Many have undertaken to draw up an account of the things that have been fulfilled among us'** (1:1). By the time Luke wrote his account Mark's was already in circulation. Matthew, Mark and John had all seen Jesus and had heard him preach, but Luke was a second-generation Christian. He could not give an eyewitness account of what the Lord had said and done in Galilee or Judea. He had to rely on the testimony of others to satisfy his curiosity, for he was born too late and too far away from the actual events to have observed what had happened.

Luke was not an apostle and it was unlikely that he saw Jesus when he was on earth. He had been converted through the ministry of those who had brought him the good news which had been preached by others. (He writes about some of these in his second book, the Acts.) As a result of his conversion his life had been completely changed and the tremendous difference Christ had made in his life had transformed him in every way. This is why one of the characteristics of Luke's Gospel is his emphasis upon life-changing events.

The message of salvation was spoken of everywhere; it was a verbal message. As few ordinary people could read, nothing was written of these events at the time and the early church was living with the expectation that the Lord Jesus Christ would return at any time to set up his kingdom and bring in the culmination of all things. But, as time went by, and many of those who had personally seen and heard Jesus began to die, and the return of the Lord did not come about, it became clear that much of the story of the Lord's ministry should be written down before it was forgotten and lost for ever.

So, Luke writes that many had **'undertaken to draw up an account of the things that have been fulfilled among us, just as they were handed down ... by those who from the first were eyewitnesses and servants of the word'** (1:1-2). Almost certainly Mark's Gospel was one of those 'many' accounts. A great many of these things, and the order in which Mark wrote them, have been included in Luke's Gospel. But there were other accounts which have not survived the centuries since that time. (And some of those which have come down to us are rather fanciful and evidently not inspired Scripture.)

With great foresight Luke realized that this would happen. So he, under the inspiration and direction of the Holy Spirit, also wrote down what he called a **'carefully investigated'** and **'orderly account'** of **'everything** [about Jesus] **from the beginning'**.

How did Luke go about his work?

Luke was concerned about 'the things ... fulfilled among us' (1:1). That was the way early Christians viewed the life and work of Jesus

— as events which were fulfilled. So many of the events concerning Jesus had been prophesied beforehand. All the way through the Old Testament we read about the one who 'is to come'.

Luke was concerned to seek out eyewitnesses in the compilation of his Gospel. These are the people who can give the most reliable testimony, because they were there and saw what happened with their own eyes, and heard what was said with their own ears.

Luke evidently received his information from the people he met. We know that he was Paul's travelling companion for much of the time from the second missionary journey right until the end of the apostle's life (see 2 Tim. 4:11). On these journeys Luke would have met many of those who had been with the Lord during his earthly ministry. Colossians 4:10,14 and Philemon 24 tell us that both Mark and Luke were with Paul. Luke may also have known Peter. So he would have met many people who could have answered his questions about the work and ministry of Jesus.

Also we know that Luke visited the Holy Land. He was present at Paul's interviews with James (Acts 21:18-25) and it is very likely that while he was there he also met Mary, the mother of Jesus. It is very interesting to notice that Luke is the only one of the four Gospel writers to record details of the birth of Jesus (and, for that matter, John the Baptist). It seems probable that Luke was not just recording hearsay testimony, but that he obtained his information from Mary herself.

Many of these eyewitnesses consulted by Luke were also 'servants of the word' (1:2). Quite a number were apostles. The Twelve were with Jesus all through his earthly ministry. They would have been glad to pass on all that they saw and heard concerning their Master.

Luke was also concerned to investigate everything carefully from the beginning (1:2). His Gospel is a well thought-out, orderly account of the ministry of Jesus. Colossians 4:14 tells us that Luke was a doctor and Luke's Gospel certainly gives many indications that its author was a medical man. He gave careful and full descriptions of diseases. He showed great interest in individual people (far more than the other Gospel writers). He included a number of stories about women, and he had a scientist's approach to investigative journalism.

Luke's desire was to write his Gospel telling 'everything from the beginning'. Mark begins his account at the baptism of Jesus.

Matthew's Gospel has only two stories relating to the birth of Jesus; he then passes on to the commencement of Jesus' public ministry. John speaks about the Word at 'the beginning' of creation and then proceeds straight away to the ministry of John the Baptist. Only Luke tells us details about the birth of Jesus and two stories about his early childhood.

Luke wanted to write 'an orderly account' (1:3). This does not necessarily mean that it is written in chronological order. But it means that it carries with it a sense of purpose. It is not just a loose collection of sayings of Jesus and stories about him.

Why did Luke write his Gospel?

He wrote it for Theophilus. We do not know who this man was but he certainly was a specific individual. His name (or nickname) means 'lover of God' or 'one loved by God'. He was obviously someone who was interested to know more about the Christian faith and he was evidently someone who was important. Luke calls him **'most excellent Theophilus'**. He uses this same title for the governor Felix (Acts 23:26; 24:3) and his successor, Festus (Acts 26:25). If Theophilus was not a high Roman official, he was certainly someone who was respected enough to have been given a courtesy title.

Luke also dedicated part two of his writings to the same person. He says, 'In my former book, Theophilus, I wrote about all that Jesus began to do and to teach until the day he was taken up into heaven' (Acts 1:1-2), and in the Acts of the Apostles Luke goes on to tell Theophilus about all that Jesus continued to do through his apostles (that is, his special messengers).

The central message of Luke's Gospel is that 'The Son of Man came to seek and to save what was lost' (19:10). John tells us that the good shepherd 'calls his own sheep by name and leads them out' (John 10:3). Jesus called Zacchæus to come down from the tree; and today the Lord calls those whom by his grace he has chosen to eternal life from before the foundation of the world.

The birth of John foretold (1:5-25)

Something new was happening. The Old Testament period had come to an end and a new age was beginning, and John the Baptist was the link between the two. He was to herald the Messiah. His role 'was not merely to announce but to "make ready", to reveal the hearts of people and measure them against the concerns of God'.[1]

Luke sets the scene

He introduces three people to us. He says these events took place in **'the time of Herod king of Judea'** (1:5) The date was about 7-6 B.C. Herod was a cruel and vindictive man. He even had many of his own relatives killed to protect himself and his power. The Scriptures tell us what kind of man he was. It was he who ordered the killing of the innocent babies of Bethlehem after he had discovered that a new 'King of the Jews' had been born there. He ordered the murder of 'all the boys in Bethlehem and its vicinity who were two years old and under' (Matt. 2:16).

But the first person we actually meet in this Gospel is a priest. His name was Zechariah, which means 'The Lord remembers'. Luke tells us that he was of the priestly division of Abijah. From the time of David, the priests were divided into twenty-four divisions, and Abijah was one of the 'heads of the priestly families' (Neh. 12:12; 1 Chron. 24:10).

Next we meet his wife. **'Elizabeth was also a descendant of Aaron.'** Priests could marry anyone, provided they were Israelite virgins. But if a priest married a priest's daughter that was considered to be a double and special blessing. It was often said of an excellent woman, 'She deserves to be married to a priest.'[2] The name 'Elizabeth' means 'My God is an oath,' or 'the absolutely reliable one'.[3]

Consider the contrast between Herod and this godly couple. Herod was a terrible character, frightened of losing his power. He was a disgrace to Israel. He tried to please God and man at the same time. However, Jesus said that anyone who tries to please two masters is doomed to failure (Matt. 6:24).

How different Zechariah and Elizabeth were from the king! **'Both of them were upright ... observing all the Lord's commandments and regulations blamelessly'** (1:6). This does not mean that they were sinless. We know that no one is without sin except Jesus, but Luke means that this elderly couple were faithful and sincere in keeping God's ordinances. Everything about these people was the very opposite of Herod.

But there was sadness in the hearts of Zechariah and Elizabeth.

'**They had no children**' (1:7). This caused great sorrow to them. Each Israelite woman longed that she would be the one chosen by God to give birth to the Messiah, but Elizabeth was barren. There was then for her apparently no possibility of producing any child — least of all the son for whom she longed. Also '**They were both well on in years**' (1:7,18).

The story opens in the temple

The temple was the place where God's presence was manifested in a very special way. Worship was offered up by thousands of priests. To make it possible for most to have the opportunity to offer sacrifices in the temple each division of priests served in there for a week twice every year. Their task was to offer incense and prayers on behalf of the Israelite people. Every day, at the morning and evening sacrifices, one of the priests was specially selected to go into the Holy Place and remain there, on his own. His task was to offer prayers and incense to God while he stood before the veil which separated the Holy Place from the Holy of Holies.

When Christ died on the cross the veil in the temple was split from top to bottom; his death has opened up the presence of God to all believers. The story of the beginning of this wonderful access to God begins with this statement that the humble, godly priest Zechariah entered the Holy Place. '**He was chosen by lot**' (1:9) to offer the incense. This was a once-in-a-lifetime experience for him. And, as it turned out, it was a far, far greater privilege than he even dreamed possible. When the time came, '**All the assembled worshippers were praying outside**' (1:10). This means that they were in the outer court of the temple. The people used to gather there to receive the Aaronic blessing from the priest when he came out from offering the incense. But on this occasion, when he came out from the Holy Place Zechariah did not say,

> 'The Lord bless you
>   and keep you
> The Lord make his face to shine upon you
>   and be gracious to you:
> The Lord turn his face towards you
>   and give you peace'

(Num. 6:24-26).

Something happened in the Holy Place to delay Zechariah: **'An angel of the Lord appeared to him, standing at the right** [south] **side of the altar of incense'** (1:11). This startled Zechariah and he **'was gripped with fear'**. But the angel said, **'Do not be afraid, Zechariah.'** He called him by his name. The angel knew him and understood his anxieties and gave him this message: **'Your prayer has been heard'** (1:13). What prayer was that? Zechariah and Elizabeth had probably long ago given up praying for a child, because such a thing was impossible. I believe the prayer that the angel was referring to was the one Zechariah had just offered. That would have been for the salvation of his people, that is, for their redemption by the Messiah.

The angel then gave Zechariah the miraculous news that Elizabeth would bear a son, and his name would be called John. John means 'the gift of God'. Hebrew names were very significant. The birth of John would, indeed, be a gracious gift of God. Geldenhuys puts it like this: 'The grace of God, soon to be revealed in the Redeemer whose coming is to be prepared by John, is the outcome of his remembrance of his covenant and of his absolute faithfulness.'[4] All three names of each of these characters were linked together.

The angel also told Zechariah that John **'will be great in the sight of the Lord'** (1:15). We all need to remember that everything that happens to us, and everything that we do is 'in the sight of the Lord' (1:6). We cannot hide anything from his all-seeing gaze. Then the angel gave more information about John. He said, **'He is never to take wine or other fermented drink, and he will be filled with the Holy Spirit even from birth'** (1:15).

The work of John was going to be like the work of Elijah (Mal. 4:5-6). John was going to **'go on before the Lord, in the spirit and power of Elijah, to turn the hearts of the fathers to their children and the disobedient to the wisdom of the righteous'** (1:17). In other words, he was going, through his ministry, to cause families to be reconciled to each other and to the Lord. But his greatest work was **'to make ready a people prepared for the Lord'** (1:17). He was going to do that by calling them to repent and be baptized.

The joyous outcome

Gabriel told Zechariah **'good news'**. This is the first time that Luke uses the word, which is connected with the word 'gospel'. John was

going to bring joy to many in Israel because he was going to be the
forerunner of Christ. However, because of Zechariah's unbelief he
had to remain silent until John's circumcision. This was in answer
to his call for a sign (1:18). How could such a godly man as
Zechariah disbelieve God? He knew his Bible. The Old Testament
details a number of people who had children in their old age (e.g. the
births of Isaac, Samson and Samuel) 'He ought to have remembered
that what God has done once, he can do again, and that with him
nothing is impossible.'⁵ I believe it was not so much his lack of faith
in God's ability as his sheer amazement that he had been chosen
which caused his unbelief.⁶

However, God tempers his justice with mercy. The dumbness is
only to be temporary. But when the people saw him come out of the
Holy Place they realized that **'he had seen a vision in the temple'**
(1:22)

All these events happened just as God said they would. His wife
did become pregnant (1:24). For five months she remained in
seclusion. She had been a laughing-stock for many years because
she could produce no child. Now she was going to shut herself away
until it became obvious to anyone looking at her that she was
expecting a baby. I wonder what she did in those five months of
seclusion? I believe she quietly waited before the Lord. Her heart
was overwhelmed with happiness. **"'The Lord has done this for
me," she said. "In these days he has shown his favour and taken
away my disgrace among the people'"** (1:25). She had waited for
many years for this moment. Now she was going to enjoy the bliss
of this miracle shut up on her own, with the Lord.

The birth of Jesus foretold (1:26-38)

Every Christmas time God's people, and many who do not belong
to the Lord, look at this story of the Annunciation (or announcement) of the birth of Christ. At the beginning and at the end of this
story we read about an angel. **'In the sixth month God sent the
angel Gabriel'** (1:26). **'Then the angel left her'** (1:38). Angels are
heavenly messengers sent from God. Gabriel came to Mary with a
divine message six months after he appeared to Zechariah with a
similar one.

How sad it is that 'clever' men and women try to say that Gabriel came with a lie! They say that Mary was not really a virgin. They say that this is a myth made up to explain for simple people the mystery of how God came down to this earth. They say that Luke was telling the kind of story that his readers would find acceptable; Jesus was really born naturally with Joseph as his real father. All this talk of a girl who was a virgin giving birth to a baby is untrue, they argue.

But what nonsense these so-called theologians make of the wonderful event of God becoming man at Bethlehem! They start off with the idea that the Bible is not the inerrant Word of God, and so they have to try to explain away all the miracles. They have to reject anything that is supernatural because it does not fit in with their way of reasoning.

But they forget a number of important things. They forget that God is God and he can do all things. Gabriel said, **'Nothing is impossible with God'** (1:38). He is the God of miracles. We learn from the Old Testament that Sarah and Abraham had a child in their old age, and they were asked, 'Is anything too hard for the Lord?' (Gen. 18:14). The psalmist said, 'Our God is in heaven; he does whatever pleases him' (Ps. 115:3). Jeremiah prayed, 'Ah, Sovereign Lord, you have made the earth by your great power and outstretched arm. Nothing is too hard for you' (Jer. 32:17).

Mary did not doubt what the angel was saying. She knew that she was a virgin. She was prepared to accept the truth of the message. Her only question was: **'How will this be ... since I am a virgin?'** (1:34).

The place of the announcement

Gabriel gave this great news in Nazareth. This was a town in Galilee; 'Galilee of the nations' it has been called. It was a place where people walked in darkness (Isa. 9:2). It was the northern part of Palestine through which foreign traders and Roman soldiers often passed. Therefore Nazareth was, in Jewish eyes, a place which was very suspect because the population had not remained pure and separate from all the other nations.

How amazing it is, then, that God's heavenly messenger was sent to this despised district! The holy city of Jerusalem was bypassed in favour of unknown Nazareth — a town which is not mentioned even once in the Old Testament Scriptures. The angel did not come to the holy temple where God dwelt among his people in a special way.

Gabriel was sent to a humble home in unimportant Nazareth, which was situated in despised Galilee.

The recipient of the annoucement

The message was given **'to a virgin pledged to be married to a man named Joseph'** (1:26). Mary was probably a teenager at the time. People were married quite young in those days. It is unlikely that she had travelled far from the area around about — except to visit the holy city of Jerusalem at feast times. She was a normal girl who lived an ordinary life, and she was engaged to the village carpenter, Joseph.

Engagement meant much more in those days than it does today. It was a binding agreement which lasted a whole year before the marriage was performed. The couple made solemn promises to each other at the ceremony and in many ways the young couple were already regarded as husband and wife. The only difference was that they did not live together during the time of betrothal, and there was certainly no question of any sexual contact until they were married at the end of the period of engagement. The law was very strict regarding this. If there was the slightest question of any immoral behaviour then the law prescribed that the woman should be stoned to death, although, in fact, on the rare occasions that unfaithfulness did occur, the husband gave his wife a bill of divorcement. This is why Joseph began to think in terms of a quiet divorce when he first learned of Mary's pregnancy (Matt. 1:19).

Another thing to notice about both Joseph and Mary is that they were descendants of the great King David. This is why they travelled to Bethlehem, the city of David, to register (2:3). Joseph appears as a descendant of David in the genealogy of Jesus in Luke 3:23-38 and Mary is listed together with Joseph in Matthew's list (1:2-16).

The angel's greeting

The angel said, **'Greetings, you who are highly favoured! The Lord is with you'** (1:28). Mary had probably never seen an angel before, but she evidently believed in their existence. Luke says that the angel 'went to her' (as a friend or relative might enter a door), as though he was a welcome guest.[7] But it was not the appearance of the angel which troubled Mary. It was the words which he spoke.

She **'wondered what kind of greeting this might be'** (1:29). The angel said, 'You are highly favoured.' This means, 'You are full of grace.'

The angel's message

Once again Gabriel came with a great message from God: **'Do not be afraid ... you have found favour with God'**(1:30). He had said the same to Zechariah (1:13). Then Mary was given this stupendous news: **'You will be with child and give birth to a son, and you are to give him the name Jesus'** (1:31). It was then that the good news dawned upon Mary that she was to be the mother of the Messiah; the one for whom all of Israel had been waiting for centuries would be born to her. She would have the privilege of giving birth to the Christ (the Greek word for the Hebrew 'Messiah') and of bringing him up in the ways of the Lord.

The name for this child had already been chosen. He was to be called 'Jesus'. It was not an unusual name. There were many children called 'Jesus' in those days. The first one of whom we read in the Scriptures was Joshua, the successor of Moses. His name means, 'God our Saviour'. Luke does not explain the significance of this name for his Gentile readers but Matthew tells us what it means. He says that Joseph was told in a dream to **'give [the child] the name Jesus, because he will save his people from their sins'** (Matt. 1:21).

Then the angel gave Mary more information about the child: **'He will be great and will be called the Son of the Most High.'** The title 'Most High' is a term often used in the Old and the New Testaments for God (Gen. 14:19; Ps. 7:10; Luke 6:35; 8:28). Jesus is declared to be the Son of the Most High. This is another way of saying he is God himself, who has come down in human form. **'The Lord God will give him the throne of his father David, and he will reign over the house of Jacob for ever; his kingdom will never end'** (1:32-33). This child is King. According to prophecy he will take the throne of his father David and reign for ever over his people. He is to be 'great David's greater Son'.

Some 1,000 years before this event God had said to David, 'The Lord himself will establish a house for you ... I will raise up your offspring to succeed you, who will come from your own body, and I will establish his kingdom' (2 Sam. 7:11-12). The Lord was not speaking about an earthly or political kingdom but 'the kingdom or rule of grace and truth established in the hearts and lives of all those who have the God of Jacob as their refuge (Ps. 46:7,11)'.[8]

So how did Mary respond to this breathtaking news? She did not doubt it. She was not like Zechariah. She did not demand a sign. She did not challenge the fact, but she did query the method.[9] She asked, **'How will this be ... since I am a virgin?'** It was a perfectly natural question to ask. Every sensible adult knows the means by which babies are conceived. But this had not happened to Mary. 'I am a virgin,' she said.

Did the angel rebuke her for asking the question? No. He explained how the miracle would take place. He said, **'The Holy Spirit will come upon you, and the power of the Most High will overshadow you. So the holy one to be born will be called the Son of God.'** This would be the work of the Holy Spirit (the Third Person of the Trinity). The Holy Spirit is the power of God working in miraculous ways. Mary was to be enveloped, as it were, in the Holy Spirit; and, as a result, God himself (Jesus) would grow within her body.

There was no intervention of any man here because the child would be born sinless. He is the holy one. Jesus never sinned (2 Cor. 5:21; Heb. 4:15; 7:26; 1 Peter 2:22; 1 John 3:5). He is the only person who was ever born without sin, lived without sin and died without sin. Even the most godly of all other people have a sinful nature within them because they are born of men. Jesus alone is the holy one.

The angel's further explanation

Gabriel continued, **'Even Elizabeth your relative is going to have a child in her old age, and she who was said to be barren is in her sixth month. For nothing is impossible with God'** (1:36-37). Mary was given this news as an example of what God can do. For the aged Elizabeth and Zechariah to have a child was an almost unheard-of thing. However, for Mary there was to be an even greater miracle. Isaiah had prophesied centuries before, 'The virgin will be with child and will give birth to a son, and will call him Immanuel [God with us)]' (Isa. 7:14). Mary responded, **'I am the Lord's servant... May it be to me as you have said'** (1:38).

We should submit to whatever God has in store for us. We should say to the Lord, 'May it be to me as you have said.' Mary was ready to be used by God — even though it meant being misunderstood, because when it became obvious that she was pregnant people would say that she had been behaving immorally.

The songs of Mary and Elizabeth (1:39-56)

The main characters in this section are Elizabeth, the wife of the priest Zechariah (who is a representative of the Old Testament), and Mary, the wife of a village carpenter (the one who ushers in the New Testament). At this point the Old and New meet. The New Testament does not blot out the Old, nor does it supersede it. It fulfils all of the Old Testament (Matt. 5:17). Those promises and blessings which had been seen in shadow form in the Old Testament are now brought into sharp focus and reality for us in Jesus Christ, in the New Testament.

Mary travelled to Judea

As soon as Mary received the angel's message she hurried away to the hill country of Judea. We do not know exactly where Zechariah and Elizabeth lived, but it was in the south of the country within fairly easy reach of Jerusalem because Zechariah, as a priest, worked in the temple.

Their home, however, was in the countryside. That means that it would have been secluded; it would have been a peaceful place. While Mary was there she and her relative Elizabeth could have many days of quiet communing together. It would have been a place where the unkind questions of prying busybodies could have been kept at bay.

Whatever the people of Nazareth had said or thought, Mary found faith in Judea; she was believed. Elizabeth had no hesitation in accepting that Mary was to be the mother of the Messiah. **'When Elizabeth heard Mary's greeting, the baby leaped in her womb.'** Not only did Elizabeth receive Mary, but the unborn John leaped for joy at the presence of the unborn Christ. Also at the same time Elizabeth was filled with the Holy Spirit. Incidentally, Luke often speaks of the work of the Holy Spirit (1:67).

What does it mean that Elizabeth was filled with the Holy Spirit?

How did the Holy Spirit show his presence? One of the things that happened was that Elizabeth spoke and called Mary's baby **'my Lord'** (1:43). Elizabeth recognized the baby as the Messiah. Paul tells us that 'No one can say, "Jesus is Lord," except by the Holy Spirit' (1 Cor. 12:3). At this point Elizabeth sang the first of five songs which Luke records in the first two chapters of his Gospel. She sang to Mary, **'Blessed are you among women, and blessed is the child you will bear!'** (1:42). Although she was elderly and six months pregnant she could sing with a loud voice. She sang of the privilege which was hers that Mary should come to her. Mary was blessed because of the child within her. The holy child was exalted above everything.

This is no suggestion of any bitterness in the voice of Elizabeth. She was thrilled that Mary had been chosen to give birth to the Messiah and that she had come to visit her with the great good news. Amazed, she sang, **'But why am I so favoured, that the mother of my Lord should come to me?'** (1:43).

Then she sang the final 'blessing' (of the three) to encourage Mary because of her faith. **'Blessed is she who has believed that what the Lord has said to her will be accomplished!'** (1:45). Faith is always commended. Abraham believed God when he was told that a child would be born to him and his elderly wife Sarah. Paul tells us that 'Abraham's faith was credited to him as righteousness' (Rom. 4:9). It is those who believe God's word, and who act upon it, who are truly blessed in this life.

The song of Mary

Those who have been brought up in the Anglican tradition will find the words of this song very familiar. It is part of the Prayer Book Service for Evening Prayer. It is called the Magnificat because, in the Latin version, the opening word is *Magnificat,* which means 'glorifies'. Mary's song is quite different from Elizabeth's. This is not a loud song of triumph and blessing, but a quiet song of peaceful acceptance and trust in God.

In this song Mary shows how graciously and humbly she accepted the privilege which was hers in bearing the child Jesus. The opening verses show her gratitude to God for all that he has done for her:

'My soul glorifies the Lord
   and my spirit rejoices in God my Saviour,
for he has been mindful
   of the humble state of his servant.
From now on all generations will call me blessed,
   for the Mighty One has done great things for me.'

There was nothing proud or boastful in her song. She showed how willing she was to be a servant of the Lord. She displayed her pleasure that, although she was only a humble maid, she had been called by God to perform such an honoured service. She realized that all generations were going to call her blessed; but most of all she acknowledged that the Mighty One had done great things for her.

Next she sang of *the holiness of God*: **'Holy is his name'** (1:49). In Hebrew thought the name stands for the person. We say, in the Lord's prayer, 'Hallowed be thy name.' That means, 'May God himself be hallowed' (i.e. recognized as the Holy One).

This song is similar to the song of Hannah in 1 Samuel 2. Mary sings of the attributes of God. She quotes a great deal from the Old Testament, especially from the Psalms. This shows what a reverence she had for the Word of God, and how it was so natural for her to quote it and make it her own, in her song — and, presumably, in her conversation as well.

She sang of *the mercy of God*. She went back to Abraham. God has

'helped his servant [i.e. the nation of] **Israel,**
   remembering to be merciful
to Abraham and his descendants for ever,
   even as he said to our fathers'

(1:54-55).

She sang that God's **'mercy extends to those who fear him, from generation to generation'** (1:50).

Next Mary sang of *the loving power of God*. **'He has performed mighty deeds with his arm'** (1:51). God is Spirit. He has no physical arms or legs, but, to help us understand, he is often depicted as though he had arms. The Jews would have remembered the many times that God showed his power. What has God done with his arm?

'He has scattered those who are proud in their inmost thoughts.
He has brought down rulers from their thrones' (1:51-52). He
did that many times in history for his people. And he 'has lifted up
the humble' (people like Mary herself). He has filled the hungry
with good things but sent the rich away empty. Both literally and
physically he has done that, and continues to do it for his people.
Those who hunger and thirst after righteousness will be satisfied by
the Lord.

Last of all, Mary sang of *the faithfulness of God.* He has kept all
of his promises. God remembers the promise which he made to
Abraham. After Abraham had been prepared to sacrifice his only
son Isaac on Mount Moriah, God said to him, 'Because you have
done this and have not withheld your son, your only son, I will surely
bless you and make your descendants as numerous as the stars in the
sky and as the sand on the seashore. Your descendants will take
possession of the cities of their enemies, and through your offspring
all nations on earth will be blessed, because you have obeyed me'
(Gen. 22:16-18).

God has kept his promise. And in Jesus this promise found an
even richer fulfilment. Through his atoning death at Calvary (pre-
figured by the sacrifice of Isaac) God has extended mercy to all those
who fear him — those who call upon his name.

A quiet ending

At the beginning of this passage Mary enters the house of her
relative, Elizabeth. It ends with Mary returning home (1:56). This
was probably just before the birth of John the Baptist.

We know what Jesus did. It all came to pass. Mary's joy at God's
blessing went on to find a richer meaning in the life and work of the
son she bore.

The birth of John (1:57-80)

When John was born Elizabeth's neighbours and relatives came and
shared in her joy. All of them were glad that 'the Lord had shown
her great mercy' (1:58). They rejoiced because Elizabeth's life had
been spared in the labours of childbirth.

The circumcision of John

All good Jews circumcised their sons on the eighth day (e.g. Phil. 3:5). Medically this is the very best time to perform circumcision. The cut heals up quickest, the smallest amount of pain is caused and the fewest complications occur if it is done on the eighth day after the birth of the boy.

Circumcision was carried out to signify the identification of the child as a member of the Jewish race. Jews today still circumcise all of their male children, but they are not sure why they do it — at least that is what one rabbi friend told me. In his epistles Paul also speaks about the spiritual significance of this rite for Christians today as they become identified as God's people (Rom. 2:29; Col. 2:11).

The naming of the child also took place at the same time. Everyone assumed that he would be called 'Zechariah' after his father, but Elizabeth was emphatic about this. She said, **'No! He is to be called John'** (1:60). Obviously Zechariah had communicated to her all that the angel Gabriel had said. So 'John', which means, 'The mercy or grace of God', was the name chosen by the Lord for this child (see 1:13).

The crowd could not understand the choice of this name, as no one in the family was called John. So they made signs to Zechariah **'to find out what he would like to name the child'** (1:62). (It may well be that they made signs to Zechariah because he was deaf as well as dumb.)

What did Zechariah write on the wax writing tablet? He did not write, 'We have discussed this together and we think it would be nice to call him John.' He wrote four words: **'His name is John.'** He meant that his name was John already. It was as though he had written, 'God himself has chosen his name; and who are we to argue?'

By this time Zechariah had been cured of his doubting. He was now able to accept the message of the angel fully. The result was that **'His mouth was opened and his tongue was loosed, and he began to speak'** (1:64)

What kind of thing did Zechariah speak about after nine months of silence? He praised God. We can imagine how thrilled he must have been to have had the use of his tongue back again. His praise of God had a remarkable effect upon everyone throughout the whole area. 'The neighbours were all filled with awe, and throughout the hill country of Judea people were talking about all these things. Everyone who heard this wondered about it, asking, "What then is this child going to be?" For the Lord's hand was with him' (1:65-66).

Zechariah's song

This is a song of hope. Elizabeth's song (1:42-45) was a song of love. Mary's song (1:46-55) was a song of faith; and now Zechariah sings a song of hope.[10] This was not a vague hope. It was not just a wish for the future. Zechariah sang of a confident hope which was sure and certain. It was something he looked forward to, because it was the fulfilment of God's promise to, and for, his people.

Zechariah was filled with the Holy Spirit as he sang. This is a prophecy which does not just predict what will happen in the future. It also 'tells forth' the wonderful workings of God in the world. It is called the 'Benedictus' because this is the opening word in the Latin Vulgate. It means, 'Praise be.'

The first part speaks of *all that God has done for his people* (1:68-75). He sings of Israel in verse 68 and also of God's people in the same verse. He sings of God raising up **'a horn of salvation for us in the house of his servant David'** (1:69). He makes reference to the **'holy prophets of long ago'** (1:70). He sings of **'our fathers'** (1:72), **'his holy covenant'** (1:72) and **'our father Abraham'** (1:73).

Zechariah is filled with joy at all that God has done. He weaves the names of his son, himself and his wife into this song. The name 'John' means 'the grace, or gift of God'. That is what the song is all about: the glory of God made known. 'Zechariah' means, 'He remembers his holy covenant.' In the song Zechariah sings that God has remembered **'his holy covenant'** (1:73). Finally 'Elizabeth' means, 'the oath of God'. Zechariah sings of **'the oath'** of God which **'he swore to our father Abraham'** (1:73).[11]

This song speaks of the power of God. Zechariah sings that God has **'come and has redeemed his people'**. The thought of God coming for his people is very precious. It speaks of God stooping down to rescue us. It tells of God drawing near to us and delivering us from our bondage. The same thought occurs in verse 78, where

Zechariah sings of Christ as **'the rising sun** [who] **will come to us from heaven'**.

The power of God is depicted as a horn of salvation. The strength of a fighting animal is in its horn. God's power and might are shown in the **'horn of salvation'** which **'he has raised up ... for us in the house of his servant David'** (1:69). Again this speaks of the Lord Jesus Christ. The deliverance of God's people is a feature of this song. It was spoken of by the holy prophets of long before (1:70) and is salvation from all her enemies (1:71,74).

The second part of the song speaks of *the mission of John the Baptist*. John was to be **'a prophet of the Most High'** (1:76). Gabriel had told Mary that Jesus would be called 'the Son of the Most High' (1:32). He also said that 'The power of the Most High will overshadow you' (1:35). John would be the prophet of the Lord God Almighty. He would be given the task of going on before the Lord to prepare the way for him (1:76). John's role was to be the herald of the King. He had to prepare the people to receive Jesus. He was going to do that by calling them to repentance and baptizing them for the remission of their sins. Through this the people would be given the knowledge of salvation (1:77).

Lastly, Zechariah sings of *hope for the future*. He speaks of Jesus as **'the rising sun** [who] **will come to us from heaven'** (1:78). God has given us Jesus because of his tender mercy. He is so gracious, loving and merciful that he gives to us the best of all gifts — his own dear Son. Malachi had already prophesied that 'The sun of righteousness will rise with healing in his wings' (Mal. 4:2) for those who revere the name of the Lord. Peter speaks of 'the morning star' arising in the hearts of his people (2 Peter 1:19); and Jesus is also called 'the bright Morning Star' in Revelation 22:16.

This godly priest sings of the light of God shining, because without Christ the world is in darkness. Not only are the people of the world in darkness, but they are also living in the shadow of death. Jesus is described as the rising sun because the only thing which can dispel darkness is light.

He sings of the coming of the Messiah who guides the feet of his people into the paths of peace. 'When he shines on them they too begin to shine ... brighter and brighter until the full day' (Prov. 4:18).[12]

John's childhood

After Zechariah's song, we are told that John **'grew and became strong in spirit; and he lived in the desert until he appeared publicly to Israel'** (1:80). His parents were very elderly, and they probably died when he was young. We know nothing else about John when he was a boy. We do not know who brought him up. We are not told exactly where he lived (except that it was in the desert). However, we are told that both physically and spiritually his development was favourable.

2.
The early years

Please read Luke 2

The birth of Jesus (2:1-20)

It is interesting to know that a copy of a national newspaper which was printed on the day of a person's birth can now be purchased from specialist companies. Anyone buying one of these can find out what was happening on the day he or she was born. Most of these things will mean nothing now — unless the newspaper was printed on one of those days when some important historical event occurred.

If newspapers had been produced in the times of the Roman Empire, and one was discovered which was printed on the day that Jesus was born (assuming that anyone knew which day that was) there would be no reference to him, to Mary or Joseph, or even to the unimportant province of Judea.

On the other hand, there would have been a great deal about Cæsar Augustus and the Roman Empire. There would be mention of the glorious peace which then existed throughout the whole of the Roman world (the *Pax Romana*) — a peace which was to last for thirty years.

Important people in the story of Jesus' birth

Cæsar Augustus was the most important person then alive. He was a ruthless man who had trodden down many in his rise to become the supreme ruler of the known world. **'In those days'** he gave an order and **'Everyone went to his own town to register'** (2:3). At least that is how they did it in the province of Palestine; it was the Jewish method of conducting a census.

Luke gives us all of these details because he is writing a 'carefully investigated' and 'orderly account' of what had happened 'from the first' (see 1:1-4). He lifts us away from Judea and gives us a world-view of these events. He also does a similar thing at the beginning of chapter 3. He is concerned that these events can be dated accurately. Scholars have worked out that Jesus was born about 5 B.C., even though Quirinius did not become governor of Syria until A.D. 6.[1]

If you are wondering why Jesus was born five years 'Before Christ', it is because the person who worked out the date for the birth of Christ (in the sixth century) was a few years out in his arithmetic. No one knows the exact date of Jesus' birth. Does this mean that special Christmas events should not be held around 25 December? Some would say, 'Yes, the church should not celebrate what was, in origin, a pagan festival.' However, I feel that if the majority of the people around us are celebrating Christmas then we should use that opportunity to tell them the real reason why Christ came to this earth (see Eph. 5:16).

Unimportant people in this story

These are Joseph, Mary and some members of a despised profession — shepherds. These shepherds were living out in the fields near Bethlehem. So far as Cæsar, or anyone else of importance was concerned, none of these people mattered. Yet God has chosen 'the weak things of the world to shame the strong. He chose the lowly things of this world and the despised things — and the things that are not — to nullify the things that are, so that no one may boast before him' (1 Cor. 1:27-29).

God chose these shepherds to fulfil his purposes and to make his good news known to the world. Cæsar Augustus, Quirinius and Herod thought that it was they who were directing events, but they were wrong. It is God who is always in control of all things (Gal. 4:4).

Mary and Joseph must have wondered why they were having to travel some eighty miles south to Joseph's home town of Bethlehem. It was at least three days' journey and Mary's time to give birth was near. However, this godly couple trusted God. They knew that

God's purpose was that his word would be fulfilled. 650 years beforehand Micah had prophesied,

'But you, Bethlehem Ephrathah,
   though you are small among the clans of Judah,
out of you will come for me
   one who will be ruler over Israel,
whose origins are from of old,
   from ancient times'

(Micah 5:2).

The birth was a very simple affair. There was no room for the parents in the inn. Many people were proud of the fact that they were descendants of the great King David, so they had returned to his city for the census. But eventually space was found for Mary somewhere, possibly in a cave attached to the inn. J. R. H. Moorman wrote, 'When Christ came among us we pushed him into an outhouse; and we have done our best to keep him there ever since.'[2] The world did not want to receive Christ when he was born, and it wants to have little to do with him now. Perhaps this is because God's people are not prepared to be like the shepherds and go and **'spread the word'** (2:17) concerning Jesus.

The heavenly messengers

Once again Luke tells us that the good news was given by angels (cf. 1:11,26). Naturally these ordinary, but surely God-fearing, shepherds were scared when the glory of the Lord shone around them. But the same message was given to them as it was to Mary: 'Do not be afraid.' This good news was not just given to the Jews or important people. It was to all, without distinction.

Clear directions were given to the shepherds so that they could find the Saviour. There may have been many babies born in Bethlehem that night but only one of them was **'lying in a manger'** (2:12). The angels spoke of glory to God in heaven, where God dwells. (The text does not say that they sang.) They told of true, lasting peace. They did not talk of the mere absence of war (the *Pax Romana*). They spoke about that peace which is known only by those who have had their sins forgiven through the precious blood of Christ. This peace is for those on whom God's favour rests.

The actions of the shepherds

The shepherds went to Bethlehem to see. They did not doubt the
words of the angel, nor were they ordered to go to Bethlehem.
However, no doubt after making suitable arrangements for the
safety of the sheep, they went to see what the Lord had spoken of,
and they found everything exactly as they had been told.

We can all picture the scene in our minds. From our childhood
we have seen many pictures of it. Yet Luke tells us nothing about the
stable. Why is that? I believe it is because he wants us to see the Lord
himself and not the circumstances of his birth. It is only Jesus who
matters. When the visitors had seen the Lord they went and told all
of their friends what had been told them concerning this child (2:17).

**'But Mary treasured up all these things and pondered them
in her heart'** (2:19). She had much to think about. There was
Gabriel's visit to her and to Joseph. There was her visit to Elizabeth.
Now there was the joy of the birth of her own son, who was also her
Saviour (1:47).

Anna and Simeon (2:21-40)

Jesus, like John the Baptist, was circumcised on the eighth day of his
life. The Jewish law prescribed that this should be done to all males
as a sign that they were true Israelites. It demonstrated their
obedience to God and their membership of the Jewish faith. As we
saw earlier, medical evidence has shown that if it is carried out
earlier or later than the eighth day then unnecessary pain and
discomfort can be caused to the baby. It was not exactly invalid if
it was done later in life but the eighth day was the day which the law
prescribed for circumcision. We know that Paul was very proud of
the fact that he was 'circumcised on the eighth day' (Phil. 3:5).

However, it is not the circumcision of Jesus which Luke emphasizes here, but the naming of the child. Naming was a very important
ceremony for Jews. We remember the crowds which gathered
around when John was named. Like his relative, Jesus also had his
name given to him from heaven. It had been **'given him before he
had been conceived'** (2:21). The name 'Jesus' means, 'God our
Saviour'.

How sweet the name of Jesus sounds
In a believer's ear!
It soothes his sorrows, heals his wounds
And drives away his fear.[3]

The time came for Jesus to be taken to the temple

This, again, was something which was done in fulfilment of the Old
Testament law. After forty days (in the case of the birth of a baby
boy) the mother had to present herself at the temple. This was to
show that her time of purification had been completed. She was to
demonstrate her thanksgiving to God by offering a sacrifice. This
would normally consist of a lamb and a pigeon. But if the family
were too poor they could offer two pigeons instead (Lev. 12:2-8). Is
that why Mary offered two pigeons? Even though they may have
been poor they still fulfilled the demands of the law; they made a
sacrifice to God.

The other reason why the family travelled the five miles from
Bethlehem to Jerusalem was to present Jesus to God. Again this was
to fulfil the demands of the law. It was the right time in the life of the
child for this to be done. Even though this child was the Son of the
Most High (1:32), Mary humbly obeyed the law of the Lord, just as
her son was to do when John demurred at baptizing Jesus later on
(Matt. 3:15).

Simeon came into the temple

Luke tells us that Simeon was waiting for the consolation of Israel
and the Holy Spirit was upon him. Three times the Spirit is
mentioned in verses 25-27. God prompted Simeon to enter the
temple just at the time when the child Jesus was being presented to
the Lord. We are told that this venerable old man took the baby (who
was now nearly six weeks old) in his arms and praised God. The
hymn which he uttered is called the Nunc Dimittis, from the opening
words of the Latin version ('[You] now dismiss').

Simeon had been waiting for 'the comfort which the Messiah
would bring to his people at his coming'.[4] The Holy Spirit had
revealed to this godly man that he would not die before he had seen
the Lord's Christ (2:26). He did not need to see the fulfilment of the

salvation of God's people; to set eyes upon the Lord's anointed was sufficient for him. No wonder he said,

> **'Sovereign Lord, as you have promised,**
>   **you now dismiss your servant in peace.**
> **For my eyes have seen your salvation'**
>
>   (2:29-30).

Simeon spoke of the wider implications of Christ's coming. He referred to the extent of the salvation Christ had brought. He said that God's salvation had been **'prepared in the sight of all people'** (2:31). It would be a light for revelation to the Gentiles, and for glory to Israel.

Luke, as a Gentile himself, was keen to emphasize the truth that salvation was offered to the Gentiles as well as to the Jews. Right at the beginning of his life upon earth Jesus is seen as one who will bring light to all. He is described as one who will light up the darkness of this world. And **'The child's** [earthly] **father and mother marvelled at what was said about him'** (2:33).

Then Simeon spoke some strange words to Mary: **'This child is destined to cause the falling and rising of many in Israel, and to be a sign that will be spoken against.'** Simeon spoke in the power of the Holy Spirit, and when the power of the Spirit of God is at work, everyone should take notice and obey. Isaiah had spoken of 'a stone that causes men to stumble and a rock that makes them fall' (Isa. 8:14). Simeon takes up this theme and speaks of Jesus as one who will be a stumbling-block to many people because they will not believe in him (1 Cor. 1:23; 1 Peter 2:6-8). He meant that no one can be neutral about Jesus.

Simeon then added, speaking to Mary, **'And a sword will pierce your own soul too'** (2:35). Mary would have to suffer because of this dear little baby. Here we have the first indication in Luke's Gospel of the death Christ would have to die. The cross would be a very painful thing for the virgin mother to bear. It would be like having one of those broad, sharp Roman swords piercing through into Mary's own soul.

Someone else was also waiting for this time

Anna, the daughter of Phanuel, of the tribe of Asher, was also in the temple at that time; indeed she seems to have lived in there. **'She** never left the temple but worshipped night and day, fasting and praying' (2:37). She is described as a prophetess (2:36); most prophets were male. She came from Asher, one of the ten tribes carried into Assyria; so she was from a tribe which many would have given up for lost. She had been a widow for very many years and now her whole time was taken up in worshipping night and day; fasting and praying. Anna was not a very likely candidate to have the honour of meeting the King of kings. But **'Coming up to them at that very moment** [God's timing is always perfect], **she gave thanks to God and spoke about the child to all who were looking forward to the redemption of Jerusalem'** (2:38).

So Simeon was waiting for the salvation of Israel, and Anna was looking forward to the redemption of Jerusalem. The Old Testament prophets had spoken of the restoration of Jerusalem. Jeremiah had written about this in his thirty-third chapter, Daniel had done the same in his ninth chapter and Zechariah had repeatedly spoken of this final and permanent redemption of Jerusalem. He had 'made it clear that he was thinking of restoration far more glorious than what was achieved when Nehemiah rebuilt the city walls'.[5]

When Anna said that through this child Jerusalem would be redeemed, what did she mean? I believe she was describing the holy city as a picture of the redeemed people of God—all those who have been washed from their sin in the precious blood of Christ. She was saying, 'Here, in this child, is the redemption of God's people.'

The time came to leave Jerusalem

When everything was done according to the law of the Lord, Luke tells us that they left Jerusalem. They returned to Galilee, to their own town of Nazareth. But they went via Egypt. Luke does not mention this, but Matthew tells us that they went south and stayed until cruel King Herod was dead (Matt. 2:19-21). It was not until Jesus was about three years old that the whole family moved back to Galilee. There **'The child grew and became strong; he was filled with wisdom'** (2:39-40). Although he was God, he developed as a child, and then grew into manhood. He passed through all the stages of man so that he could sympathize with us in all our infirmities.

'And the grace of God was upon him.' He knew the blessing and power of God in his life.

The boy Jesus in the temple (2:41-52)

Since medieval times numerous fanciful stories have been circulating which tell of Jesus performing amazing miracles when he was a young boy. Yet the Bible tells us nothing about any such happenings. Indeed we are specifically told that the water which Jesus turned into wine at the wedding in Cana was his first miracle (John 2:1-11). He was then a man of at least thirty years old.

Mary and Joseph were devout

They both obeyed the law of God (2:41). The Old Testament declared that all adult males should attend three feasts each year. These were Passover, Pentecost and Tabernacles (Exod. 23:14-17; Deut. 16:16). For Mary and Joseph this meant travelling the long journey to Jerusalem. As these three journeys were very costly in time and money, those living at some distance from Jerusalem normally only attended one of the three festivals — the Passover, which was the most important feast of all. It commemorated the deliverance of the children of Israel from the slavery of Egypt and spoke of redemption through the blood of a lamb.

Jewish families always did things together, so Jesus would have accompanied his parents to Jerusalem. If only fathers and mothers today would likewise give a lead to their children in attending to the things of God, the nations would be much stronger and more blessed.

Today, when a Jewish boy reaches his thirteenth birthday, he normally has his Bar Mitzvah (a special religious ceremony which initiates him into the Jewish religion). Through this rite he becomes a 'son of the law' (or a 'son of the commandments'). He becomes an adult Jew, so far as religion is concerned, at his Bar Mitzvah, even though he may be only thirteen years old.

As this story, recorded by Luke in this chapter, is the only one about the boyhood of Jesus, there must be some special reason for its inclusion. It may well be that we have been given this incident to show that as Jesus was twelve years old he was nearing that time when he would become responsible for his own religious development.

Jesus was in the correct place

After the feast was over the people started to return home. Everyone went on foot. Those going on a journey find it is more helpful and more interesting to walk with a crowd. Conversation helps the journey along. No doubt all the many people from Galilee moved off together in a group.

When travelling in a large party the custom was that the women and children would move off first. Obviously the children were inclined to walk more slowly than the men so it was only sensible that they should set the pace. Then, bringing up the rear, would come the men.

In which party would Jesus have travelled? He was still, technically, a boy, but he was almost a man — so far as religious duties were concerned. No doubt some of the boys, particularly the younger ones, preferred to walk near their mothers, but many of them would feel more grown up by walking with the men.

All through that first day's walk home both Mary (with the women and children) and Joseph (in the group with the men) thought that Jesus was with the other group. Luke tells us, **'Thinking he** [Jesus] **was in their company, they travelled on for a day'** (2:44). It was only at the end of the day that both Mary and Joseph realized that Jesus was missing. John Blanchard comments: 'A Christian can make the same kind of careless mistake with regard to his spiritual condition.' He goes on to say, 'Never be satisfied with "supposing" that the Lord is with you in life's decisions and directions.'[6]

When Mary and Joseph could not find Jesus they went back to Jerusalem to look for him (2:45). It took three days to find him. One day had been spent in travelling north from Jerusalem. A second day was used up in returning back to the holy city and a third day was taken touring around the capital. It was on this third day that they found Jesus, in the temple courts.

He was sitting among the religious teachers, listening to them and asking them questions (2:46). Luke tells us that **'Everyone who heard him was amazed at his understanding and his answers'** (2:47). So we see that already, by the age of twelve, Jesus was beginning to make an impact, because of his grasp of spiritual truths.

Naturally his parents were anxious. Joseph said nothing. Indeed we have no recorded words of Joseph anywhere in the Bible. What we do know is that he was a good husband to Mary and he was a good 'legal' father to Jesus too. He always tried to do the right thing (cf. Matt. 1:19) and he faithfully passed on the messages from the angel. However, although he was one of those firm, silent types, who gave good support, he kept somewhat in the background himself.

But we can imagine how Joseph and Mary must have felt — thinking that they might have lost Jesus. So when they eventually found him, Mary rushed up to him and said, **'Son, why have you treated us like this? Your father and I have been anxiously searching for you'** (2:48). She tried to scold him, mildly, but it seems that this astonishing scene in the temple had taken some of the sting out of her tongue.

At this point we read the first recorded words of Jesus: **'Why were you searching for me?'** he asked. That is a very telling question. Why did they want to find him? Did they not realize that, although formerly they had been responsible for his religious upbringing, now he was to be responsible for himself?

The next thing that Jesus said was, **'Didn't you know I had to be in my Father's house?'** Jesus seems to be saying, 'Why were you searching for me? Didn't you realize that I would be in the right place, my Father's place, the holy temple in Jerusalem?' Jesus was contrasting Mary's 'your father and I' with his own phrase, 'my Father's house'.

It was not so much the temple building which was important; it was that which the temple symbolized — his Father's presence. Even at the age of twelve Jesus 'was deeply conscious of the unique relation between himself and his Father in heaven'.[7] Although this was the first utterance of Jesus that we know of, in it he spoke of his future task. He said, 'I had to be in my Father's house.' Hendriksen says that 'His entire life was controlled by this divine "must".'[8]

Luke often refers to this divine compulsion. Jesus must preach (4:43). He must suffer (9:22). He must go on his way (13:33). He must stay at the home of Zacchæus (19:5). He must be delivered up to be crucified and rise again (24:7). He must suffer these things and enter his glory (22:37; 24:26), and he must fulfil all the Old Testament prophecies concerning himself (24:44).

But Mary and Joseph **'did not understand what he was saying to them'** (2:50). This was a further aspect of the sufferings of Jesus. They did not understand what he meant and also his disciples often misunderstood what he was saying and doing. This must have saddened Jesus, but, even so, he was obedient to his parents. He went down to Nazareth with them. He knew it was right to obey his parents — even if they did not understand everything about him.

What an example Jesus is to adolescents today! They so often believe that their parents do not understand them — or even care about them. But when they feel like that they should do as Jesus did. They should obey their parents, because their parents have lived longer than they have and have had more experience of life. They know its dangers and challenges.

Next we read that Mary treasured all these things in her heart (2:51). In Luke 2:19 the evangelist has already told us that Mary 'treasured up all these things and pondered them in her heart'. That was when the shepherds had left the manger to spread the word concerning what they had been told about this child. His mother kept thinking about these until after the death of her son. Then when Jesus rose from the dead she understood what it all meant. She had told many people about her thoughts at the time, and perhaps she even spoke to Luke himself. In any case this sentence could only have come from Mary, for no one else could have known what she had thought during these occasions.

Jesus grew

Verse 52 is very similar to the words spoken about the boy Samuel: 'And the boy Samuel continued to grow in stature and in favour with the Lord and with men' (1 Sam. 2:26). Although Jesus was God, like any other human being, he still needed to mature. He grew in wisdom. The experiences of life taught him wisdom. The example and teaching of his parents and of others helped him to develop in this way. And the wisdom of God, his Father, grew continually within him.

Jesus also grew in stature. If a child does not increase in size, in the right proportion and rate of growth, then there is something wrong with him. Jesus grew in the normal way. Like Samuel, Jesus grew in favour with God and men. It is not good for people just to make progress in religious matters, if their fellow men do not accept them. Jesus increased in favour with his fellow men, as well as with God.

During this period of a further eighteen years or so (until Jesus was about thirty) various family events took place. Joseph seems to have died during these years; we hear no more of him. And Jesus appears to have taken over the family business; he was called 'the carpenter' from Nazareth (Mark 6:3). A village carpenter would have been involved in building houses, making all kinds of furniture and household requirements, and in the construction of agricultural implements like ploughs and yokes. It is no wonder that Jesus showed that he had an intimate knowledge of such things. In his parables, 'He spoke about houses built on sand or upon a rock; of a person who "turned his hand to plough"; of the taking up of his yoke — a yoke which is easy and thus makes the load light; and so on.'[9]

Also during these eighteen years Mary gave birth to a number of other children. This means that Jesus had several younger brothers. His would have been the task of helping to bring them up, especially after the death of Joseph, when he was the eldest male in the household.

All throughout this formative period of his life Jesus matured, and his desire was to do his Father's will. We too should want to grow like that. We should desire to 'grow in the grace and knowledge of our Lord and Saviour Jesus Christ' (2 Peter 3:18). And we should want to please our heavenly Father in all we do and say and think.

3.
Preparing the way

Please read Luke 3

The ministry of John (3:1-20)

Whenever a king announced that he was going to undertake a long journey, servants would be sent before him to prepare the way. They would literally mend the roads, or see that someone else repaired them. And they would make sure that every member of each local population showed enthusiasm for the ruler when he passed by. John the Baptist had a similar task. He was to 'prepare the way of the Lord'. He had to prepare the people to receive the Messiah.

The timing of John's ministry

Luke lists for us one Roman emperor, one Roman governor, three Roman-appointed tetrarchs and two Jewish high priests. What an array of important people! Yet what does Luke want us to notice about these superior men? He wants us to observe that **'The word of God came'** (3:1). However, the word of God did not come to any of these splendid people. The word of God came to the son of an ordinary, elderly priest. It came to a man who was living out in the desert — to John, son of Zechariah.

So, if our attention is to focus on John in the desert, why does Luke tell us about these other dignitaries? It is because he wants to establish at what point in history John began to preach about the coming of the Messiah. This is the beginning of the gospel. If we look at the time when each of these 'important' people held office, then we can work out that John started his ministry between the years A.D. 26 and 29.

Luke's historical information tells us what the world was like when John and, shortly afterwards, Jesus began their work. Tiberius Cæsar ruled in Rome; he was a tyrant who ended his life in debauchery on the Isle of Capri. Pontius Pilate was governor of Judea; he was a rather foolish Roman official who lacked any backbone — as we can see from the way he allowed the Jewish crowd to sway him and make him pass the death sentence upon Jesus, whom he knew to be innocent.

Herod was tetrarch of Galilee. This Herod was the one who ruled during most of the lifetime of Jesus. He was a son of Herod the Great, who had caused the babies of Bethlehem to be slaughtered when Jesus was a baby. He was only interested in the entertainment value of Jesus (see 23:8). Philip and Lysanias, like Herod, each ruled over a fourth part of Herod the Great's old kingdom. Although Herod called himself 'king' he had to remember that the real power rested in Rome with Cæsar.

Finally, Annas and Caiaphas were the high priests. Under the system of religious organization which God had set up there was only to be one high priest at a time. So why does Luke write about the high-priesthood of Annas and Caiaphas? It was because there were, in effect, two high priests at that time. Annas had held this office for a while, but he had displeased Rome, and Cæsar had replaced him with his son-in-law, Caiaphas. When Luke wrote, **'during the high priesthood of Annas and Caiaphas'**, he was merely reflecting what was actually happening. Although Caiaphas was officially the high priest, Annas was still the 'power behind the throne'.

So when John began to preach there was a cruel tryrant ruling Rome, a weak governor in Judea and three of 'power-crazy' Herod the Great's sons ruling the land, while the religious affairs of the country were in the hands of two scheming high priests who were ruling contrary to God's Word.

The calling of John

It was into such a situation that God called John to minister. Just like Jeremiah, and many of the Old Testament prophets (see Jer. 2:2;

Ezek. 1:3; Hosea 1:1; Joel 1:1) the word of God came to him. He was called to be a herald of the King, a voice calling in the desert to **'prepare the way for the Lord'** (3:4). John was the fulfilment of Isaiah's prophecy which had been made some 700 years earlier (Isa. 40:3-5). His task was to make straight paths for the Lord. People's lives were wrong; they were crooked. They needed to be put right, and John's task was to call people back to moral ways.

He used great boldness in his work. He called everyone to turn from their wrong ways and return to the Lord and to his ways. Repentance means a complete turn around — a change of heart, mind and will. And John said that not only should people repent, but that those who changed their ways should make a public declaration of that change by being baptized in the river Jordan.

However, John did not baptize everyone who came out **'to be baptized by him'** (3:7). He said to many, **'You brood of vipers! Who warned you to flee from the coming wrath?'** Matthew's account of this shows that these words were especially addressed to the Pharisees and Sadducees (Matt. 3:7). Why did he call them a brood of vipers? He said it because vipers are very vicious. They attack anyone who walks near to them. I have a friend who trod on one while on holiday on the Greek island of Patmos and it bit him. His leg quickly swelled up and, had he not been given the antidote within an hour, he might well have lost his life. So when John called the religious people a brood of vipers he was using very descriptive language which showed what he thought of them.

He said to them, **'Produce fruit in keeping with repentance'** (3:8). He meant that there must be some evidence of repentance before anyone can be baptized. Jesus himself said, 'By their fruit you will recognize them' (Matt. 7:16). People who are not living lives which are glorifying to God have not repented of their sin; therefore such people should not be baptized.

Why was it, then, that religious people wanted John to baptize them? They wanted to undergo this rite because it seemed the thing to do. Previous to John's preaching it was only non-Jews who were baptized. Jews did not need to do such a thing because of their membership of the Jewish race. They relied upon the fact that they could say, **'We have Abraham as our father.'** However, John told them that such a pedigree, without repentance, counted for nothing. He said, **'I tell you that out of these stones God can raise up children for Abraham'** (3:8).

Then John gave a solemn warning to them all. He said, **'The axe is already at the root of the trees, and every tree that does not produce good fruit will be cut down and thrown into the fire'** (3:9). He was talking about destruction — cutting down unfruitful trees — and casting them into the fire. Jesus spoke about the fires of hell, and by 'hell' Jesus meant a complete and permanent separation from God and all his blessings.

Here John is declaring that 'The axe is already at the root of the trees.' He was talking about unfruitful people, those who were not living valuable lives. John said that the only fruitful people are those who have acknowledged their sinful ways, confessed their transgressions to God and sought and obtained his forgiveness and have gone on to glorify him by the way they live their lives.

Action is demanded

When John the Baptist preached the gospel to the crowds on the bank of the River Jordan they cried out, **'What should we do then?'** (3:10). Tax collectors came to John and said, **'What should we do?'** (3:12). Also many soldiers approached him and said, **'And what should we do?'** (3:14). If a person is to follow Christ then he or she must make a specific response.

In a very real sense it is true that we can do nothing to save ourselves. Only a human being who is without sin can bring about our redemption. That is why God's Son had to come down to this earth. Yet, when our eyes are opened to see the enormity of our sin, we have to do something about it. It is when, in the power of the Holy Spirit, a preacher issues a call to repentance, that seekers are deeply moved and convicted of their sin and they want to do something to get rid of it.

Some textbooks give the impression that John only spoke in a censorious voice. They say things like this, 'John was harsh and stern in his preaching. He spoke of the anger of God with evil-doing, not of his love for evil-doers.'[1] It is true that this harsh element featured very strongly in the preaching of John, but that is not the whole picture. Luke tells us that John preached **'a baptism of repentance for the forgiveness of sins'** (3:3).

John was looking forward to the time when Jesus, the spotless Lamb of God, would offer up himself as a sacrifice to take away sin. He said that religious people had to repent. He also said that Jews, who were resting on the fact that they were sons of Abraham, had to repent. In fact he was saying that everyone who has ever lived (apart from the Lamb of God) is a sinner in the eyes of God and needs to be forgiven. And when anyone truly repents then there must be a public demonstration of that repentance.

Baptism is a way in which new converts can show to everyone that they have repented of their sin and that they are determined, henceforth, to live their lives for God's glory. However, baptism is an outward sign. It can be false. It can mean little, and it can be undergone just because it is the thing for people to do at a certain age.

John spoke seriously to all those who wanted to live for God. He told them to **'produce fruit in keeping with repentance'** (3:8). He meant that all those who say they have turned their backs upon sin and want to turn towards God must show some evidence of a complete change in the direction of their lives. John Blanchard says, 'Christians are expected to have the highest living standards in the world.'[2]

Three illustrations of fruit-bearing

First of all Luke tells us about a general enquiry from the crowd: **'What should we do then?'** (3:10). In answer John gives a very practical suggestion. Israel was a theocracy. It was ruled by God. This meant that there should, by rights, be no poor people. If God's injunctions were followed to the letter, then those who possessed little would automatically be cared for by those who had more.

John illustrated it like this: **'The man with two tunics** [a kind of undershirt worn by males and females] **should share with him who has none, and the one who has food should do the same.'** No one needs two tunics. He cannot wear both at once. He should be taught to share what he has with those who are in need.

John the Baptist does not say that the state should step in and deprive the rich person of his property. Nor does he tell the man with no tunic that he must help himself to that which belongs to his neighbour. Neither does he in any way condone anyone's refusal to work in order to earn money so that he can purchase life's necessities. What he is advocating is a voluntary sharing of possessions.[3]

Giving hospitality is a practical example. All church members should ask themselves, 'How often do I invite anyone home for meals or coffee?' and, 'What kind of people do I ask to my home?

Are they only those who are well off enough to ask me back?' Jesus
has something to say about such people (see 6:32-36).

Next Luke tells us that tax collectors came to be baptized. They
said, **'Teacher ... what should we do?'** (3:12). Tax collectors were
despised for two reasons. They were usually Jews who were
collaborating with the Roman occupation forces, and it was gener-
ally recognized that tax collectors were dishonest. After Zacchæus,
a chief tax collector, had met with Jesus, he declared, 'If I have
cheated anybody out of anything, I will pay back four times the
amount' (19:8).

So when tax collectors came to be baptized and they asked,
'What should we do?' John told them to make sure that their house
was in order. He said, **'Don't collect any more than you are
required to'** (3:13). This is how we should all show our repentance
from sin and our desire to live for Christ. We should live our lives
in an open, honest way. We should be above reproach. No one
should be able justly to charge us with even so much as stealing a
paper clip, or five minutes' time from our employer.

Thirdly, some soldiers asked him, **'And what should we do?'**
(3:14). These were probably Jewish soldiers who had been enlisted
to help the tax collectors in their work. They were noted as being
cruel, ruthless and arrogant. Yet they too came under conviction of
sin and they were bold enough to ask John what they should do.

He said, **'Don't extort money and don't accuse people falsely
— be content with your pay'** (3:14). They seem to have been
obsessed with money. They were those who got money out of
people for a living, and they used threats to get it. They were none
too particular about how they obtained their cash. They would lie
and cheat to extract it from citizens. And when they got their own
pay packet from their work, they complained about it.

Is John saying that it is always wrong to ask for more pay? No.
He is saying, 'A fair day's work for a fair day's pay.' Jesus told a
parable about a generous landowner who paid the same amount of
wages to those who were engaged near the end of the day as to those
who had worked hard all day (Matt. 20:1-16). Acquiring more and
more money should not be the objective of life. Paul said, 'The love
of money is a root of all kinds of evil' (1 Tim. 6:10).

To all kinds of people John was saying that true repentance
means giving our whole life over to God and obeying the rules of his
kingdom, not ours.

Was John the Christ?

Luke tells us that they were all **'waiting expectantly and were all wondering in their hearts if John might possibly be the Christ'** (3:15). They were on 'tiptoe of expectation' is how Hendriksen translates this phrase. They had heard John's wonderful teaching. They had been touched in their hearts with the message of God. And now they wondered if John the Baptist was the long-awaited Saviour.

It is good when people start thinking about spiritual things. We live in an age when most people do not want to think. They just want to fill their lives with activities and their minds with noise. But these people started wondering. Bishop Ryle says, 'Thoughtlessness about spiritual things is one great feature of unconverted men. It cannot be said, in many cases, that they either like the gospel, or dislike it. But they do not give it a place in their thoughts.'[4]

John said, 'No. I am not the Christ, I am not even fit enough to be a slave of Christ. The one who is coming is much more powerful than I am. I am not worthy even to take off his sandals. I baptize you with water, but he will baptize you with the Holy Spirit.' John's baptism symbolized repentance from sin, but the baptism of the Holy Spirit symbolizes the power of God upon our lives.

Finally, John speaks about the fire of Judgement Day. He likens this to the separation of wheat from chaff. At the harvest-time, the culmination of all his efforts, the farmer threshes the wheat in order to separate the wholesome from the useless. The wheat is gathered up into a safe place and the chaff is burned with unquenchable fire. John said this harvest-time is going to be good news! (3:18). Judgement actually came upon the Jewish nation in A.D. 70. Titus and the Roman armies destroyed Jerusalem and the whole land so that not one stone was left standing upon another.

This teaching of John declares that the Judgement Day is good news to all who believe in Christ. However, it is terrible news to all those who fail to respond to the gospel message. How important it is, then, to warn everyone to **'flee from the coming wrath'**! (3:7). All of God's people should be busy telling this message to everyone because God is certainly going to bring judgement upon this world (2 Peter 3:10-13).

John continued to denounce sin

John was bold in his declaration of evil. He even rebuked the king. Herod had left his own wife and taken the wife of his half-brother, Philip. (This was not Philip the Tetrarch of Iturea and Traconitis, but another half-brother who was a private citizen.) This was sinful not only because it was an adulterous act, but it was incestuous as well. Under the Mosaic law it was forbidden to marry one's brother's wife (Lev. 18:16). Herod's action went to show that when people are intent upon sin they care nothing for the laws of God and his kingdom.

Luke gives this as only one illustration of the sinful ways of the king (3:19). And, as a result of his preaching, John ended up in prison. It may well be that Herodias (Herod's new wife) demanded that he shut John up. She may also have demanded that the prophet be executed, but Herod was too scared to do this in case some terrible punishment came upon him (Matt. 14:5).

John the Baptist was fearless in his denunciations of wrongdoing. But this was not the totality of his work; he also received all those who truly repented of their sin. He pointed them towards Jesus, who would one day die for their sin (John 1:29). He was so concerned to do God's will that nothing else mattered to him. Oh, that we would live our lives with the same desire!

The baptism of Jesus (3:21-38)

In this passage Luke tells us about the commencement of the work of Jesus as the Messiah. Throughout the Old Testament we read of the coming of God's chosen one, whom he has appointed (and anointed) to be the deliverer of his people. In Hebrew the word for this one was 'Messiah' but the Greek translation of this word is 'Christ'. That is why Jesus is called the Christ. He is, and always has been, the Messiah, but he commenced his earthly ministry as God's chosen one when he was baptized by John in the River Jordan.

Jesus was baptized

Jesus was baptized when all the people were being baptized; it was not a private ceremony (3:21). When Jesus came to be baptized John tried to put him off. He said, 'I need to be baptized by you, and do you come to me?' (Matt. 3:14). John meant that he knew that Jesus was so good and holy, while he, in comparison to the Lord, was far too unworthy to baptize him. But if Jesus was sinless why did he need to be baptized?

Jesus said to John, 'Let it be so now; it is proper for us to do this to fulfil all righteousness' (Matt. 3:15). He meant that *it is the right thing for anyone to do*. Baptism is God's divinely appointed initiation ceremony. Secondly, Jesus was baptized *to show that he is God's appointed one*. John said, '"Look, the Lamb of God, who takes away the sin of the world! This is the one I meant when I said, 'A man who comes after me has surpassed me because he was before me.' I myself did not know him, but the reason I came baptizing with water was that he might be revealed to Israel." Then John gave this testimony, "I saw the Spirit come down from heaven as a dove and remain on him. I would not have known him, except that the one who sent me to baptize with water told me, 'The man on whom you see the Spirit come down and remain is he who will baptize with the Holy Spirit.' I have seen and I testify that this is the Son of God"' (John 1:31-34).

Another reason why Jesus was baptized was *so that he could be completely identified with man's sin and failure*. He was the only person who has lived a perfect life on this earth. Therefore Jesus did not need to be baptized because of his sin, because he had none. What he was showing publicly through his baptism was that he was to be our substitute for sin and he would die for us. It all became much clearer after Calvary. Paul explains that 'God made him who had no sin to be sin for us, so that in him we might become the righteousness of God' (2 Cor. 5:21).

The baptism of Jesus was also *an example to all of his followers*. Jesus, by submitting to baptism, was showing to us all that we should not be ashamed of passing through the waters of baptism. After all, God himself has ordained this ceremony for us. When Jesus ascended up into heaven, after his death and resurrection, he told each of his disciples to 'Go and make disciples of all nations, baptizing them in the name of the Father and of the Son and of the Holy Spirit' (Matt. 28:19). That command still holds good today for all who wish to follow Jesus.

Next let us notice that *Jesus was praying in connection with his baptism*. Prayer was a vital part of Jesus' work. Luke emphasized

again and again that Jesus prayed. After Jesus had been healing the
sick he 'often withdrew to lonely places and prayed' (5:16). Before
he chose his twelve special disciples Jesus spent whole whole nights
praying to God (6:12). In Luke 9:18 we read that 'Jesus was praying
in private,' and we also read similar comments about the prayer life
of Jesus in Luke 9:28-29; 11:1; 22:32,41; 23:34,46.

Bishop Ryle wrote, 'A baptism without prayer ... is a baptism on
which we have no right to expect God's blessing.'[5] The devil always
attacks those who witness to their Lord in baptism. This means that
much prayer always ought to be made when anyone is baptized.
Jesus felt it necessary to pray; and so should we.

God showed his approval

As Jesus was praying, heaven was opened. This is a way of saying
that God opened up a way between himself and mankind. He
fulfilled all righteousness and when prayer was made, heaven was
opened.

We cannot expect God to reveal himself to us unless we do the
right thing, in the right way, with the right motives. We so often
worry and fret about things, when all we need to do is to keep God's
commands. Prayer should be our constant occupation; it is not just
something that we do when we have a great need.

Luke tells us next that the Holy Spirit descended on Jesus in
bodily form, like a dove at, or shortly after, his baptism. This was to
show that Jesus had upon him, and within him, the power of God.
It showed that God, the Father, authenticated the ministry of Jesus
and approved of him. So why did the Holy Spirit appear as a dove?

Probably the first thing that anyone notices about a dove is that
it is white. Therefore, in the Scriptures, a dove is a symbol of purity.
Hendriksen says that 'To save us from our sin Jesus himself needed
to be pure.'[6] Jesus was sinless, and remained so throughout his
whole time upon the earth. Secondly, a dove is a symbol of gentle-
ness, meekness and graciousness. Jesus was eminently gentle, meek
and gracious. He said, 'Take my yoke upon you and learn from me,
for I am gentle and humble in heart, and you will find rest for your
souls' (Matt. 11:29).

But it was not only a dove which descended upon Jesus from
heaven; a voice was also heard (3:22) — the voice of God the Father.
We are not sure who heard this voice. Jesus certainly did, but we do

not know whether anyone else heard it, except John the Baptist. In John 1:32,34 we read, 'Then John gave this testimony: "I saw the Spirit come down from heaven as a dove and remain on him... I have seen and I testify that this is the Son of God."'

On two other occasions God spoke from heaven concerning Jesus. At the transfiguration God said, 'This is my Son, whom I have chosen; listen to him' (9:35), and in the temple area during the final week of his earthly life, Jesus prayed, 'Father, glorify your name!' The answer to that prayer was a voice from heaven which said, 'I have glorified it, and will glorify it again' (John 12:28).

The voice of God confirmed that Jesus is God's Son, in other words, God himself. He is the beloved Son of God. In Psalm 2:7 we read that God said, 'You are my Son; today I have become your Father,' and in Isaiah 42:1 we read the words of God:

'Here is my servant, whom I uphold,
   my chosen one in whom I delight;
I will put my Spirit on him
   and he will bring justice to the nations.'

Jesus is declared to be the one whom the Father loves. His life, from the time of his birth until his baptism, had been pleasing to God and this would also be true of the life which he would lead in the next three years or so. So here, in this one verse, we have the Trinity spoken of: Jesus the Son, God the Father and God the Holy Spirit. God the Father and God the Holy Spirit both testify that God the Son is the beloved one in whom the Father is well pleased!

The earthly line of Jesus

Luke is the only Gospel writer to mention the age of Jesus at the commencement of his ministry. He says that Jesus was about thirty years old. Thirty was a very significant time for Jewish males. Levites began their service in the temple at this age (Num. 4:47). Joseph became 'prime minister' of Egypt at thirty (Gen. 41:46) and David started to reign as king at the same age (2 Sam. 5:4).

'**Jesus himself was about thirty years old when he began his ministry**' (3:23). The evangelist was 'laying emphasis upon the personality which he had already described in chapters one and two'.[7] Luke has already shown us glimpses of Jesus before he was born (1:31-33), when he was forty days old (2:22), when he was twelve years old (2:43), as he was growing up (2:52) and finally as he was baptized (3:21). And here we read, 'Jesus himself'. He was writing about Jesus, who at this point commenced his earthly public ministry. 'The fact that Jesus had a family tree shows that he was not a figment of the imagination or a kind of mystical half man-half god.'[8]

Luke then gives us a long list of names. We have a similar genealogy of Jesus in Matthew. But Matthew starts with Abraham and traces the line of Jesus through David up to Joseph, the husband of Mary, and on to 'Jesus, who is called Christ' (Matt. 1:2-16). Luke, on the other hand, starts with Jesus, **'the son, so it was thought, of Joseph'** (3:23). He then traces the ancestors of Jesus back through David to Abraham, and then beyond to **'Seth, the son of Adam, the son of God'** (3:38).

Why do each of these evangelists adopt different methods of showing their ancestry of Jesus? It seems that Matthew, writing for his Jewish readers, was tracing the 'legal' lineage of Jesus; that was through his earthly father (women did not have family trees of their own). But Luke is concerned to show the ancestry of Jesus through his mother, Mary. The stories in the opening chapters of Matthew seem to be looked at from the viewpoint of Joseph, while the stories in the opening chapters of Luke appear to have come from Mary herself, or her friends. Even though there are some differences in these lists both of them show that the ancestry of Jesus was through King David. Both his earthly father and his mother numbered this great king among their forebears. Remember that Gabriel said that Jesus was to be given the throne of his father David and reign for ever (1:33).

What do we notice about all of these names in Luke 3:23-38? Firstly, we know very little about most of them. A few were famous but many were unknown. Yet they all took their place in the Messiah's line. It is an encouragement to us, when we feel that no one cares about us, to realize that we never know what part we may be called upon to play in God's divine plan.

A second thing to notice is that all of these, except the Lord himself, are now dead. Bishop Ryle says, 'They all had their joys and sorrows, their hopes and fears, their cares and troubles, their schemes and plans, like any of ourselves. But they have all passed away from the earth, and gone to their own place. And so it will be with us. We too are passing away, and shall soon be gone.'[9] How we need to be ready to leave at a moment's notice, whenever our Lord calls us!

A third thing to notice is that Luke's list goes back to 'Adam, the son of God'. Adam was made in God's likeness (Gen. 1:26). And Jesus is, by his very humanity, also God's Son. Now all of us are sons of Adam. 'But the line was not continuous. It was broken by the Fall. No other man has ever come into the world bearing the likeness of a son of God, for by Adam's sin every one of his descendants forfeited that sonship.'[10]

4.
Christ begins his public ministry

Please read Luke 4

The temptations of Jesus (4:1-13)

Is it sinful to be tempted? No, because Jesus himself was tempted on at least three occasions, and we know that he was without sin. It is not wrong to be tempted, but it is sinful to give way to the temptation.

It is always the devil who tempts us and he always makes the temptation appear to be exciting. He knows our weak points. If we are hungry, he tempts us with forbidden fruit. If we are feeling weak, he promises us power; and if we are feeling unnoticed he promises that we will gain the applause of the crowd. He tells us that we can gain all of these things if we will only submit to him.

He never tempts us to do something which has no attraction for us. When Satan comes to us with a proposition that is wrong, we must say, as Jesus did, 'Get thee behind me Satan' (4:8, AV). C. H. Spurgeon said, 'Learn to say "No"; it will be more use to you than to be able to read Latin.'[1]

Jesus in the desert

When the Lord was baptized he began his public ministry. Luke says that he was **'full of the Holy Spirit'** (4:1). He continually mentions the Holy Spirit in his Gospel and, in addition, he does so fifty-seven times in Acts. Jesus was led into the desert. This was possibly the same desert where John had lived for many years in his youth (1:80). Jesus fasted in this desert. He wanted to free his mind from the desires of the body so that he could concentrate upon the needs of the spirit. In the Scriptures fasting often goes hand in hand with prayer. In the desert the Lord prepared himself for the work which was ahead of him. Paul did the same thing when he was called to serve the Lord (Gal. 1:15-17).

There is no escape from the devil. He knows that deep down we are all proud in our hearts, and he gives us the opportunity to be in the limelight. All we have to do is to bow down to him first! So often he catches us out. To use the words of T. S. Eliot, we do 'the right deed for the wrong reason'.[2]

The first temptation: the satisfaction of physical needs

Naturally, after forty days of fasting, Jesus was hungry (4:2). So the devil came and reminded him of the power which he possessed. He said to the Lord, 'You can turn these stones into bread'; and Jesus, conscious of his hunger, and looking at the smooth round pebbles, was tempted to see them as small loaves of bread.

Satan said, **'If you are the Son of God'**. He used the same ploy which he had used many years before when he spoke to the first Adam in the Garden of Eden. He had said to the woman, 'Did God really say, "You must not eat from any tree in the garden?"' (Gen. 3:1). God himself had just declared, at the baptism of Jesus, 'You are my Son' (3:22) and then Satan craftily said, 'If you are the Son of God'.

One of Satan's tricks is to make God's people doubt God's word. He tries to make us question the Bible — and this is a very subtle temptation. Many so-called theologians doubt that this book is the Word of God. They say, 'It contains the word of God, but there are errors in it.' They say, 'We must place alongside of the Bible the wisdom of men and the culture in which we live.' But God's believing people have to turn their backs on all such ideas because Satan is behind all false teaching.

When Jesus was tempted to turn the stones into bread, he quoted Scripture at Satan. He said, **'It is written'** (4:4). We should always remember that if God has written something in his Word then it must be true and it must be relevant for our needs today. Jesus quoted the law of the Lord. He referred to the book of Deuteronomy and said, **'Man does not live on bread alone'** (Deut. 8:3). He meant that there is a spiritual dimension in all of us and that must be fed. None of us must neglect to feed our souls by prayer and the study and meditation of God's Word.

The second temptation: the satisfaction of worldly ambition

Jesus was tempted to receive the authority and splendour of all of the kingdoms of the world. If he would but bow down and worship the devil, then Satan would give them to him. The Evil One was speaking the truth up to a point. He is the 'ruler of the kingdom of the air' (Eph. 2:2). He is the leader of 'the spiritual forces of evil in the heavenly realms' (Eph. 6:12), and 1 John 5:19 tells us that 'The whole world is under the control of the evil one.' But that does not mean that the devil has the power to hand over the authority and splendour of the world to whomsoever he pleases. The truth is that 'Satan exercises a very powerful influence for evil over the lives of all those wicked people and spirits that acknowledge him as their master.'[3] But the devil is a liar; he cannot pass his power on to others.

To answer Satan, Jesus quoted from Deuteronomy 6:13. He said, 'It is written'. Those who have seen the film *Lawrence of Arabia* know that for desert people, 'It is written' means, 'It is unalterable and it must be carried out' — rather like the law of the Medes and the Persians in the time of Daniel! Jesus said, **'It is written: "Worship the Lord your God and serve him only."'** There is only one worthy of spiritual worship. He is the Lord God Almighty. We should take care that we bow down in worship to none other. Many young people today listen to the voice of the Evil One and bow down to him by taking drugs, getting hooked on alcohol and becoming involved in occult practices. All of these things are foolish and we should do everything in our power to encourage people to refuse to bow the knee to Satan and all his evil host.

The third temptation: to worldly acclaim

The devil led Jesus to Jerusalem. We do not know whether this was achieved literally, in his thoughts or by a vision, but the devil organized it so that Jesus stood on the highest point of the temple. Perhaps he meant to imply, 'If you do as I say, then you can be the highest of all; even higher than the temple of God and everything it stands for.' Next the devil said, **'Throw yourself down from here for it is written,**

> "He will command his angels concerning you
>> to guard you carefully;
> they will lift you up in their hands,
>> so that you will not strike your foot against a stone'"
>>>>>> (4: 10-11).

Even the devil can quote Scripture; this is from Psalm 91:11-12. We, too, must be well versed in the Bible, but, unlike Satan, we must not quote it out of context. Satan tempted Jesus to do this so that he could achieve quick results and effortlessly receive popular support.

However, Jesus was not taken in by Satan's quick and easy way to success. He again quoted from Deuteronomy. He said, **'Do not put the Lord your God to the test'** (Deut. 6:16). No one should try to make bargains with God; they should obey him. I often tell the children at school that Jesus was not an acrobat or a conjurer. He never performed miracles just to entertain people, so that they could say, 'How wonderful this man is!' Jesus only performed miracles to help someone or to teach something.

The devil's reaction

When he saw that he had failed, the devil went away. But he only went for a little while (4:13). He was busy watching Jesus for every opportunity he could get to tempt him again. His great aim was to defeat Jesus.

What Satan tried to do to the Lord, he will attempt on us. We should remember these scriptures: 'We do not have a high priest [Jesus] who is unable to sympathize with our weaknesses, but we have one who has been tempted in every way, just as we are — yet was without sin' (Heb. 4:15); and 'Because [Jesus] himself suffered when he was tempted, he is able to help those who are being tempted' (Heb. 2:18). The way to victory in the Christian life is the way of suffering and obedience. Jesus went that way, so we should gladly follow him knowing that he is with us all of our days.

The rejection of Jesus (4:14-30)

I have a friend who says, 'I'm a Christian but I never go to church.' But that is just like someone saying, 'I believe in education, but I don't go to school.'⁴ Such people are really turning their backs upon the Lord Jesus Christ; they are rejecting him because he does not measure up to their expectations of a Saviour.

Jesus went to the northern district

He had been brought up in Nazareth, in the region of the Sea of Galilee and he seems to have established his headquarters in the lakeside town of Capernaum. It was here that Jesus did much of his teaching and performed many of his miracles. Luke tells us that he returned to Galilee in the power of the Spirit (4:14). After the baptism of Jesus and the temptations there appears to have been about a year which Luke covers briefly in the section related in verses 14-15. Mark or Matthew do not record anything about this year of obscurity. Only John tells us some of the happenings between the temptations and Jesus going to Nazareth (see John 1:19-4:42).

The Nazareth synagogue

The whole village would have remembered Jesus as the one who 'grew in wisdom and stature, and in favour with God and man' (2:52). In this incident we have a glimpse of something that Jesus did every Sabbath day. He went to worship God in the synagogue. Synagogues came into being when the Jews were deported to Babylon many hundreds of years before. Because they were unable to go to the temple at Jerusalem, they formed meeting-places for worship where they lived. So in every town, wherever there were at least ten adult Jewish men, a synagogue was established. It did not have to be in a special religious building. It was the people who made up the synagogue. The word itself merely means 'a meeting-place'.

There is nothing in the Scriptures to say that Jesus only went to 'good' synagogues. His concern was to meet with God's people. He did not first find out who was preaching or wait to see how he was feeling. Nothing stopped him. He did not take the Sabbath day off sometimes. He certainly never said, 'I'm too tired, I have work to do at home which must be done,' or 'My friends have invited me out.' **'As was his custom,'** he went into the synagogue on the Sabbath day (see Heb. 10:25).

As Jesus was a visitor who had grown up in the town, the officials of the synagogue gave him the honour of reading the Scriptures. We do not know what the appointed reading for the day was, but Jesus unrolled the scroll until he found Isaiah 61:1-2. He then read,

'The Spirit of the Lord is on me,
 because he has anointed me
 to preach good news to the poor.
He has sent me to proclaim freedom for the prisoners
 and recovery of sight for the blind,
to release the oppressed,
 to proclaim the year of the Lord's favour'

(4:18-19).

At that point, Luke tells us that **'He rolled up the scroll, gave it back to the attendant and sat down'** (4:20). This was a sign that he was going to speak to the congregation. His sermon was, as all true sermons should be, an explanation of what the Scriptures meant both for the original hearers and the people of that day.

Every Jew knew that Isaiah 61 referred to the coming of the Messiah. That is why **'The eyes of everyone in the synagogue were fastened on him'** (4:20). They had heard of the signs and wonders which he had been doing in the area of Capernaum (4:23). It was no wonder that they were eager to hear what he had to say. How they must have been amazed when they heard him say, **'Today this scripture is fulfilled in your hearing'** (4:21). The Lord applied Isaiah 61 to that very day in which they were living.

What did Jesus mean by saying, 'Today this scripture is fulfilled'? Isaiah spoke of a time coming when good news would be preached to the poor, prisoners would be set free, the blind would be made to see again, the oppressed would be released and the year of the Lord's favour would be proclaimed. Jesus said, 'The time has come.' He meant that the people of those days were living in the period of God's graciousness. That same day of grace is with us still.

Those who heard Jesus preach on that day had heard of the blind regaining their sight, deaf people hearing and the lame being made to walk again. However, Jesus was referring to something much deeper. He was talking about spiritual bondage. He meant that because of sin, and Satan's power, many people were being held as captives, many were longing to be freed from the bondage of their emotions and their guilt. He declared that he had come to set men free. In other words, he was saying that he was the Messiah—God's chosen, anointed one. He had come to usher in the period of God's grace.

There is great significance in this action of Jesus in stopping at the place where he did. He rolled up the scroll in mid-sentence. Isaiah said, 'To proclaim the year of the Lord's favour and the day of vengeance of our God' (Isa. 61:2). What Jesus meant was that he had come to the earth on this first occasion to save people from their sins. He had come in grace and mercy to repentant sinners. But one day, and we do not know how soon it will be, he is coming again. On that occasion it will be to bring in a day of vengeance.

The effect of his message

Everyone thought it was marvellous. **'All spoke well of him and were amazed at the gracious words that came from his lips'** (4:22). We have the same kind of statement in verse 15 where we read that **'Everyone praised him.'** But a little later on the Lord said, 'Woe to you when all men speak well of you, for that is how their fathers treated the false prophets' (6:26).

The people said, **'Isn't this Joseph's son?'** (4:22). They could hardly believe that someone who had grown up among them could speak so well. Perhaps it had not sunk in that Jesus was, in effect, saying, 'I am the Messiah — God's chosen one.'

Then Jesus went on: **'Surely you will quote this proverb to me: "Physician, heal yourself! Do here in your home town what we have heard that you did in Capernaum"'** (4:23). He knew that what they really wanted was to see some excitement. They wanted to have miracles in Nazareth — preferably right there in their own synagogue; and they wanted them right then. But Jesus did few miracles in his home town (Matt. 13:58). He was not interested in entertaining people. He did not use gimmicks to attract people to God. He was concerned that their hearts and their lives should be changed. He wanted them to be more concerned to do God's will, rather than getting some temporary thrill. Brian Edwards, in his book on *Revival* has written, 'It is not our happiness that God is concerned with, but our holiness... The first work of the Spirit is not to tell us that we can be happy but that we must be holy — because God is.'[5]

Next Jesus reminded his congregation of two incidents in their history. The first was where Elijah was fed by a very poor widow woman, and the second was where Elisha was used by God to cleanse a very rich man from his leprosy. The meaning which Jesus was conveying from these incidents was not lost on the crowd. Both the poor widow and the rich general (who was, in fact, also poor, but in health) were Gentiles. Luke used this story of Jesus in the synagogue at Nazareth to show that the Lord did not come only to bring salvation to the Jews, but that he is the Saviour of the world.

The people of Nazareth were very angry. Luke writes, **'All the people in the synagogue were furious when they heard this. They got up, drove him out of the town, and took him to the brow of the hill on which the town was built, in order to throw him down the cliff'** (4:28-29). Eventually Jesus was killed by his fellow countrymen, but it did not happen in Nazareth. His hour had not come. The narrative continues, **'But he walked right through the crowd and went on his way'** (4:30). No one could take his life from him until God's appointed time. God has a time and a purpose for all things and no man, however religious or powerful, can alter that time.

Those who lived in Nazareth rejected Jesus because he did not measure up to their ideas of what a Saviour should be. Those who reject him today are just as foolish, even more so, if they have heard the gospel message of the cross proclaimed in all its fulness.

The authority of Jesus (4:31-44)

In these last fourteen verses of Luke 4 we have several instances of the authority of Jesus. In verses 31-32 we read of the authority of his preaching. In verses 33-37 we learn of his authority over evil spirits. In verses 38-39 Luke tells us about his authority over a high fever; and in verses 40-41 we read about his authority over various kinds of sickness. Finally in verses 42-44 we discover the secret of his authority.

His authority in preaching

When Jesus left Nazareth, **'He went down to Capernaum'** — down because that town was about 700 feet below the level of the Mediterranean Sea. When he arrived he went into the synagogue

and on the Sabbath he began to teach the people. This synagogue
was the one which had been built by a Gentile, a Roman centurion.

While Jesus was in the synagogue he preached to the people and
the people were amazed at his teaching, because his message had
authority (4:32). People were compelled to listen to him and to
acknowledge that there was something very commanding about his
words and the way in which he spoke them. Mark adds that 'The
people were amazed at his teaching, because he taught them as one
who had authority, not as the teachers of the law' (Mark 1:22). 'He
spoke as the lover of men, as one concerned with the everlasting
welfare of his listeners and he pointed to the Father and his love.'[6]
Everything which he said, and the way in which he declared it, was
a great contrast to the preaching of the religious teachers of his day.

We find the same things today when we consider how the
'professional' religious people speak. Writing in the *Daily Mail* on
28 April 1990, Paul Johnson outlined the state of Christianity in this
country, as he saw it. He wrote that most of the 'leaders of the
mainstream churches ... are much more interested in politics ... than
they are in upholding Christian morals or the tenets of the Christian
faith... They [the professional church leaders] still hang on tightly to
their privileges and maintain the carve-up of religious television and
radio they operate among themselves. They are determined to stop
outsiders homing in on their "joint monopoly".'[7]

His authority over evil spirits

'In the synagogue there was a man possessed by a demon, an evil
spirit' (4:33). This poor man cried out at the top of his voice, 'Ha!
What do you want with us, Jesus of Nazareth? Have you come
to destroy us? I know who you are — the Holy One of God'
(4:34). He recognized who Jesus really was, and he was not ashamed
to declare it to all. He said that Jesus was 'the Holy One of God'. This
assertion was perfectly correct. He perceived what many did not
grasp.

Another incident like this one is found in Acts 16. There we read
of a poor girl who kept following Paul and his friends. She had a
'spirit' within her which predicted the future. She shouted out,
'These men are servants of the Most High God, who are telling you
the way to be saved' (Acts 16:17). How strange it is that people

reject the Lord Jesus Christ and yet the demons believe that there is one God — and shudder because of it! (James 2:19).

However, Jesus, just like Paul, refused to accept the testimony of the evil spirit, and commanded him to leave the poor man. **'Be quiet!'** said Jesus, sternly. **'Come out of him!'** (4:35). **'Then the demon threw the man down before them all.'** We would have thought that the force of this fall would have done harm to the man, but Jesus had control of that aspect of the deliverance as well. Luke tells us that the demon **'came out without injuring him'**.

The reaction of all the people in the synagogue was one of amazement. This is the question to which they wanted an answer: **'What is this teaching?'**(4:36). They had not heard or seen anything like it in their lives before. They said, **'With authority and power he gives orders to evil spirits and they come out!'** The result was that **'The news about him spread throughout the surrounding area'** (4:37).

His authority over fever

Jesus and his disciples went to the home of Simon Peter and Andrew. When they got there they found that Simon's mother-in-law was suffering from a high fever. From this section we learn that Simon had a mother-in-law. This means that he was married — unlike the pope of the Roman Catholic Church. Simon's wife's mother was ill. Both Matthew and Mark say that she had a fever but this is not accurate enough for Dr Luke. He said that she had a *meghalo* fever — a high fever.

When we are on holiday in Greece it is always my job to go to the supermarket before breakfast. I ask for *Ghala parakalo* (Milk, please). It is often the case that when you ask for something in Greece you are, in return, met with a question. Invariably when you ask for *Ghala* you are asked, *'Meghalo ee Meekree?'* (Do you want a big or a little one?) Simon's mother-in-law had a big fever and they asked Jesus to help her.

Then Jesus came and took up the stance of a doctor. Luke used a medical term when he wrote, **'He bent over her'** (4:39). At that point Jesus healed her. Just as he had rebuked the evil spirit and caused him to come out of the man and leave him unharmed, so he rebuked the fever in Simon's mother-in-law and it left her. The cure was so complete and immediate that **'She got up at once and began to wait on them.'**

His authority over various kinds of sickness

We read, **'When the sun was setting, the people brought to Jesus all who had various kinds of sickness'** (4:40). The Sabbath day ended as sunset began. While it was the Sabbath the people could not journey more than half or three quarters of a mile but now the Sabbath had come to an end. That is why Luke wrote, 'When the sun was setting'. It seems that they could hardly wait for the Sabbath to finish before they brought their friends to Jesus for healing.

Luke tells us that Jesus went round each one of them, laying his hands on them and healing them. It must have taken a long time to lay hands on every one of them but Jesus did just that. 'He imposed no condition upon them. He did not enquire about their family life. He asked nothing about their past history. He healed without reference to anything in them but their need.'[8]

Again, **'Demons came out of many people, shouting, "You are the Son of God"'** (4:41). But for the third time Jesus rebuked them. He would not allow them to speak, because they knew he was the Christ. He refused to accept any testimony from demons. Even when they spoke the truth he forbade them to continue because he knew how dangerous it was to allow Satan and his evil hosts to speak at all.

The secret of the authority of Jesus

'At daybreak Jesus went out to a solitary place.' Mark adds these words: '...where he prayed' (Mark 1:35). Jesus regularly needed to get alone with God in prayer. He knew that wherever he was he could quickly speak to his Father in an emergency, but he also knew that this was no substitute for being alone with his Father. He often spent all night alone with God in prayer.

On this occasion Jesus was disturbed in his praying. **'The people were looking for him and when they came to where he was, they tried to keep him from leaving them'** (4:42). They wanted Jesus to stay with them. When he was on earth he could only be in one place at a time. He had to keep moving onwards, otherwise he would not have fulfilled his mission to all of the people. But now that he has gone up into heaven and the Holy Spirit has come in his place, his presence can be known and felt in many places at the same time.

Not only did Jesus spend much time in prayer; he went out preaching **'the good news of the kingdom of God'** (4:43). The kingdom of God is the reign of God. This is something that is present now. It should be our desire to long for it to be more widely known. We should work and pray to this end. Not only is the kingdom of God something which is here with us now, but it is also something which is yet to come. In the Lord's Prayer we pray, 'Thy kingdom come.'

This chapter in Luke's Gospel is rounded off with this statement: **'[Jesus] kept on preaching in the synagogues of Judea'** (4:44). Luke was writing for Gentiles, so he called the whole land 'Judea'. The secret of the authority of the Lord was that God was with him; he spent much time with his Father. In the strength of that relationship he could go about healing and teaching and drawing all sorts and conditions of men into the kingdom of God; he brought many under his kingly reign.

Jesus still has authority today. He is Lord and he is King. He has the power to heal from all kinds of sicknesses and diseases, especially the devastation wrought by the deadly affliction of sin.

5.
The Lord deals with people

Please read Luke 5

In this chapter Luke tells us about the Lord's dealings with four people: Peter (5:1-11), a man with leprosy (5:12-16), a paralytic (5:17-26) and Levi (5:27-32).

A miraculous catch (5:1-11)

Jesus was standing by the Lake of Gennesaret, or, as it is often called, the Sea of Galilee. It is about thirteen miles long by seven miles wide and was the home district of most of the disciples of Jesus. In fact at least four of them actually worked on it: Simon Peter and his brother Andrew and James and his brother John were all fishermen.

Because Jesus was there (his fame had spread), he attracted a great many people. Luke says that they were **'crowding round him and listening to the word of God'** (5:1) but after a while, standing by the lake became impractical. Because of the crowds, Jesus got into one of the empty boats on the shore-line. He chose Simon's boat and **'asked him to put out a little from the shore'** (5:3). He then resumed his teaching. He did not need a particular building in which to preach. So if he was happy to preach from a boat, then we should be glad to use whatever facilities are available to us.

When the boat was a little way from the shore Jesus sat down in it. He had done the same thing in the synagogue at Nazareth (4:20). This action was an indication that he was going to preach God's Word. However, Jesus did not just use a boat because the crowds were growing. He chose this 'pulpit' so that he could reach more people. Whenever I swim out a long way on holiday I can always hear voices on the beach — especially my young daughter's. Sounds carry a long way over the water.

The Lord's dealings with Peter

Luke does not tell us what effect the preaching had; from verse 4 onwards, the crowds just fade out of the picture. Although Peter must have heard everything that Jesus said, we are not given any indication that the sermon had much effect upon him. Nevertheless, Jesus was interested in capturing Peter.

He asked Peter to put out a little from shore (5:3). He also made a request from a Samaritan woman. He asked her to draw water from a well so that he could drink (John 4:7). This was remarkable because no normal Jew would speak to a Samaritan; and certainly not a woman — especially one of ill repute. But in order to reach her mind and heart, Jesus asked her to do him a favour.

After Jesus had finished his sermon, he rewarded Simon. He said, **'Put out into deep water, and let down the nets for a catch'** (5:4). Can you imagine the scene? Here was Jesus, a wandering preacher and miracle-worker, telling Peter, who was an expert fisherman, to start fishing — in deep water. Peter said, **'Master, we've worked hard all night and haven't caught anything'** (5:5).

He knew that it was *the wrong time* to go fishing. Many hours before he and his colleagues had hauled their boats up onto the beach. They had washed their nets and hung them up to dry, to stop them from rotting. They had listened while Jesus had first of all preached to the crowd on the beach (5:1). Peter had been there while Jesus preached again from the boat (5:3).

While all this had been going on time had been passing. By now it may have been nearly midday. The sun would have been high in the sky. Every fisherman knew that fish did not stay near the surface, where they could easily be caught. No experienced fisherman would set out to work while strong sunlight was beating down upon the water. He and his colleagues had tried fishing at the right time and they had caught nothing. Surely it was crazy to go fishing at midday.

Peter did not hesitate because he was a slacker; he had worked hard and had caught nothing.

The trouble was that Peter also knew that it was *the wrong place* to fish. He would have no chance of catching anything in deep water. His prey could easily escape from the nets. The shallows and the night-time were the right places and the right time to get a successful catch. And, in any case, there were no fish to be had. Peter had proved that from his own experience.

He also had another problem which would have tried his faith. The other fishermen, who were probably dozing up and down the shore-line, would have been watching him. They would have thought him crazy to go out fishing at midday; especially so if they knew that he was doing it because a preacher had said that he should.

Moreover, on top of all that, *Peter would have been very tired.* He had been fishing all night long. He did not give up halfway through the night. He had persevered. That is why he said to Jesus, 'We have worked hard all night.'

However, he had only hesitated for a moment and then said, **'But because you say so, I will let down the nets'** (5:5). Peter may not have been fully committed to following Jesus at this point but he made one of the most important decisions of his life when he agreed to do as Jesus said. It was because Jesus said so that Peter obeyed. He had come to realize that Jesus is Lord of all things and he was prepared to cast everything upon him. That is why he called him **'Master'** (5:5). That is the term which is used for the captain of a great ocean-going liner. Peter accepted that Jesus was the captain of his soul.

The outcome was that, contrary to all expectations, **'They caught such a large number of fish that their nets began to break'** (5:6) and they had to signal to their partners in the other boat. They did not shout to them. They just beckoned them. When they loaded all the fish into both boats the catch was so great that the ships began to sink under the weight of it all. **'When Simon Peter** [Luke used his full name] **saw this, he fell at Jesus' knees and said, "Go away from me, Lord; I am a sinful man!"'**(5:8). When he saw for himself the greatness of the power of Jesus, he felt very unworthy.

Many years earlier Abraham had experienced the same thing. He had said to the Lord, when pleading for the city of Sodom, 'I am nothing but dust and ashes' (Gen. 18:27). He felt that God was so powerful and holy that in contrast he was worthless. Job also felt so undeserving before God that he said, 'I despise myself and repent in dust and ashes' (Job 42:6). Isaiah was so overwhelmed when the holiness of God was revealed to him that he said, 'Woe to me! ... I am ruined! For I am a man of unclean lips, and my eyes have seen the King, the Lord Almighty' (Isa. 6:5).

Peter did not really want Jesus to go away from him. He desired to be with his Master always, but he felt so unworthy to be a follower of Jesus. He believed that it would not be right for the Lord to have mercy upon such a vile character as himself.

The miracles which Jesus had performed (especially on Peter's own mother-in-law) had certainly touched his heart. He had been moved by these things, but now something new happened: he experienced the mighty working power of Jesus in his own life. That was the final thing which made Peter reach that point where he handed the whole of his life over to the Lord. Jesus was no longer Peter's Master; he was now his Lord. Luke tells us, **'When Simon Peter saw this, he fell at Jesus' knees and said, "Go away from me, Lord; I am a sinful man!" For he and all his companions were astonished at the catch of fish they had taken, and so were James and John, the sons of Zebedee, Simon's partners'** (5:8-10).

'Then Jesus said to Simon, "Don't be afraid; from now on you will catch men"' (5:10). It would seem that Jesus had previously called Peter and Andrew to follow him. We read of this in Matthew 4:18-20 and Mark 1:16-18. But their obedience had only been partial. Every now and then they returned to their homes and their fishing. 'They did not follow him in a complete and unconditional manner.'[1] However, since this incident that half-hearted way of following Jesus was over. Peter had a completely new attitude, and he would follow the Lord wherever he would lead him.

Why did Jesus say, 'Don't be afraid?' Because Peter had been fearful of committing the whole of his future to the care of the Lord, but now he realized that he need have no fear. Jesus had demonstrated that he knew all things and he had the power to perform all things.

What happened to all of those fish which they caught? We are not told, but I am sure that Jesus, who instructed his disciples to pick up twelve basketfuls of crumbs which remained after the feeding of the 5,000, would not have left them to rot and go to waste. They would have been given to the families of the fishermen whom Jesus was calling away. Peter would know that as Jesus had met his needs, so the Lord would also provide for the needs of his family.

No one who leaves everything to follow Jesus will lose out by it. Nor will their families suffer by their departure. Those who trust in the Lord will have each and every one of their needs supplied. They have but to trust everything into his care and control and leave all things in his hands as they follow wherever he leads them.

Jesus finally tells Peter of his new career: **'From now on you will catch men'** (5:10). Peter had been used to catching live fish and allowing them to die so that they could be sold for food. But in future he was going to be used by the Lord to catch dead men and women so that they could be made alive by the power of Christ.

Jesus still calls people like Peter today. There is a feminine version of the name Peter; it is Petra. God is calling both men and women to leave everything and commit the whole of their lives to him so that they can go out and become 'fishers of men'.

Two remarkable healings (5:12-26)

Luke demonstrates in these verses some of the wonderful variety there is in the healing power of Christ. He cured a man who was so full of leprosy that no one would dare to touch him, and he made a paralytic walk again.

A leper

Whenever anyone caught leprosy they had to stay away from other people. Leprosy is a dreadful skin disease which starts with spots and boils and gradually spreads until the sores begin to bite into the body of the afflicted person. In the end the hands and the feet of the sufferer become useless and life itself becomes a great burden. Under the Old Testament law a leper was obliged to cry out, 'Unclean! Unclean!' (Lev. 13:45-46) wherever he went. No one would be allowed to touch him for fear of catching and passing on the disease. This man in Luke 5:12-14 was so far gone that Luke, the doctor, describes him as being **'covered with leprosy'**. Such a person was an outcast from society. He would have to depend upon the charity of others. If no one left food or drink out for him he would starve.

It was while Jesus was in one of the towns of Galilee that this leper saw him (5:12). **'He fell with his face to the ground and begged him, "Lord, if you are willing, you can make me clean"'** (5:12). The man in all his desperation approached Jesus. He was not ashamed to beg from the Lord. He believed that Jesus could meet his need. The only question in his mind was, 'Will Jesus be willing to make me clean?'

So when Jesus saw the faith and the humility of the leper he reached out his hand and touched him. It is interesting to notice that Jesus had to reach out. The man was so humble that he kept himself at a distance from the Lord. But no one who desires the Saviour's blessing is so far away that he is beyond the Lord's reach. The sister of Corrie Ten Boom said, when she was in the horrible concentration camp of Ravensbruck, 'There is no pit so deep that he is not deeper still.'

Despite this man's leprosy Jesus was willing to touch him. It had probably been many years since anyone had touched this poor man. Does this mean that Jesus broke the Mosaic law? I think not. It is God's law, and it must be obeyed. Jesus reached out to touch the leper, but by the time his hand reached him I believe the man had already been cleansed of his defilement. Dr Campbell Morgan says, 'He did not touch the leper, he touched a cleansed man. Word and work synchronized. As soon as the "I will" was across the lips of Jesus, his cleansing power had operated... He touched him to show that he was clean.'[2] Luke puts it like this: Jesus said, **'"I am willing ... be clean!" And immediately the leprosy left him'** (5:13).

After the healing, Jesus told the cleansed leper to go and show himself to the priests. This was what was required by the law (see Lev. 14:2-32). But that was not the only reason Jesus sent him to the priests. If he did as Jesus told him he would be enabled to go back into society and take his rightful place once more.

Then Jesus told the man, **'Don't tell anyone'** (5:11). Presumably this was because Jesus did not want the people to start proclaiming him as the Messiah. But Jesus *was* the Messiah, the long-awaited deliverer who had been sent from heaven to set his people free. Why did he not want this to be known at that time? It was because he did not want people to start proclaiming him as the Christ; they had a wrong idea of the task of the Messiah. They saw him merely in human, political terms. They were looking for a Messiah who would be their deliverer in the sense that he would drive out the Romans from their shores. They were looking for an earthly ruler, who would again set up the kingdom of Judah — like King David of old. But Jesus was to say, 'My kingdom is not of this world' (John 18:36).

The cleansed leper went to the priests, but he did not keep his mouth shut. I am sure he tried to do what Jesus had said, but we can imagine what people would have said: 'How have you become clean?' The story would seep out quite quickly.

Luke tells us that **'The news ... spread all the more, so that crowds of people came to hear him and to be healed of their sicknesses'** (5:15). Who can blame these people? I am sure I would have done the same thing if I had a dreadful disease; I would go to see this wonder-worker. Certainly if I had been the man who had been cleansed I do not think I would have been able to keep quiet about it. I would have been so excited I would not be able to refrain from telling everyone I met.

How strange it is that crowds do not flock to hear of Jesus today! Everyone who is outside of Christ is in just as dire, filthy and dangerous a state as that leper. They are dead in trespasses and sins (Eph. 2:1). But Jesus is alive today; he is able and willing to help anyone who comes to him and seeks his healing power. They have but to say, 'Lord, if you are willing, you can make me clean.' It is then that Jesus will stretch out his loving hand and heal them of all their diseases. This may not happen in the sense of physical ailments; it may not be God's will to heal them at that time. However, it is always so in the spiritual sense.

Henry Twells wrote,

Thy touch has still its ancient power
No word from thee can fruitless fall;
Hear, in this solemn evening hour,
And in thy mercy heal us all.[3]

We then read that Jesus was so busy that he had to get alone with God in prayer. The more active he was, the more he needed to withdraw to a lonely place to pray. This is a sensible thing for anyone to do. With all the stress of modern life, each of us needs to spend time on our own, and with God, relaxing. However, it is not just that it is a sensible thing to do; it is a strengthening thing to do as well. How often do we each withdraw from everyone and everything in order to pray to our Father? It is the secret of a successful Christian life to spend much time alone with the Lord. It is the secret of a prosperous church that much of its programme is given over to prayer.

A paralysed man

When Jesus healed this man he had an audience. **'Pharisees and teachers of the law'** were watching (5:17). These were the religious experts of the day. The Pharisees were the group which called themselves 'the separated ones'. They considered themselves to be vastly superior to others. They regarded themselves as more holy than ordinary Jews. There were also teachers of the law, or scribes, watching. These were the ones who considered that they knew everything about the law. They would be able to tell whether things were being done in accordance with the teaching of the Hebrew Bible and Jewish tradition. Luke says that they came **'from every village of Galilee and from Judea and** [even] **Jerusalem'** (5:17).

We read of them that they **'were sitting there'**. They had obviously heard about Jesus and they had come to see and hear him for themselves. Had they come to rejoice in the wonders of God's power working through him? Had they come so that they could rejoice because people were being healed from their sicknesses? No. They had come to judge. They 'were sitting there'. However, despite their judgemental attitude, **'The power of the Lord was present for [Jesus] to heal the sick.'**

This is the scene: Jesus and these religious leaders were all gathered in a house. Apparently the Lord was busy healing those who came to him with various illnesses. Then there was a slight disturbance. Some men —Mark tells us that there were four of them (Mark 2:3) — carried a paralysed man on a mat, a kind of stretcher. They had tried to take him into the house through the door because they wanted to lay him before Jesus so that he could heal him. However, they had a problem. They could not get in because of the large crowds around the doorway. But they were not put off by this. They took their friend up onto the flat roof of the house and made a hole in it. This sounds drastic to us but holes in those roofs could easily be repaired. They were only made of clay and sticks, and, in any case, no rain fell during the whole of the dry season. And they **'lowered [the paralysed man] on his mat through the tiles into the middle of the crowd, right in front of Jesus'** (5:19). This must have astounded the crowd, but when Jesus saw the faith of these determined people he did something about it. He rewarded their zeal. He saw how they all (including the paralysed man) were certain that Jesus could heal and he commended them for their faith in him.

Then Jesus said something very remarkable. He said to the man, **'Friend, your sins are forgiven'** (5:20). This man had been brought to Jesus so that he could be made to walk again. He did not come to have his sins forgiven. He, and the religious people, knew that only God could forgive sins. He must, therefore, have been astounded that Jesus pronounced his sins forgiven.

Why did Jesus forgive his sins? He did this because he knew that sin is the root cause of all the world's ills. He knew that sin forms a barrier to God's blessing. Yet this was the statement which caused so much trouble. The Old Testament plainly declared that only God can forgive sins. Even the Messiah (according to rabbinic thinking) could not forgive sins. But Jesus declared the man's sins forgiven; and they were. These haughty religious people did not rejoice in the man's healing; they murmured about the claims that Jesus was making for himself.

We do not know whether this man's illness was caused by his sin. In John 9:3 Jesus makes it clear that illness is not always caused by sin. However, what matters is that the man's sins were cleansed, and we should accept that as a true occurrence.

While all this was going on, **'The Pharisees and the teachers of the law began thinking to themselves, "Who is this fellow who speaks blasphemy?"'** (5:21). Jesus did not guess what they were thinking; he knew. 'We can keep nothing secret from Christ,' says the saintly Bishop Ryle.[4] He saw everything. 'Nothing in all creation is hidden from God's sight. Everything is uncovered and laid bare before the eyes of him to whom we must give account' (Heb. 4:13).

But the Lord said, **'Why are you thinking these things in your hearts? Which is easier to say, "Your sins are forgiven," or to say, "Get up and walk?"'** Obviously it is easier to say, 'Your sins are forgiven,' because people cannot disprove that. But for someone like this man to get up and walk is an act which requires a miracle. Then Jesus said, **'But that you may know that the Son of Man has authority on earth to forgive sins...'** (5:24).

Jesus called himself the Son of Man as an alternative to using 'the Messiah'. The Son of Man is spoken of in Daniel 7:13. There he is the one who is to come in great power and glory at the end times. But

Jesus uses the phrase some eighty times concerning himself. He wanted to show that he is identified with man and that he is the link between man and God.

Jesus did not finish his sentence. **'He said to the paralysed man, "I tell you, get up, take your mat and go home." Immediately he stood up in front of them, took what he had been lying on and went home praising God'** (5:24-25).When once his sins were forgiven his limbs were freed too. As a result of this miracle everyone declared, **'We have seen remarkable things today'** (5:26).

The man could walk again. 'In Hebrew "walking" is a standard metaphor for a man's way of life and behaviour (see Ephesians 4:17).'[5] When Christ comes into our lives we are given the power and the desire to 'walk in newness of life' (Rom. 6:4). There is nothing which Christ cannot do today to heal any of us from whatever sickness or trouble we are experiencing. He may not cure us from our physical affliction, but he will certainly heal our spiritual ailments. He is, after all, the Great Physician.

From the old to the new (5:27-39)

In these thirteen verses at the end of Luke 5, Jesus is dealing with the need for all things to become new.

Levi was called to follow Jesus

Levi, the tax collector, was also called Matthew (see Matt. 9:9). There was nothing wrong with the job itself, but many people despised those who collected taxes. In the days of Jesus tax collectors were seen as those who collaborated with the enemy. They collected money on behalf of the Romans. One of their tasks was to collect the Poll Tax. William Barclay, writing in 1975, said that 'The Poll Tax was something which all men from 14 to 65, and all women from 12 to 65, had to pay simply for the privilege of existing.'[6]

But this and other forms of tax led to abuse by the tax collectors. This is how the system worked: they were the ones who decided how much tax each individual should pay. They agreed to hand over to the authorities a certain sum from their district, but the Romans left it to each collector to work out how he collected it. Because these foreign conquerors were not interested in fairness, the system laid itself open to much misappropriation. In fact each time tax collectors are mentioned in the Gospels the question of the abuse of the system is raised.

But Levi would not only be regarded as a collaborator with the enemy and a cheat; he would have been thought of as a sinner. He, like prostitutes and thieves, would have been an outcast from all religious society. Levi would have been used to being shunned by all respectable citizens. So it must have been absolutely amazing for him to see Jesus approaching such an outcast and to hear him say, **'Follow me.'**

Much to the amazement of everyone, Levi obeyed the call of Jesus and his obedience was complete. **'Levi got up, left everything and followed him'** (5:28). He obeyed without question. He did not raise any objections. He did not say, 'Let me first go and bury my father' (cf. 9:59). Neither did he say, 'First let me go back and say goodbye to my family' (cf. 9:61). 'He got up, left everything and followed him.'

Levi understood the implications of his actions. If the fishermen (in 5:11) had afterwards discovered that following Jesus did not work out, they could have returned to their former occupations without too much difficulty, but Levi could not. If he discovered that he could not continue with his discipleship of the Saviour there was no way that he would be allowed to return to his tax-collecting. He knew that once he 'left everything and followed [Jesus]' (5:28) that would be the end of his career as a civil servant. There would be no going back to his old way of life. Yet despite all of this, Levi left everything behind him and followed the Lord.

I know a mother who said to her daughter, 'I don't mind you becoming a Christian, but don't let it rule your life.' To really follow Jesus does mean that we let him rule our lives. It means that the whole of our old way of thinking and behaviour has to be left behind and we need to become new men and women who are under Christ's control.

Following his commitment to Jesus, Levi made a great public display of his decision by holding a huge banquet for the Lord, at his house. He left everything connected with his former life behind him, but that did not mean that he turned his back upon his former associates. He invited many of his friends to feast with his new Lord. The result was that **'A large crowd of tax collectors and others**

were eating with them' (5:29). Levi wanted to share his happiness with his former colleagues and acquaintances.

Concerning this kind of witness Bishop Ryle says, 'There is no grace in the man who cares nothing about the salvation of his fellow men... The soul that has been truly called of God will earnestly desire that others may experience the same calling. A converted man will not wish to go to heaven alone.'[7] J. John, a present-day evangelist, puts it even more bluntly when he writes in a prayer letter, 'I cannot believe in the salvation of anyone who does not strive for the salvation of his neighbour.'

Objections raised

When Levi was converted some people objected. Whenever anyone makes a public stand for Christ, there is always opposition. This happens after someone has witnessed to his faith in baptism. It happens when a school child becomes a Christian and starts to tell his or her school friends about the difference Christ has made. It happens when anyone turns his back on his old way of life and finds joy in following the Lord. Satan uses all kinds of tricks to turn such people aside from Christ. He gets someone, perhaps a very close friend, to whisper to them, 'Don't let it rule your life.'

'The Pharisees and the teachers of the law who belonged to their sect complained' to the disciples of Jesus (5:30). They did not go straight to the Lord. They tried to undermine the faith of his followers. Satan always attacks the weakest people first. He tries to discredit the Lord in the eyes of new Christians.

The questions asked by the religious leaders concerned the character of Jesus. If Jesus was such a holy person why was he mixing with ungodly people? 'The Rabbis taught that it was forbidden for the learned to recline at table in the company of the ... rabble, the disreputable ones.'[8] These religious people were casting doubt upon the actions, and therefore on the person of Jesus. They were saying, in effect, 'The Son of Man would not enter into a covenant relationship with sinners.' To eat at the same table as someone meant that a covenant existed between the two parties. We can see that illustrated when Joseph ate at a separate table from his brothers when they visited him in Egypt (Gen. 43:32).

In regard to their questions, Jesus himself took over and answered them. He said, **'It is not the healthy who need a doctor,**

but the sick. I have not come to call the righteous, but sinners to
repentance'(5:32). He was saying that those who considered
themselves righteous would not seek cleansing from sin. The self-
righteous have no place in Christ's kingdom. Jesus came for those
who had seen the awfulness of their lives without God and had
admitted their sin, and confessed it. Those were the ones whom
Jesus came to save.

He was saying also that sinners are the people who need help. It
is not the person who is perfectly healthy in every way who goes to
see his doctor. It is those who are sick. Jesus acknowledged the
Pharisees' assessment of the people at the feast. He said, in effect,
'I know they are sinners.' Dr Campbell Morgan imagines Jesus
replying like this: '[I do this] because sinners are the very people I
want to reach, and I want to reach them because they are sinners,
because the malady of sin saturates them. I am here as the great
Physician to deal with that very malady.'[9]

Did the explanation which Jesus gave silence them? No. Having
failed on that point, they tried another tack. They said (directly to
Jesus this time), **'John's disciples often fast and pray, and so do
the disciples of the Pharisees, but yours go on eating and
drinking'** (5:33). They criticized the disciples of Jesus. They said
John's disciples fasted. But in saying this they forgot that John had
a different task from Jesus. John's was a much more solemn ministry
than the message which Jesus came to bring. In any case, John may
have been shut up in prison by this time, so it was perfectly natural
that his disciples should be fasting in sorrow because he had been
taken away from them.

Jesus answered this criticism by saying, **'Can you make the
guests of the bridegroom fast while he is with them?'**(5:34) He
meant, 'What is wrong with being happy?' It was the religious
people who laid down the rules about so much fasting. The law of
Moses only prescribed one day a year for solemnity and fasting.
That was the Day of Atonement, a day when everyone spent all day
in the synagogue lamenting their sins. But the Pharisees fasted every
Monday and every Thursday and they wanted to impose their views
on the disciples of Jesus. In addition the Pharisees prayed three or
four times every day even though it was not commanded in the Old
Testament. Jesus was not saying that they should not pray as often
as this; his concern was that they should not demand that others
follow their pattern of prayer.

In effect, Jesus was saying, 'These are all man-made rules.' And then he quickly added, 'There will be a time for fasting.' He likened himself to a bridegroom at a week-long wedding feast. Naturally everyone is happy during a wedding. **'But,' said Jesus, 'the time will come when the bridegroom will be taken from them; in those days they will fast'**(5:35).

The phrase which Jesus used, 'taken away', is a very strong one. It was fulfilled when Jesus was cruelly arrested and put to death. By using this figure Jesus, for the first time, refers to his death. I wonder if the disciples remembered these words of the Lord when, after his (the Bridegroom's) crucifixion, they all did fast in sorrow.

A parable

Jesus explains his mission to them by using a parable. This is in two parts. Both speak about new and old things. The first talks about putting a new patch on an old garment. Jesus asked, 'What is the point in sewing an unshrunk piece of new cloth in the hole on an old piece of material?' Everyone knew that the new piece of cloth would not be suitable. It would soon shrink and leave the stitches around it showing. Warren Wiersbe comments on this: 'Jesus did not come to patch up the old religion of Judaism by sewing his new teaching upon it.'[10] He came to fulfil the old religion by dying on the cross and creating a new and certain way for man to reach God. The old could never take anyone to heaven but Christ can. He has opened up 'a new and living way' for his people.

In the second part of the parable Jesus talks about the folly of putting new (unfermented) wine into old wineskins. These containers were whole goatskins which had been turned inside out and sewn together, in order to make a leather bottle. As the new wine matured, it increased in volume. This meant that it had to be put into a new wineskin because that would expand as the wine fermented. But if new wine was put into an old wineskin there would soon be trouble. The old wineskin would be hard and brittle and would have already expanded to its fullest extent. Any new wine put into such a skin would make it enlarge so much that it would split and all the wine would be lost.

In giving this illustration Jesus showed his concern about those who said, 'The old is better.' Maybe that may be the case with wine (I have no knowledge of such things), but it is not so with religion.

Jesus said, 'The old must go. I have come to bring a new way.'

Is it not amazing that so many people cling on to the old ways, which can bring no real blessing? Jesus said, 'Leave the old and cling to the new.' In another place he said, 'I am that new way; the only way to God' (see John 6:35-40). He wants his people to leave their old ways and follow him. He then promises to give them a new and much more satisfying and fulfilling life.

Campbell Morgan, commenting on this section, says it is 'a satirical condemnation of these men'. It was as though Jesus was saying to them, 'You are satisfied with this old; you have been drinking the old, and you are drunk; and you are saying, "We like the old best!" That,' writes Dr Morgan, 'is why they crucified him!'[11]

6.
The Master Teacher at work

Please read Luke 6

Sabbath observance (6:1-11)

When I was a boy Sunday was a rather miserable day. It was a day when I was not allowed to go out to play with the other children, I was not allowed to listen to the radio (there was no television when I was very young) and I had to wear my Sunday best clothes. Sunday was a day of prohibitions. But is that what the Bible meant when it said, 'Remember the Sabbath day by keeping it holy'? (Exod. 20:8-11).

Orthodox Jews today still do no work from sundown on Friday evening to sundown on Saturday evening. Any electricity used in a Jewish home has to be on a time-switch, because operating a switch is work. No work of any kind is done on the Sabbath; keeping the Sabbath holy is an important part of the Jewish religion.

By the time of Jesus the religious leaders had worked out many rules to ensure that the Sabbath was kept correctly. They were sticklers for the letter of the law. They were just like Mrs Proudie, wife of the Bishop of Barchester, and the Reverend Obadiah Slope: their 'hobby' was observing the Sabbath.[1] The Pharisees were very particular about Sabbath observance (the fourth Commandment) but they had little concern for keeping the tenth Commandment. 'They were notorious for covetousness (see Luke 16:14).'[2]

In this chapter Luke shows how Jesus took the Old Testament law and amplified it. Nowhere does the Lord say that God's Word has been superseded by his own teaching, but everywhere he shows

how the tradition of the Jewish teachers had fallen far short of what
God intended. Jesus said, 'The Sabbath was made for man, not man
for the Sabbath' (Mark 2:27). He meant that God never intended that
the Sabbath should be an intolerable burden, rather it should be a
blessing for a man. 'It should be for his spiritual, mental and physical
restoration.'[3]

Jesus in a cornfield

**'One Sabbath Jesus was going through the cornfields, and his
disciples began to pick some ears of corn, rub them in their
hands and eat the grain'** (6:1). This was not stealing. Deuteronomy 23:25 tells us that this kind of thing was perfectly in order.
Anyone could do it to satisfy his hunger. It was only a theft if
someone picked a farmer's grapes and put them in a basket, or
started cutting down standing corn with a sickle (Deut. 23:24-25).

While the disciples of Jesus were rubbing the ears of corn in their
hands a group of people appeared, and we are not surprised to learn
that they were Pharisees! These visitors said, **'Why are you doing
what is unlawful on the Sabbath?'** In attacking what the disciples
of Jesus were doing, they were implying that Jesus was wrong in
letting them do it.

The Great Synagogue (a great council) held many years before,
had devised a formula to interpret the phrase: 'You shall not do any
work.'[4] This test consisted of thirty-nine provisions. Among these
rules for the Sabbath were included reaping and threshing; both of
these were designated as 'work'. So they concluded that the disciples had picked some corn (that was reaping, they said), and they had
rubbed it in their hands (that, they decided, was threshing). Furthermore they had thrown away the husks (that was described as
winnowing) and then they had eaten the grain (therefore this meant
that they had prepared food). No wonder the Pharisees were cross;
they had spotted 'four distinct breaches of the Sabbath in one
mouthful!'[5]

However, Jesus had an answer to their complaint. He referred
them to one of their favourite ancestors. He said, **'Have you never
read what David did when he and his companions were
hungry?'** (6:3). Notice how he said, 'Have you never read?' Fancy
asking them that! 'These men were fighters for the law, these men
knew all about the law; these men boasted themselves in their

knowledge of their Old Testament Scriptures. These men could tell how many letters there were in the Pentateuch, where the middle letter was, they were careful about the yod and tittle.'[6]

Of course they had read the story of David eating the consecrated bread, as recorded in 1 Samuel 21. They also knew that only priests could eat the old loaves of bread when they were replaced in the Holy Place (Exod. 25:30; Lev. 24:5-9). David was not a priest, but he was God's appointed leader of the people, and he was hungry. It was David's hunger which qualified him to eat the consecrated bread. Jesus was concerned about the Sabbath meeting man's needs, not their man-made traditions. The Pharisees did not dare suggest that their revered and respected forebear, King David, broke God's law. This is why Jesus added, **'The Son of Man is Lord of the Sabbath.'** The Sabbath was not designed to harm man, but to nourish him. Jesus is saying that the Son of Man (the Messiah, the Son of David) is the one who also reigns supremely over the Sabbath and every ceremony connected with this holy day.

Jesus in the synagogue

'On another Sabbath [Jesus] went into the synagogue and was teaching' (6:6). It was probably the synagogue at Capernaum where Jesus went and taught on that Sabbath. **'And a man was there whose right hand was shrivelled'** (6:6). Dr Luke emphasizes that it was his right hand which was incapacitated. When we consider how much we use our right hands (unless we are left-handed) we can imagine how many things this man was prevented from doing.

But he was not the only one in the synagogue that day; the Pharisees and the teachers of the law were there also. Luke tells us that they **'were looking for a reason to accuse Jesus, so they watched him closely to see if he would heal on the Sabbath'** (6:7). They were not concerned about the state of the man; they may even have arranged for him to be there. They were looking at Jesus. They knew that Jesus never turned away anyone who came to him for help and they wanted to see if he would heal the man on the Sabbath day. Their own man-made rules and regulations were much more important to them than the needs of this disabled man.

'But Jesus knew what they were thinking' (6:8). He always knows everyone's innermost thoughts. He sees the real motives for all actions. He has eyes 'like blazing fire' (Rev. 1:14). He can see deep down into souls. And he **'said to the man with the shrivelled hand, "Get up and stand in front of everyone"'** (6:8). The man obeyed Jesus. **'He got up and stood there.'** Jesus wanted everyone to see what he was going to do.

The Lord then turned to the crowd and said, **'I ask you, which is lawful on the Sabbath: to do good or to do evil, to save life or to destroy it?'** (6:9). Had the Sabbath day been given to them in order to put restrictions on the people and be a burden to them? Or was it to be a blessing to them? It was obviously the latter. The rabbis did not object to healing being done on the Sabbath if there was any danger to life. Even their own man-made rules said, 'Wherever there is doubt whether life is in danger this overrides the Sabbath.'[7]

Therefore, Jesus puts this challenge to them: 'What happens to this man if I do not heal him?' He is implying, surely, that it must be sinful to leave him in his pitiable condition while there is the opportunity of healing him. In fact Jesus, who knew what they were thinking, must have meant, 'Are you trying to destroy life?' The target of the Pharisees was not the man with the shrivelled hand, but Jesus himself. Geldenhuys says, 'What is indeed unlawful on the Sabbath is to attempt to slay an innocent person, as the Pharisees and Scribes were engaged in doing by watching Jesus with murderous intent.'[8]

Jesus waited for his critics to answer him, but no answer came. So **'He looked round at them all'** (6:10). But still no one spoke up. Then he said to the man, **'Stretch out your hand.'** That certainly concentrated everybody's attention on the man's useless, shrivelled hand. It was as though he were saying to the people, 'Look at this poor hand. Here am I with the ability and desire to heal and to make it whole again. Do you think that it is God's will to keep this man waiting one more day — just because this is the Sabbath?' David Gooding says, 'God in his great compassion had instituted the Sabbath so that men's hands might rest and regain strength for further work, not so that it might prolong their disability to do any work at all. Christ, who in his compassion had stretched out his own hand and touched the leper (5:13), now bade this man stretch out his own hand, and healed him.'[9]

Luke tells us that the man **'did so, and his hand was completely restored'** (6:10). What did the people do then? Normally there would have been excitement and joyful thanksgiving at Jesus performing a healing miracle. But on this occasion, The Pharisees and teachers of the law **'were furious and began to discuss with one another what they might do to Jesus'** (6:11). With this statement Luke leaves the story. It is the first hint that we have in this Gospel that Jesus' life was in danger.

The implications for us

We must beware of letting our traditions override the clear teaching of God's Word. And we must remember God's teaching concerning the Sabbath day. He has never abolished that command to keep the Sabbath day holy, and to refrain from our daily work. Saturday is the seventh day, the Sabbath day which is kept free from work by strict Jews, but the early Christian church changed the day of rest from the seventh to the first day, which is called the Lord's Day. The Lord's Day is the day of resurrection. That is why every Sunday should be an Easter Day for us. Campbell Morgan says that man was created on the sixth day of creation. This means that man's first full day on earth was the Sabbath, the day on which God rested from all his labours. That is why we keep the first day of the week as the new 'Sabbath'.

While every day should be holy and dedicated to the Lord's honour, we all need one day's rest in seven. This, after all, is the divine order of things. I once heard Enoch Powell say in a radio programme, when he was a very busy Member of Parliament, that at midnight on a Saturday evening he stopped doing any of his normal weekday work, and however urgent it was, he never looked at it again until after midnight on Sunday evening. He added that he did not do this so much for religious reasons; rather it was common sense and it worked. He was much more refreshed for the new week if he had enjoyed a completely free Sunday.

The Lord's Day should be dedicated to the worship of God and fellowship with his people. Jesus went into the synagogue on the Sabbath day, and so should we delight to be in church with God's people. This means that we should prepare for the Lord's Day on Saturday evening. Late-night parties on Saturday night should be 'out' for those who wish to honour the Lord.

When Jesus said, 'The Sabbath was made for man' (Mark 2:27) he did not mean that the Sabbath was made for man to do what he liked on it. He meant that the Sabbath was given to benefit man. It was not designed for shopping, painting garden fences or catching up with the work which had not been finished during the week. The Sabbath is designed to provide a day in which the believer can have a complete break from all the routine of the workaday week.

The twelve apostles (6:12-16)

Jesus had a very important task to perform. So what did he do? He prayed about it; but how different was his prayer-time to ours! He went out to a mountainside (6:12). He knew that certain people were determined to stop his work (6:11), but that did not prevent him from proceeding and appointing others to help him and carry on after he had gone. He got away from all the worries and cares of this life, and went somewhere where he could be alone.

If we are trying to study, we do not want interruptions from other people. If we are reading a difficult section in a textbook and making notes on it, nothing distracts us more than for someone to ask us something which could easily have waited until later. If our thoughts are interrupted then, not only will we feel all churned up inside, but it will take us precious time to get our minds back to what we were thinking about before.

Jesus wanted to be alone with his Father. When we were younger we may have valued spending time alone with our fathers. Some earthly fathers fail their children, but God, the perfect, ideal Father, never does that. Therefore, Jesus wanted to spend as much time as possible consulting and communing with him.

Although Jesus is God in human form, in his humanity he needed to spend time with his Father. If we had the same overwhelming desire to often get alone with God, we would be much more sure of what God wanted us to do, and we would be men and women who are far more consecrated to God and the work of the gospel.

We have many examples of Jesus wishing to be alone with his Father. In Luke 5:16 we read that 'Jesus often withdrew to lonely places and prayed.' In 9:28 Luke tells us that Jesus 'took Peter, John and James with him and went up onto a mountain to pray'. In Luke 11:1 we find that 'One day Jesus was praying in a certain place ... [and] one of his disciples said to him, "Lord, teach us to pray, just as John taught his disciples."' And we know that, on the Mount of Olives, just before Jesus was arrested, 'He withdrew about a stone's throw beyond [his disciples], knelt down and prayed' (22:41).

How Jesus prayed

He spent the night praying to God (6:12). He did not say, 'I'm tired. I've been busy all day. I have a lot on my mind.' In fact it was because he had such important work to do that he prayed; and that prayer lasted all night. Dr Sangster said, 'If you are too busy to pray, then you are too busy.'[10] Richard Cecil commented, 'The Christian will find his parentheses for prayer even in the busiest hours.'[11]

Jesus spent all night praying to God. He did not spend the time worrying. This is what we do when we have a problem. Jesus took his concerns to his Father. He knew that he had to choose certain people to carry on his work when the time came for him to leave this earth. Prayer is not just talking to God. Prayer is being in that frame of mind where we are able to listen to what God has to say to us.

What did Jesus do at the end of his prayer?

He chose twelve disciples. A disciple is a follower who is also a learner. Jesus had attracted very many disciples as he ministered in Galilee and Luke tells us that **'When morning came [Jesus] called his disciples to him and chose twelve of them, whom he also designated apostles'** (6:13). This means that they were chosen by Jesus not merely to learn from being his companions; they were to pass on the Lord's teaching to others. An apostle is one who is sent with a special message.

Who were the twelve whom he chose? We can easily name some. There were Peter, James and John, and there was Peter's brother, Andrew. Then there was Matthew, who is sometimes called Levi. And, of course, there was Judas Iscariot, the one who became a traitor (6:16). Jesus chose these special disciples to be with him, to learn from him and, later on, to continue with the work of the building up the church. There are four separate lists in the New Testament: here, in Matthew 10:2-4; Mark 3:16-19 and in Acts 1:13. Each list starts with Peter (or his other name, Simon), and they all end with Judas Iscariot (except Acts, which lists only the first eleven and refers to a time after the death of Judas).

Some of these disciples wrote, or contributed to, books in the New Testament. Matthew and John wrote Gospels and Peter wrote two epistles and probably supplied much of the material for Mark's Gospel. As for the others, we know little about them. Andrew was someone who kept in the background, but we do read of him bringing people to Jesus, including his own brother (see John 1:41). The only other one of whom everyone has heard is Judas. He betrayed Jesus, and then hanged himself. Why did Jesus choose Judas? He was the only one who came from Judea. He was the one who kept the money and begrudged it being wasted. And, eventually, he betrayed his master for thirty pieces of silver. We do not know why Jesus chose Judas, but we can say this, the Lord knew exactly what he was doing; and we should never query his actions.

It is significant that there were twelve disciples. Twelve was a very meaningful number for Jews. There were twelve tribes of Israel; this is because Jacob had twelve sons. Jesus was establishing a new Israel, and these twelve men were his own apostles sent out to do this work. The new Israel would be 'built on the foundation of the apostles and prophets, with Christ Jesus himself as the chief cornerstone' (Eph. 2:20). The apostles' doctrine was that which Jesus was to teach to these twelve men; it was to be foundational of everything in the kingdom of God. In symbolic form John tells us that the heavenly city of God has 'twelve foundations, and on them were the names of the twelve apostles' (Rev. 21:14).

However, these twelve were all very different from each other. None was famous in the land. There were no university scholars among them, except Paul, who came later, and was added to the apostles. There were some businessmen. Some were tradesmen. Some we know nothing about at all. But we do know that they had very different temperaments. Peter was very impetuous, and somewhat unreliable; he even denied that he knew Jesus at the time of his arrest. Some were prone to quick tempers; John and James were possibly called 'sons of thunder' for that reason. One was an underground revolutionary who wanted to see the Romans driven out and the kingdom of Judah set up again as it had been under King David. But many were so ordinary and so quiet that we know nothing about them.However, we do know that Jesus prayed for them in his high-priestly prayer. John records it in his Gospel (John 17:9). He tells us that Jesus prayed, 'I pray for them. I am not praying for the world, but for those you have given me, for they are yours.'

God calls ordinary people to do special tasks. He called a Northamptonshire cobbler, William Carey, to start the modern missionary movement. He called little Gladys Aylward to take the gospel to China in the 1930s. And he has called countless people who have remained unknown, to work quietly for him in his kingdom.

God uses different temperaments to perform his work. It would not do if we were all placid and calm. Nothing new would ever be attempted. It would not be good if we were all workers and there were no visionaries. It would not be helpful if everyone was to the fore, in the limelight, all of the time. There would be nobody in the background quietly getting on with the work. God calls all sorts and conditions of men and women to serve him in his kingdom.

God's blueprint for blessing (6:17-26)

The Lord went down from the mountain, where he had been praying, and he stood on a level place (6:17). Some people say that this passage in Luke is not the sermon which Jesus delivered on the mount (as recorded in Matthew chapters 5-7). But Jesus could still have been on the mountain. He could have just come down a little way to where there was a level place on the side of the mountain. However, it does not really matter whether that was the same occasion or a later one. Jesus must have often repeated the same teaching.

The Lord took the twelve with him, and they were to remain with him during the rest of his public ministry. His message, in the Beatitudes, or 'Blessings', was primarily addressed to the wider circle of his disciples in the hearing of a much larger number of people **'from all over Judea, from Jerusalem, and from the coast of Tyre and Sidon'** (6:17).

What had attracted all these people? Why had they travelled such long distances (from the south and from the north-west)? They had come **'to hear [Jesus] and to be healed of their diseases'** (6:18). Wherever there is some spectacular happening, the crowds will begin to gather. Luke tells us that everyone **'tried to touch him, because power was coming from him and healing them all'** (6:19). Jesus did not disappoint them. The Lord performed many miracles that day, but he wanted to do more for the people than give them temporary blessings. He wanted to turn the whole of their idea of blessing on its head. He wanted them to stop thinking of temporary benefits, and to start thinking of eternal blessings.

Warren Wiersbe says, 'To most Jewish people, the word "blessing" evoked images of a long life, wealth, a large family, a full barn, and defeated enemies. God's covenant with Israel did include such material and physical blessings (Deut. 28; Job 1:1-12 and Prov. 3:1-10), for this was how God taught and disciplined them. After all, they were "little children" in the faith, and we teach children by means of rewards and punishments. With the coming of Jesus, Israel's childhood period ended, and the people had to mature in their understanding of God's ways (Gal. 4:1-6).'[12]

The blessings promised

Jesus said, **'Blessed are you who are poor, for yours is the kingdom of God'** (6:20). We should care for the poor; God has a special concern for those who have little, or nothing, of this world's goods. But that is not what the Lord was teaching here. He was speaking about those who are poor in spirit (see Matt. 5:3). He means that people who are not spiritually proud or self-sufficient are especially blessed by God. His teaching is always against those who boast of their own goodness and righteousness. 'Jesus is saying that there is special blessing in store for those who do not trust in themselves.'[13] The poor in spirit are those who lean only upon God, because they acknowledge that there is no goodness or cleverness within them at all. Those whose hope is in God alone will receive the blessing of God.

Then he said, **'Blessed are you who are hungry now, for you will be satisfied'** (6:21). Again Jesus is not talking about those who are starving because they have no physical food, but about those who are starving spiritually. Matthew puts it like this: 'Blessed are those who hunger and thirst for righteousness, for they will be filled' (Matt. 5:6). The picture here is of someone who is fainting for lack of food and drink. He or she is in a desperate way. But the sustenence these people are seeking is spiritual food and drink. Jesus is saying that those who long after God will find him and be satisfied. The psalmist draws a picture of a thirsty deer when he says, 'As the deer pants for streams of water, so my soul pants for you, O God' (Ps. 42:1).

The Lord went on to say, **'Blessed are you who weep now, for you will laugh'** (6:21). Jesus is always concerned about those who are sorrowful. He himself wept at the grave of Lazarus (John 11:35); he has great sympathy and compassion for all who mourn.

Throughout the Scriptures the teaching is always that those who weep in the work of the Lord will gain joy at the end (see Ps. 30:5). Matthew says, 'Blessed are those who mourn, for they will be comforted' (Matt. 5:4). The mourning spoken of here is mourning for sin. We sometimes mourn because of the awful cruelty of people around us. Occasionally we cry out to God because of the greed and injustice of those selfish people in the world who care little for the pain which they cause others. But how often do we cry out to God because of the sin, godlessness, greed and selfishness which lie within our own hearts?

Jesus says, 'Blessed are you who weep now [because of your sin], for you will laugh.' Before any of us can know the joy of the Lord, we have to know the vileness of our own hearts. Before we can experience the joy of God's salvation, we have to acknowledge and confess our sin before him. No one can become a Christian until he or she is first of all made aware of the evil which is within his or her own heart.

Believers in the Lord Jesus Christ also need to be aware of their unworthiness. There is a sense in which we all ought to feel poor in spirit. Dr Martyn Lloyd-Jones was one of the most powerful preachers of this century, but listen to part of a letter he wrote to a friend in 1943: 'When I read the New Testament and think of the things that have been experienced by God's people in the past I feel ashamed. It is all there for us in all its wealth and fulness and yet my life seems so weak and poor and barren. I have undergone considerable searching of spirit along that very line during the past few months. I praise God for the fact that I have had a clearer view than ever before of my own unworthiness and utter inadequacy. But still I rely over-much on myself. How foolish does sin makes us. What utter fools we are.'[14]

Lastly Jesus says, **'Blessed are you when men hate you, when they exclude you and insult you and reject your name as evil, because of the Son of Man. Rejoice in that day and leap for joy, because great is your reward in heaven. For that is how their fathers treated the prophets'** (6:22-23). Persecution does not sound a very blessed thing, yet Jesus said, 'You will be persecuted because of righteousness' (Matt. 5:10). Those who work in our church coffee bar find that they are sometimes insulted and hated, just because they are Christians. Jesus was saying, 'If you do the right thing you will suffer for it.'

Christians today are beginning to find that there are certain occupations in which they cannot in all conscience work. Christian doctors and nurses are having to say, 'I will not take part in abortions.' It seems that the time will one day come when they will find themselves out of work if they continue with that stance. There is increasing pressure upon Christians to conform to the demands of their employers rather than stand by the teaching of the Bible. One of our local councillors told me that he considered it a shop manager's right to dismiss any of his staff who say they will not work on a Sunday. Every week we discover that Christians are increasingly being 'marginalized' because of their beliefs. What does Jesus say about this? He said, 'Rejoice in that day and leap for joy.'

How can we rejoice when we are being persecuted for righteousness? We can rejoice because we know that we are receiving the same kind of treatment as true prophets of God have received down through the ages — and especially the Lord Jesus Christ himself. We should be glad to follow the Lord's example. 'When they hurled their insults at him, he did not retaliate; when he suffered, he made no threats. Instead, he entrusted himself to him who judges justly' (1 Peter 2:23).

The woes predicted

Matthew makes no mention of these four woes; not in this form, anyway. They are the exact opposite of the four blessings. The poor are blessed because they will receive their reward in the kingdom of God (6:20). But the rich have already received their comfort (6:24). Paul Getty was the richest man of his time, yet, judging by appearances, it seems that he gained very little satisfaction through all his money.

In 1990 my family took a boat trip from the Greek island of Levkas to sail around the island of Scopious. This is a small island which was owned by Aristotle Onassis. He was a very wealthy Greek shipowner. But both he and his daughter are now dead and the whole place now belongs to his young granddaughter. He had tremendous wealth but where did it get him? All he has to show for it is a grand mausoleum on a beautiful, peaceful island that no one is allowed to visit!

If we were to have everything we wanted, we might be tempted to believe that we had no need of God. But think of the rich person who does not know Christ when he comes to the end of his days. He will only inherit hell. But what a contrast with those who are hungry and thirsty for righteousness! They will, eventually, be satisfied (6:21). On the other hand, those who are well-fed now will one day go hungry (6:25). They have obtained their satisfaction now. They care little for the afterlife. The sad thing for them is that they will end up with nothing, because they had their reward while they were on earth.

In a similar way, Jesus says that those who weep now will eventually be filled with laughter (6:21), but those who laugh now will mourn and weep in everlasting punishment because of their sins (6:25). 'Let us eat, drink and be merry, for tomorrow we die,' is a very sad saying.

Then Jesus says that those who are hated by men will be loved by God (6: 22-23), but those who are proud because all men speak well of them will be dismayed at the end; they will prove to be false prophets (6:26).

Jesus says, 'Woe to all of those who think of themselves first, rather than seeking first the kingdom of God and his righteousness' (Matt. 6:33). Jesus uttered this teaching 2,000 years ago but it is still so relevant today. Woe to any who ignore it, or who think they know better than Jesus!

Love your enemies (6:27-38)

Whatever did the Jews of Jesus' day think when the Lord said, 'Love your enemies'? The Jews then were very conscious of their enemies. They lived in an occupied country. Rome demanded obedience from them and made them pay taxes for the privilege of having an army of occupation wandering all over their country. Rome was hated, and so were all who served her.

The importance of love

Popular songs have always been full of love. However, the kind of love that Jesus was speaking of in this passage was not that earthly, sexual *(eros)* love. He was speaking of *agape* love, which is 'love even of the unworthy, love which is not drawn out by merit in the beloved but which proceeds from the fact that the lover chooses to be a loving person'.[15]

Jesus had been addressing his disciples, but now he turns to the whole crowd. **'I tell you who hear me: Love your enemies, do good to those who hate you, bless those who curse you, pray for those who ill-treat you'** (6:27). He was reminding them all of their law in Leviticus 19:18 where it said, 'Love your neighbour.'

Loving one's neighbour is quite easy — if your neighbours are nice and helpful and understanding. But how can anyone like their neighbours if they are continually holding noisy parties which carry on well into the early hours of the morning, or they are the kind of people who leave great piles of rubbish around, causing the value of everyone's property to drop considerably? But God's Word does not say that we should like our neighbours. Jesus said that we should love them. He said that we should do positive good to those who hate us, and we should bless those who curse us. We should also pray for those who ill-treat us. The Lord was talking about the attitude which we should have towards our fellow men and women.

The Jews interpreted the teaching of Leviticus 19:18 in their own way. It says, 'Do not seek revenge or bear a grudge against one of your people, but love your neighbour as yourself. I am the Lord.' The Jews knew this command but they decided who their neighbours were. For them neighbours were certainly not the kind of people whom they regarded as sinners — prostitutes, tax collectors and Samaritans, to name but a few. The Jews loved their neighbours all right, but, for them, their neighbours were the ones who thought and acted as they did.

However, Jesus was clearly teaching that our neighbours are all those who are around us. He was to bring out this teaching much more powerfully when he told the parable of the Good Samaritan in Luke 10:25-37. The Lord also highlighted the fact that the Jews had only taken part of Leviticus 19:18 and had bent it to suit their own ends. The Old Testament law declared that Jews should treat their neighbours as they would like to be treated themselves. God sealed his statement with, 'I am the Lord.' In other words, God was saying to the Jews, 'Do as I command you, if you regard me as your Lord.'

Then Jesus gave some illustrations of what he meant. He said, **'Give to everyone who asks you.'** The Lord was talking about those who ask because they are so poor. It was part of Jewish custom to give alms to those in need. Therefore Jesus was saying that we should all share our substance with those who are less well off than ourselves. 'This is how you should show love,' is what he was really saying to them.

Next Jesus said something very startling. He said, **'If anyone takes what belongs to you, do not demand it back'** (6:30). On the face of it Jesus appears to be saying that we should give everything away, and end up without even the clothes we are wearing. But that is obviously not the case. 'It is characteristic of Hebrew style that a startling statement is made in order to shake people, to arouse them from their lethargy.'[16] The Lord was talking about our attitude to others. **'If someone** [forcibly] **takes your cloak, do not stop him from taking your tunic'** (6:29). He means that we must not be angry with such people, but show them love, even though they are treating us badly.

The Golden Rule is: **'Do to others as you would have them do to you.'** This kind of saying would not have been entirely new to the Jews; it was widespread in the world of those days. But when others used it, they always put it in a negative form. Jewish writers, Plato, Aristotle, Socrates and Seneca all said something similar. And, even in the Hindu *Mahabharata*, Confucius says, 'Do nothing to your neighbour which afterwards you would not have your neighbour do to you.'[17]

But Jesus takes this negative saying and puts it in a positive form. No one else seems to have done that. He says, 'Do to others as you would have them do to you.' Leon Morris writes, 'It is not enough that his followers refrain from acts they would not like done to them. They must be active in well doing.'[18] Jesus means, 'Do not treat your neighbour with anything less than genuine love.'

Spot the differences

The Lord went on to explain how we can attempt to put this teaching into practice. Firstly, love must be unconditional. That is what God's love for us is like. We do not deserve the least of all his mercies, yet he saw us when we 'were dead in [our] transgressions and sins' (Eph. 2:1) and he stooped down and saved us. When we consider God's love in carrying out this tremendous act we realize that we should love others just as God has shown his love to us.

Secondly, we should love others without expecting anything in return. **'If you love those who love you, what credit is that to you?'** asks Jesus (6:32). Even those whom the Jews called 'sinners' loved those who loved them, did good to those who did good to them and lent money to those whom they trusted to repay them in full without delay or argument. If we only behave as the people of the world behave, what difference is there between Christians and non-Christians?

Thirdly, we should treat everyone in a godly way. We should love our enemies; and that takes a great deal of grace. We should have a positive attitude of love towards those who dislike us because Christ commands us to love our enemies.

But Jesus takes this teaching even further. He said that we should lend to our enemies without expecting anything back. That takes a great deal of courage because the worldly person only loves his friends. He only does good to those who are in a position to do good to him in return. He only lends to those who are in a position to pay him back, or those who own a house which can be possessed and sold off to pay the exorbitant rate of interest he has charged on the loan.

Fourthly, Jesus said, 'Love, do good and lend to all those who are in need.' If we do this then our reward will be great. The Lord is teaching us that our goal should not be to gain treasure on earth. We should be those who are storing up for ourselves 'treasures in heaven, where moth and rust do not destroy, and where thieves do not break in and steal'. He added, 'Where your treasure is, there your heart will be also' (Matt. 6:19).

If you behave like this, says Jesus, **'You will be sons of the Most High'** (6:35). The Lord is not teaching that unselfish love makes people God's sons. Rather it is those who love unselfishly who show that they are sons; they do this by their actions and their attitudes.

The fifth thing to notice in this section is that Jesus adds this wonderful command: **'Be merciful, just as your Father is merciful'** (6:36). In Matthew's account of this Jesus said, 'Be perfect ... as your heavenly Father is perfect' (Matt. 5:48). We are called upon to be imitators of God. God's people should seek to live as he lives. We see God in Jesus Christ. That is why he says, 'your Father' on this occasion and not 'my Father'. Peter explains it like this: he tells us that we should be holy as God is holy (1 Peter 1:16).

Some practical lessons

Jesus said, **'Do not judge, and you will not be judged'** (6:37). He did not mean that we should have no discernment, rather that we should not have a judgemental attitude towards other people, especially those we do not like. Then he amplifies this by saying, **'Do not condemn, and you will not be condemned'** (6:37). We have so much to be grateful for that we should not be those who carry out witch-hunts against others. We need to take note of what Paul said in Romans 12:17-21.

Lastly, in this section, Jesus says, **'Give, and it will be given to you'** (6:38). He has said, 'Don't judge' and 'Don't condemn'. Now he gives a positive command: 'Give.' This is what we should do to everyone. He does not say, 'sell,' or 'charge for'. He says, 'give', and he means, 'Give as God has given to you.' We should give of our love, our time and our substance. We should give to everyone who is in need and we should give secretly, not making a show of our good works (otherwise we will have our reward on earth by gaining men's praise). We should give generously. We should not be reluctant, keeping our hand on the scales in order to weigh them down. We should not make it seem that we are giving more than we really are. We should give **'a good measure, pressed down, shaken together and running over'**. In those days people wore their robes with a belt around their waists. Above the belt was a loose piece of their garment; this could be used to form a pocket for carrying things in. Jesus said that when Christians give they should pour their gift into the lap of the recipient, and keep pouring until the lap is filled right up.

Jesus taught that God will bless us by using the same standard which we use to give to others. This does not mean that God will accept anyone just because he is generous to the poor. Jesus was not speaking to unbelievers; he was teaching those who belonged to him. He has already taught that he accepts only those who have wept because of their sin (6:21). Those who confess their sin and repent of it will come to faith in Christ. It is those who are truly his who will be blessed abundantly. But those who are generous with the wealth that God has given to them will be blessed with a similar measure. Paul taught, 'Remember this: Whoever sows sparingly will also reap sparingly, and whoever sows generously will also reap generously. Each man should give what he has decided in his heart to give, not reluctantly or under compulsion, for God loves a cheerful giver' (2 Cor. 9:6-7).

Actions speak louder than words (6:39-49)

Blindness is an awful affliction. The world of a blind person is a dark one. But it is not only the physically blind who are handicapped; many religious leaders also have difficulty with their sight. Jesus told a parable about this. He asked, **'Can a blind man lead a blind man?'** (6:39). The obvious answer is, 'No. They will both fall into a pit.' In those days many of the roads and paths of Palestine were full of ruts and holes; they had many dangerous places in them. It would have been difficult to have avoided falling down while walking along such roads. Everyone would have had to have walked carefully, making sure where they put their feet. It would have been quite easy to have fallen into a large hole, or pit. Obviously, people who lived near such dangerous pathways would have needed to have clear sight, and they would have needed to watch all the time where they were going.

In telling this parable Jesus was pointing out that blind people need others to guide them; and those who undertake this work must have good eyesight themselves. They need to be clear-sighted in order to lead the blind person into safe and right paths. The dangers are obvious, and the guide needs to be able to see all the hazards in the pathway. A guide who is blind himself is worse than useless; he is a liability. He is likely to lead another blind person into danger and even to death.

Who was Jesus talking about when he spoke of blind leaders? He was clearly referring to the Jewish religious teachers and the Pharisees. The Lord meant that those who claimed to be religious leaders were blind themselves to the truth of God. They were unable to see the truth because they were not serving God; they were serving themselves. One of the other Gospels records the words of Jesus when he spoke about the Pharisees. He said, 'They are blind guides' (Matt. 15:14).

Today there are many who claim to be servants of God, yet they are blind to the reality of new life in Christ. Satan has blinded their minds so that they do not realize that there is a judgement day coming in which Jesus will come as Judge and make a great division between those who know him as their Saviour and Lord (Jesus calls these 'sheep') and those who have rejected his gospel (he calls them 'goats' — see Matt. 25:31-46).

How awful it is to listen to the preaching of a man who may be clothed in gorgeous priestly robes, but who does not speak the truth of God! David Gooding says, 'It is a pathetic thing to listen to a man who has no personal experience of Christ's salvation trying to instruct others like himself in the gospel of Christ.'[19]

Jesus then amplified this teaching by saying, **'A student is not above his teacher, but everyone who is fully trained will be like his teacher'** (6:40). How did a student learn in those days? There were no libraries, or audio and video tapes, to learn from. He had to find a rabbi, and learn from him. This meant that no one could learn more than his teacher knew himself. So everyone needed to have the best teacher he could find. And when a student had finished his training he would then have known as much as his teacher; he would be like him.

When Jesus spoke this parable he was condemning the Pharisees and scribes. He was saying that they were not only blind themselves, but they were useless teachers who led their students astray. For us this means that the most important teacher anyone can have is the Lord Jesus Christ. Those who truly learn from him will be like him and show forth his glory as they go about their daily lives.

Then Jesus took his teaching further. He turned to someone who, while not totally blind, had defective eyesight. The Lord goes on to paint a picture of an 'eye-doctor with a plank in his eye, performing surgery on a patient with a speck in his eye!'[20]

What did Jesus mean by saying this? It is not possible for anyone to have something as large as a plank in his eye. Of course, the Lord was using the figure of speech called 'hyperbole'. The *Concise Oxford Dictionary* defines 'hyperbole' as 'exaggerated statement not meant to be taken literally'. We can illustrate this for those who understand the game of cricket. We can say that a bowler missed the stumps 'by a mile'. When we use this phrase no one thinks that we mean the bowler was 1,760 yards out in his aim. Everyone knows that we mean he was some way off the target — perhaps as much as ten inches! Or someone measuring cloth may say that she has cut off 'miles too much'. She is using hyperbole. She means that she has cut off much more than she needs.

So when Jesus spoke about a plank in someone's eye, he meant that it is hypocritical for anyone to go around criticizing others for their faults, 'while remaining blind to [his] own considerable fault'.[21] Once again Jesus was teaching about the evil of having a wrong attitude towards others. The message for us is that we must see that we are living a godly life before we go around castigating others for their misdeeds. And when we do have to point out the faults of others, we should do it in a caring and loving manner.

The way to tell what kind of persons we are is by the fruit we produce in our lives. He means by 'fruit' the effects that our actions have upon our surroundings. Jesus said, **'No good tree bears bad fruit, nor does a bad tree bear good fruit. Each tree is recognized by its own fruit. People do not pick figs from thorn-bushes, or grapes from briers. The good man brings good things out of the good stored up in his heart, and the evil man brings evil things out of the evil stored up in his heart. For out of the overflow of his heart his mouth speaks'** (6: 43-45).

Jesus meant that if a person has evil stored up in his heart then sooner or later that evil will be revealed; it will come out of his mouth, or it will be seen through his actions. Those who truly belong to the Lord, who have had their sins forgiven and have been given a new heart, will speak to the glory of God. Those who still belong to the Evil One have never been to the foot of the cross for Christ's forgiveness. They will discover that, however much they try to avoid it, they will sooner or later speak evil things (either by the words they use or by the way in which they live their lives). Just as it is in the nature of an apple tree only to produce apples, so it is in the nature of a person who does not know God (even if he or she is a kind person who is full of good works) only to engage in activities which will not bring glory to God. The way in which someone lives his life will declare loudly whether his testimony is true or not.

Lives built without a foundation

There are many religious people who build their lives without true foundations. Jesus illustrates this last saying by telling the story of the wise and foolish builders. This parable comes both at the end of the Sermon on the Mount (Matt. 7:24-29) and the Sermon on the Plain (Luke 6:46-49). Jesus rounds off his teaching by talking about the importance of having good foundations for our lives. The Lord put this illustration in this place so that he could sum up his teaching. He wanted his hearers to go home thinking about these things. We need to make sure that we grasp the teaching firmly in our minds; it is foundational to our understanding of our Christian living.

The parable concerns two people. Both of them hear what Jesus said. Jesus said that the wise man hears his words (6:47) and the foolish man also hears his words (6:49). Both call him, **'Lord, Lord'** (6:46). They mean by stating this, 'You are the one who owns my allegiance.' And so that there can be no misunderstanding, they repeat the word to emphasize that they mean it: 'Lord, Lord.'

Both of them built a house which was beautiful to look at. We presume that they had all the latest gadgets in them. Both of these houses had to face up to a great storm beating upon them. Perhaps both of these men built their houses in the same area, even near to each other.

What is Jesus teaching by this story? He is saying that all of us are building houses. We are all building as we all live our lives. All of us have different faces (even twins), different fingerprints and different personalities. Yet there is something which is common to all of us. All of our lives are built upon some kind of foundation. The thing to ask ourselves is, 'On what kind of foundation am I building my life?'

The first man (the wise man) **'dug down deep and laid the foundation on rock'**. He was not afraid of hard work. He may not have liked digging down deeply but he did it because he knew that it was necessary to build his life on a good strong foundation. The wise man is aware of the dangers of life. He does not just live for today. He thinks of the stresses and strains which will be thrust upon his life. He knows that one day there is a judgement coming upon all of us. The wise man in the story made plans for the future so that when the floods did come they could not shake his house. Why was that? It was **'because it was well built'** (6:48).

How did the foolish man build his house? He built his house upon the ground. He did not bother about a foundation. His attitude was slovenly. He said, 'Let us eat, drink and be merry for tomorrow we die.' He cared nothing about the future. He was lazy.

So many people do not think about what will happen in the day of testing. They think only of today. They say, 'There is plenty of time to think of eternity.' But, of course, **'The moment the torrent struck that house, it collapsed and its destruction was complete'**

(6:49). In the end there was nothing left to show for all of the foolish man's effort. The house of his life was completely destroyed because he did not take the trouble to lay a solid foundation for his life.

What does this story teach us about our lives today? It shows us the difference a foundation makes. The difference between having a foundation for our lives and not having a foundation depends on our attitude to Jesus and his words. The wise man not only said, 'Lord, Lord,' but he heard the words of Jesus and put them into practice (6:47). He took notice of Jesus. He had a right attitude towards Jesus, and he did what he said.

The foolish man also said, 'Lord, Lord'. He heard the words of Jesus but he did not put them into practice (6:49). There are many instances of people like this in Scripture. The Lord said to Ezekiel, 'My people come to you, as they usually do, and sit before you to listen to your words, but they do not put them into practice. With their mouths they express devotion, but their hearts are greedy for unjust gain' (Ezek. 33:31). James also writes about the same attitude. He says, 'Do not merely listen to the word, and so deceive yourselves. Do what it says' (James 1:22).

We need to remind ourselves that the storms of life will come to us all. The torrents which struck the two houses battered them both with the same force. There is no one who has a smooth pathway throughout the whole of his life without times of sadness and testing. These things can either make us or break us. Malcolm Muggeridge, the journalist and broadcaster who died in 1990, said that the richest times in his life were those when pain and suffering came. The person who has no solid foundation for his life will not survive in times of severe testing. If we have failed to listen to Jesus, and put his words into practice we too shall fail.

It is not sufficient just to say, 'Lord, Lord,' and think that a profession of religion is the same thing as a possession of Christ. The Lord Jesus Christ will say to us, **'Why do you call me "Lord, Lord", and do not do what I say?'** (6:46). We need to have a personal acquaintance with the Lord if we are going to stand up under severe testing. We need to be those who do what he says.

The storms of life will come upon us all, and the storm of death will as well. But it is not only the storms of life which will batter us, there is the storm of the Judgement Day too. None of us will escape that awesome day. 'We will all stand before God's judgement seat'

(Rom. 14:10). How will we fare then? Will the 'house' of our lives collapse because it did not have Christ as its foundation? The thing that will be asked of each of us then is, 'On whom did you build your life?' John Newton sums it all so well:

'What think you of Christ?' is the test,
To try both your state and your scheme;
You cannot be right in the rest,
Unless you think rightly of him.
As Jesus appears in your view,
As he is beloved or not,
So he is disposed to you,
And mercy or wrath are your lot.[22]

7.
People whose lives the Lord touched

Please read Luke 7

A soldier's faith and a widow's need (7:1-17)

In the opening verses of chapter 7 Luke relates two stories to show what Jesus taught about the conditions on which a person can be saved. In the first incident we see Jesus restoring to full life a slave who **'was sick and about to die'** (7:2), and in the second story we see Jesus actually bringing back to life **'a dead person'** (7:12), one who was in the process of being carried outside of the town to be buried.

The centurion's slave

The centurion was probably a Roman soldier who had a hundred men under him; that is why he was called a centurion. He belonged to that group which was the backbone of the Roman army; they were ruthless and hard fighting men. They were the kind of people who would inspire courage and confidence in the soldiers under their command. But, strangely enough, almost everywhere in the New Testament where we read about centurions they are spoken of favourably (see Luke 23:47; Acts 10:1-2; 22:26; 23:17,23; 24:23; 27:1,43).

This centurion was obviously a Gentile and was probably serving in the forces of 'King' Herod Antipas, the ruler of Galilee, but he was so different from the average Roman officer. It seems that he treated his slaves well (7:2) and he was upset because this slave was near to death. The slave was 'paralysed and in terrible suffering' (Matt. 8:6). Someone had told the soldier about Jesus so he sent someone to ask the Lord to come to his house and heal his servant (7:3).

First of all the centurion asked some Jewish elders to bring Jesus to the boy (7:3). He had evidently won their confidence. Most Romans despised the Jews and regarded their religion as contempt-ible because only one God was worshipped. But somehow there had been established a trust and understanding between this centurion and the Jewish religious leaders.

The elders came to Jesus greatly commending this particular solider. They pleaded earnestly, **'This man deserves to have you do this, because he loves our nation and has built our synagogue'** (7:4-5). We do not know whether he had started to worship God himself, but he had certainly paid a considerable sum out of his own pocket to have the synagogue built — possibly the one on the site of the ancient synagogue, the ruins of which tourists can see today.

The elders said, 'This man is worthy.' So Jesus went with them to the home of the centurion (7:6). However, when he got near to the house he received another communication from the soldier; this one was sent by friends. It was quite different from the one brought by the elders. Their estimation of the centurion had been, 'He is worthy.' But his own estimation of himself (brought by his friends) was, 'I am not worthy.'

As important as he was in Roman eyes, he said to Jesus, **'Lord, don't trouble yourself, for I do not deserve to have you come under my roof. That is why I did not even consider myself worthy to come to you. But say the word, and my servant will be healed. For I myself am a man under authority, with soldiers under me. I tell this one, "Go", and he goes; and that one "Come", and he comes. I say to my servant, "Do this", and he does it'** (7:6-8).

He respected the customs of the Jews. He knew that Jesus, a Jew, would not be allowed to enter the house of a Gentile, so he said, 'I do not deserve to have you come under my roof.' He was so humble that, rather than complaining about the injustice of Jewish customs, he accepted them and graciously put things the other way around by saying, 'I am not worthy for you to enter my house.' He grasped the point that it is the worthiness and authority of Jesus which matters more than any ability that men have. He says, 'I know what authority is; I am a Roman soldier, drilled for many years in the discipline of the army.' He could have said, 'I am in authority over a hundred men.' Instead he said, 'I myself am a man under authority.' Then he goes on to illustrate the point about the one in authority who has power to give orders which must be obeyed.

Therefore, he says, 'You only have to say the word, and my servant will be healed.' Luke tells us that, **'When Jesus heard this, he was amazed at him'** (7:9). Only on one previous occasion is it recorded that Jesus was amazed. That was at the unbelief of the people of Nazareth (Mark 6:6). But here, Jesus is amazed at the faith of this Gentile soldier. So he turned to the crowd and said, **'I tell you, I have not found such great faith even in Israel'** (7:9). **'Then the men who had been sent returned to the house and found the servant well'** (7:10).

It was not the great things that the centurion had done, or the fact that the elders had said, 'He is worthy', or the centurion's deep humility which brought about the miracle. It was the man's faith in Jesus which was the key to the whole thing. His good works showed his belief in God. His humility indicated his deep trust. Jesus acted when he saw his great faith. The Lord did not see the lad who was ill, nor, apparently, did he set eyes on the centurion himself, even though Matthew's account says that 'A centurion came to Jesus asking for help' (Matt. 8:5). How can this be explained? It seems that Matthew gives an abbreviated version of this story. He does not contradict what Luke wrote. Matthew obviously meant that the centurion said these things through the various groups of elders and friends who did come to Jesus.

The widow's need

Luke immediately follows this incident with a contrasting story. In the earlier story we learnt that the centurion had achieved much; he was a man of deep humility and he had a rich faith. But what do we know about this widow? Only that she lived in Nain, which was about six miles south-east of Nazareth. But this town and, indeed, this story, is only mentioned on this one occasion in the Scriptures. We know too that she had no husband, and was therefore poor. She had no job, because widows were unlikely to be able to obtain any work, and now tragedy had struck her. She no longer had a son. Her only means of livelihood had gone because this lad was her only son (7:12). Luke often points out touching aspects of a story like this. We shall see this again later on when we read the story of the raising from the dead of Jairus's child, where Luke tells us that she was his only daughter (8:42). Now, with the death of this widow's son, the family line had come to an end.

Luke puts this story at this point to show the other side of God's love. 'If you have many good works to your credit and good resources like the Centurion, or nothing at all like the widow, it makes no difference: for salvation is not of works, whether many or few, whether good or bad; it is by grace, through faith, it is the gift of God.'[1]

In this incident there are two processions. One was joyful, as it approached the town and was about to enter it with Jesus. They were glad because they had seen many great things which were happening in those days. But look at the other crowd. It was mournful. It consisted of a sad group of people who had come out from the town to bury the mortal remains of a poor widow's son. The mother, the chief mourner, was at the head of the column. Following next were men who were carrying the basket in which the dead body was lying. Also nearby would have been professional mourners. Leon Morris tells us that 'Even the poorest in Israel [had to] have not less than two flutes and one wailing woman.'[2] Behind this grieving group there came a large crowd of sympathizers; they wanted to be with this poor widow in her time of great need.

Sometimes the only thing that any of us can do to comfort bereaved persons is to be with them. They cannot cope with words, but our presence is a great comfort to them (see Ezek. 3:15). However, as comforting as the presence of friends can be, the greatest blessing that anyone can experience is to know that the Lord is with them in their sorrow. How often at funeral services do we hear the lovely words of King David, who said in his beautiful psalm,

'Even though I walk
    through the valley of the shadow of death,
I will fear no evil,
    for you are with me'

(Ps. 23:4).

What happened when the two crowds met up? Was there any resentment on the part of the mourners? I well remember in 1958 when my father, my sister and I stood in a wet, cold cemetery in Kent. As the minister said the words over my mother's coffin, the thing that I recall most clearly was the sound of children's happy voices wafting over the churchyard. It did not seem right to me, in my time of grief, that people should be enjoying themselves when I was so sad.

As the two crowds met we read, **'When the Lord saw...'** This is the first time Luke calls Jesus 'the Lord'. He went straight up to the woman and **'his heart went out to her'** (7:13). He was filled with compassion and said, **'Don't cry.'** This is what we too say in similar circumstances, but unlike us, Jesus had the power to do something which could bring joy into the sadness. He went up to the coffin and touched it.

Those carrying the body stood still as Jesus addressed the dead body: **'Young man, I say to you, get up!'** No sooner had Jesus spoken these words than the dead man sat up and began to talk. Some say that Jesus was so marvellous because he had perceived that the lad had just fainted and the Lord woken him up.[3] What nonsense! This action of Jesus was not merely to detect a fluke of dying nerves; it was a great miracle borne out of tender love for a broken-hearted woman. We can sense the compassion of the Lord as Luke tells us that Jesus gave the lad back to his mother (7:15).

Naturally the effect of this miracle upon the people was tremendous. They had read of incidents like this in the Old Testament. Elijah and Elisha had brought back to life the sons of widows, but nothing like that had happened since those days. But in the Gospels we have records of Jesus bringing back three people to life from the dead. There was this young man, there was the daughter of Jairus and there was the brother of Mary and Martha. No wonder the people were filled with awe, and praised God! They gave the glory where it belonged, and they said of Jesus, **'A great prophet has appeared among us... God has come to help his people'** (7:16). After such an event it is not surprising that the news about Jesus spread throughout the countryside.

Some lessons for us

When we consider these two miracles we can see that God is sovereign. We do not read that the widow of Nain had faith in Jesus.

She may well not have known who he was. But God is in control of all things and he heals whom he will. He chooses to heal some, and he allows others to remain ill. This is not because he wishes to reward some and punish others. It is because he chooses to act, or not to act, as it pleases him. He knows what is best for his people. Some people he heals and some he gives grace to witness for him through their pain and suffering. Either way the Lord is glorified.

We should remember that 'Spiritually speaking, each of us is in one of these two crowds [that were outside of the town of Nain]. If we have trusted Christ we are going to the city [of heaven]; (Heb. 11:10,13-16; 12:22). If we are "dead in sin" we are already in the cemetery and under the condemnation of God (Eph. 2:1-3; John 3:36). We need to trust in Jesus Christ and be raised from the dead (Eph. 2:4-10; John 5:24).'[4]

How Jesus dealt with doubt (7:18-35)

When things go wrong it is not unusual for us to doubt that we are true Christians. Satan takes our circumstances and tempts us to unbelief. When this happens let us remember that doubt is not the same as unbelief. 'Doubt is a matter of the mind: we can't understand what God is doing and why he is doing it. Unbelief is a matter of the will: we refuse to believe God's Word and obey what he tells us to do. "Doubt is not always a sign that a man is wrong," said Oswald Chambers, "it may be a sign that he is thinking.'[5]

John had doubts

John the Baptist had been shut up in prison for about eighteen months. Imagine what an awful trial this must have been to a man like John, a man of the desert. The inactivity of imprisonment must have been a great burden to him. But he knew that he had to diminish so that Christ could become greater (John 3:30). Therefore, he surely saw his imprisonment as part of God's plan for his people. He knew that he would probably be executed for his outspokenness, but he realized that this did not put an end to the kingdom of heaven which he had been sent to proclaim (Matt. 3:1). He just longed to hear news that Jesus was continuing with the work which he had announced.

Because John had spoken of the imminence of judgement (3:9), he was no doubt patiently waiting to hear of the judgement of God falling upon the nation of Israel (rather like Jonah at the end of his work — Jonah 4:5). But what did John hear about the ministry of Jesus? He heard, not of a proclamation of judgement; but of a ministry of mercy. He, therefore, became uncertain of what was happening. So he sent two messengers to Jesus to ask, **'Are you the one who was to come, or should we expect someone else?'**(7:20). There is an important principle here. When we are perplexed we should take our burden directly to the Lord. We do not need to send two messengers. We can go straight to God via the throne of grace, by means of prayer.

Yet when the messengers came to Jesus, the Lord seemed to keep them waiting for an answer while he carried on with his healing work (7:21). It was not that Jesus was rude, or that he wanted to keep them waiting because he considered their question an impertinent one. He wanted them to observe what he was doing. He **'cured many who had diseases, sicknesses and evil spirits, and gave sight to many who were blind'** (7:21).

Then he said to the messengers, **'Go back and report to John what you have seen and heard: The blind receive sight, the lame walk, those who have leprosy are cured, the deaf hear, the dead are raised, and the good news is preached to the poor.'** These are the kind of things which Jesus read about from the scroll when he was in the synagogue at Nazareth (4:18). These wonderful things are prophesied in Isaiah 35:5-6 and Isaiah 61:1. However, Jesus puts them in reverse order.

John had heard about these healings. He may even have heard about the raising up from death of the son of the widow of Nain. Certainly Luke tells us that **'This news about Jesus spread throughout Judea** [which may have been where John was imprisoned] **and the surrounding country'** (7:17). But the greatest thing which Jesus says is left until last. He said, 'The good news is preached to the poor' (7:22). He meant by this that those who are poor in spirit (those who acknowledge that they are sinners) have the good news of salvation preached to them. In other words, John had preached one part of the message; he had concentrated upon the fact that the Messiah would come to judge sinners. Following the ministry of John, Jesus had come and enlarged upon John's preaching by preaching the gospel of God's mercy to those who repented of their sin, those who had faith in Christ.

Although John's message did contain a call to repentance, it was mainly concerned with judgement — that which will be carried out at the second coming of Christ. At the first coming of Jesus, as a baby at Bethlehem, he came to preach the good news of salvation to all, whoever they are. He preached to sinners who are in need of a Saviour. Then Jesus said, **'Blessed is the man who does not fall away on account of me'** (7:23). The Lord was conveying to John, 'You may not understand everything but you will be blessed if you cling on to me.' He was saying to all who would follow him, 'Listen to the message of those who have seen and heard what I am doing. I am God's anointed Son. Do not reject me if you want the blessing of God on your lives.'

The crowds questioned

Jesus then proceeded to ask the crowd what they went out to see concerning John the Baptist; the Lord was concerned with their sight. He knew the people's sight was defective; they could not see clearly; perhaps they could not see at all. He said, 'Did you see a reed shaken by the wind?' The answer was, 'No.' They saw a man who was as strong as an oak tree, someone who would never compromise his faith in order to please anyone. Next he said, 'Did you see a man dressed in fine clothes?' Again the answer was, 'No.' They saw John wearing 'clothing made of camel's hair, with a leather belt round his waist' (Mark 1:6). John could have dressed in beautiful clothes and lived in a fine palace, but he chose to turn his back upon the friendship of influential people and the enjoyment of wealth. Lastly, Jesus asked, 'Did you see a prophet?' This time the answer was, 'Yes.' Only the man they saw was more than a prophet: he was the prophet whose coming and work had been foretold 400 years before. Malachi had spoken the Word of God when he said, **'I will send my messenger ahead of you, who will prepare your way before you'** (7:27).

Jesus then went on to commend John the Baptist to them. He said, **'I tell you, among those born of women there is no one greater than John'** (7:28). John was great because God had caused him to be born into the world to prepare the nation to receive the Messiah. He was great because he carried out the work which God had called him to do, and he did it despite the opposition of men. He was great because he was prepared to suffer for his faith.

This message brought a division between the people: **'All the people, even the tax collectors, when they heard Jesus' words, acknowledged that God's way was right, because they had been baptized by John'** (7:29). The people had submitted to baptism. They had humbled themselves and confessed that they were sinners in need of cleansing. These people had acknowledged that God's ways were right.

'But', Luke tells us, **'the Pharisees and experts in the law rejected God's purpose for themselves, because they had not been baptized by John'** (7:30). How sad it is to read that these experts in the Scriptures rejected God's purpose for themselves! Leon Morris says, 'They were very good at understanding the minutiæ of the law without ever coming to grips with its essential message. They were concerned about the law of God but not about the will of God.'[6]

The people of the day

Jesus then turns his attention to the state of the people. He said, **'To what, then, can I compare the people of this generation? What are they like?'** He said that the people were like children. Children can be lovely, but they can also be sulky and difficult. What is more, they can be happy one minute and miserable the next. Jesus said the people of his day were childish. They were like children, playing in the market-place. some of whom wanted to play at weddings. This group said, 'We'll play the flute for you.' But when they did the others decided that they did not want to join in; they would not dance. Why did they not want to dance? It was because they wanted to play at funerals. They said, 'We'll sing a dirge.' But then the others, when they heard it, refused to cry. This kind of childish behaviour is very annoying because no one will agree to join in with what anyone else wants to play. All they can do is quarrel with one another.

The Lord said to the crowd, 'You complained about John the Baptist, and also about me.' John had turned his back on all the comforts of life. He lived in the desert. He did not eat bread or drink wine, so the people declared that **'He has a demon'** (7:33).

On the other hand, Jesus lived a normal village life, mixing with everyone. So the crowd said of him, **'Here is a glutton and a drunkard, a friend of tax collectors and "sinners"'** (7:34). We have already seen that it was considered to be a dreadful thing, in the eyes of the religious experts, to be a friend of 'tax collectors and "sinners".'

What answer did Jesus give to the charge about John and himself? He said, **'Wisdom is proved right by all her children'** (7:35). The *NIV Study Bible* notes explain this very clearly: 'In contrast to the rejection by foolish critics, spiritually wise persons could see that the ministries of both John and Jesus were godly, despite their differences.'[7]

A tale of two sinners (7:36-50)

This section is about two people. One was a very sinful woman; she had probably been a prostitute. The other was a very pious person; he was one of the special group of people called Pharisees.

One of these characters had just received the gift of spiritual sight. The other was totally blind. Jesus had dealt with the sin of one of them, but the other remained in the bondage of his iniquity. Yet despite all of these things, Jesus was interested in them both. This incident probably took place somewhere in Galilee, very likely in the town of Capernaum.

A Pharisee's house

This is another story which only occurs in Luke's Gospel, although there are similar stories in the other Gospels. Simon's house would have been a respectable one; Simon was a respectable man. He was a Pharisee, a supposedly holy person. 'Luke names them twenty-eight times in the course of his gospel, and every time they are seen in hostility to Jesus.'[8] Houses like Simon's would have had a very open aspect to them. This is how the woman could have wandered into it unnoticed.

I remember visiting a house in ancient Pompeii which was built on a very open-plan system. That house would have been erected not many years after the time of Christ. And, although it was in Italy, it was probably built in a similar style to Simon's house at Capernaum. Often in Greek villages our family has walked at night down to a taverna for our evening meal. In doing so we have passed many families eating their main meal of the day in the shade of their verandas. It is not uncommon for people to stop and chat with them while they are passing. People come and go all the time. In our Western world we think of a dining room as something which is private, a place which is reserved just for our family and our guests. But in the heat of the Middle East, and in the time of Jesus, anyone could, and did, wander through houses when people were having their meals.

On this particular occasion Simon, the Pharisee, invited Jesus to have dinner with him (7:36). This may have been mere curiosity, but I think not, because he did not extend to this visitor the usual common courtesies. In the heat of the day it was refreshing to receive a bowl of cool water and have a servant wash off the dust and sweat from sticky feet. After a hot summer's day, perhaps when we have been walking for long distances, we like to sit with our feet in a bowl of warm water. But Simon did not even offer Jesus water, let alone provide a servant to wash his feet. It was also customary to greet an honoured guest with a kiss — especially one who had been addressed with the title 'teacher', or rabbi (7:40). But Jesus did not receive any kiss. So in addressing Jesus as **'teacher'** Simon was not really sincere; it was almost a sarcastic use of the word. Neither did Jesus have oil poured on his head. This was also a sign of welcome; and it refreshed the most important part of the body — the head (see Ps. 23:5).

So we can only conclude that Simon invited Jesus into his house to try to trap him into saying or doing something which would give this Pharisee the ammunition he needed to 'prove' that Jesus was not a man of God. Jesus must have known what was in Simon's mind; he certainly knew what he was thinking according to verse 39. Why, then, did Jesus accept this invitation to dinner? I believe it was because he was interested in Simon. He knew that this Pharisee was blind to spiritual truth and he wanted to bring him to that point where he would acknowledge his sin and repent of it. This is why Jesus joined the others, in reclining at the table with them.

Several times we read about Jesus accepting invitations to meals. He also asked questions in order to bring people out. He even asked, on one occasion, for a woman to draw him some water (John 4:7). Yet often we are very reluctant to go where the ungodly assemble. We would feel ashamed if the people at our church knew that we were joining in with their activities. Our method is to invite the unconverted to a religious meeting! Jesus never did that. Instead he got alongside of them and drew them by the power of his words.

A woman enters

This woman had lived a sinful life. Everyone, and certainly Simon, knew who she was. It is very likely that she was a woman of the streets, a prostitute, and she came from the lowest dregs of society. Her house was probably on the other side of the town — the poorer side. Any person who willingly associated with her would have been suspect immediately. In our days often people in the public eye, notably religious people and politicians, have been forced to resign their office for consorting with women of ill repute.

The woman, whose name we do not know (but it was almost certainly not Mary Magdalene), had heard that Jesus was eating in the Pharisee's house. Knowing this she came to him. It must have cost her a great deal to have gone to Simon's house. She would have known of his reputation for high moral standards. She must have been aware that she would probably be driven away because people would assume that she had come for immoral purposes. However, that was not the case. She had come to see Jesus; she was so determined to meet him that she plucked up her courage and entered the house.

She came to show the Lord love which was real — not the kind of degrading 'love' which she had previously dispensed. But why did she want to show love to Jesus? It can only have been because a complete change had taken place in her life. She was no longer the person she had been. It seems that she had heard Jesus speak and, as a result, had been completely changed.

What was Jesus' reaction to her presence? We are told in verse 47, **'Her many sins have been forgiven.'** The Lord used the past tense in saying this. Perhaps it was only the previous day that she had been brought to repentance and faith in the Lord, but her sin was something which had already been dealt with. This is why Jesus said to her, **'Your faith has** [already] **saved you; go in peace'** (7:50).

Jesus was reclining at the table on his left arm, with his legs stretched out behind him; that was the custom. This explains why the woman stood behind the Lord. But what was she doing? She was weeping. She wept because of the great joy she had experienced since her sins had been washed away. She provided the water of her tears, when Simon had not bothered to make any available to Jesus. She let down her hair to wipe his feet. In those days no self-respecting Jewish woman would let down her hair in public, but she was so overcome with joyful emotion that she cared nothing for the conventions of the day. She only saw her Lord, and she wanted to show her love for him as she had shown it to no other man before.

Next she kissed his feet. She was too humble to kiss his head, so she showered kisses upon his feet; this was in place of the kisses which Simon had not placed upon his face. Finally, she poured perfume on his feet. This was not like the cheap olive oil which Simon would normally have poured on the head of his guests. The perfume used by the woman was a very expensive liquid. It was a perfumed ointment which she would have kept in an alabaster jar hung around her neck.

Mary of Bethany later on was to perform a similar act, just before the crucifixion of Jesus (John 12:3). By breaking the neck of the jar and pouring the perfume on him the woman showed very great love to her wonderful Lord and Saviour. This act of love showed her complete allegiance to Jesus because once opened, the thin neck of the bottle could not be stopped up again; it had to be broken. In pouring the oil on Jesus the woman would have had to give the whole contents of the jar to the Lord.

The astonishment of Simon

This act by the woman, and the acceptance of it by Jesus, was what Simon had been waiting for, because he had been hoping that Jesus would play into his hands. We read, **'He said to himself, "If this man were a prophet, he would know who is touching him and what kind of woman she is — that she is a sinner"'** (7:39). But Jesus did know who she was, and he knew what Simon was thinking as well. He turned to the Pharisee and said, **'Simon, I have something to tell you.' 'Tell me, teacher'**, he said (7:40). Can you hear the contempt in the voice of this religious man, as he says, 'teacher'?

Jesus told a story: **'Two men owed money to a certain money-lender. One owed him five hundred denarii, and the other fifty. Neither of them had the money to pay him back, so he cancelled the debts of both.'** Then Jesus questioned Simon directly. He said,

'Now which of them will love him more?' Then Simon replied, 'I suppose the one who had the bigger debt cancelled.'

He was a little grudging with his answer. Perhaps he saw that he was falling into a trap. We can imagine Jesus pausing before simply saying, 'You have judged correctly' (7:43). The meaning of the parable must have been obvious: the woman was like the man who owed 500 denarii. This was a very large sum, something like eighteen months' wages. A denarius was a coin worth about a day's wages. [9]

Simon certainly understood the meaning of the story. Jesus had explained that the woman had been forgiven her many sins (7:47) — 500 denarii's worth. That is why she was weeping; she was full of gratitude to the Lord. That is why she washed, kissed and anointed the feet of the Lord. But she did not do this in order to obtain forgiveness. She did it out of gratitude because of her sins which had already been forgiven her. Jesus said, 'Your faith in me has been the means of your salvation. You may now go in peace' (see 7:50).

However, the other guests began to say among themselves, 'Who is this who even forgives sins?' (7:49; cf. 5:21). Their folly was that they asked the wrong question. They were the ones who were blind. They could not see who Jesus really was. They did not understand that Jesus was God himself come to this earth in human form. They never asked, 'Who was it who owed the fifty denarii?' That was only a small debt in comparison to the woman's debt of 500 denarii. The sin which 50 denarii represented was only little in comparison with the sin of the woman, which was represented by 500 denarii, but it was still sin.

The sad thing about this story is that Simon and his friends thought that they were not sinners. They thought that because they were religious and respectable, they were pleasing God. But the awful thing is that no one who is unforgiven will ever reach heaven. We do not know whether Simon ever did repent of his sin, but we do know that all who reject Christ, all who refuse to weep because of their sin will, if that attitude keeps up to the end of their days, die without Christ and, therefore, without hope.

8.
Questions of faith

Please read Luke 8

Listen carefully (8:1-21)

Jesus often compared our physical senses to our spiritual ones. In the previous few chapters he has been dealing with blindness. Now the emphasis changes to hearing; the words 'hear' or 'listen' occur nine times in this passage. The Gospel of Mark tells us that Jesus said, 'Consider carefully what you hear' (4:24); and in this parallel passage we read, **'Consider carefully how you listen'** (8:18).

Crowds gathered

The crowds either wanted something for themselves, or they desired to bring their friends and relations to the Lord for healing. Or maybe they just gathered to receive some free entertainment. As the Lord had probably been active for over two years by now, it is not surprising that many people had heard of his work. However, Jesus not only carried out a healing ministry, he proclaimed **'the good news of the kingdom of God'** (8:1). In fact, from this point onwards, he concentrated upon his teaching work. He taught about the rule of God in the hearts and lives of all those who would become subjects of the kingdom of God. The only way in which people could enter that kingdom was through faith in himself. It is a spiritual kingdom; not an earthly one. It is something which is in operation now, but it is also something which will one day come about in very great power. We sing:

Jesus shall reign where'er the sun
Doth his successive journeys run:
His kingdom stretch from shore to shore,
Till moons shall wax and wane no more.[1]

'Also some women who had been cured of evil spirits and diseases' went with him (8:2). They had experienced the wonder-working power of Jesus in their own lives and they wanted to show their love and loyalty to the Lord. Mary Magdalene had almost certainly not been a wicked woman but she had been delivered from seven demons. She had probably been suffering from some kind of mental or physical affliction. She, like Joanna, the wife of Chuza (8:3), was to be present at the empty tomb on the first Easter Sunday. Joanna came from a well-to-do home. Her husband was the manager of Herod's household (the person in charge of all the financial affairs of the king). Another of the women was Susanna, who is mentioned nowhere else in the Bible, and in addition to these ladies there were also many other women with them (8:3).

These women were helping to support Jesus and the twelve **'out of their own means'** (8:3). Being women they were not allowed to preach, but they were able to supply the daily necessities of Jesus and his disciples. Jesus was not ashamed to accept charity — and from women! Most of us would rather give help to others than humble ourselves to accept it, but Jesus had a different attitude to giving and receiving. He knew what a privilege it is for humble people to be able to help others. One day I was visiting a lady who has to spend much of her time in a wheelchair. As I spoke to her she confided in me that when people come to see her they often assume that they have come to do something for her. They seldom realize that there are things that she can do for them if they would but be humble enough to receive them. Luke so often mentions the important part that women played in the work of the gospel. In fact there is no record in Scripture of any lady being an enemy of the Lord.

An important parable

Jesus told them the parable of the sower (8:5-8). This same parable is also found in Matthew 13:1-23 and Mark 4:1-20. Everyone would have known that farmers scattered their seed on the soil by hand, having first ploughed the soil to make ridges so that the seed could fall into the ground. However, the success of the seed depended upon the condition of the soil.

Some of the seed fell upon the hard pathway which ran through the fields. That seed did not germinate; it was trampled upon by the feet of passers-by and the birds ate it up. Some of the seed fell where there was only a thin covering of soil over rock, but because there was not sufficient soil and moisture the plants did not grow well enough to produce a crop. The seed sprouted up quickly, and then, just as rapidly, withered away. Some of the seed fell on ground which on the face of it looked all right, but there were weed seeds in it. These weed seeds grew up quickly, took up most of the available moisture, minerals, light and air, and therefore choked the wheat plantlets. But some seed fell on good ground. That seed grew and produced an excellent crop. Matthew and Mark say that some of it produced thirty seeds for each one that was planted, and some gave sixty seeds for each one. All three Gospels say that, of this which was sown on good ground, up to one hundred times as many seeds were produced from each one which was shown. Such an increase is unknown, even today. What Jesus was speaking about was even more powerful than the wheat seed. He was talking about the Word of God (see 8:11).

After Jesus had told this parable he called out, **'He who has ears to hear, let him hear'** (8:8). He wanted everyone to know that they could hear the message of God if only they had ears to listen. Jesus often pleaded for people to hear, understand and put into practice what he said. In addition to the nine times this command to hear is mentioned, Luke also repeats these words of Jesus in 14:35. And John takes it up in the last book in the Bible. He tells us that the Lord said, 'He who has an ear, let him hear what the Spirit says to the churches' (Rev. 2:7,11,29; 3:6,13,22).

Hearing the message of God is vital for each one of us, but we need to 'consider carefully how [we] listen' (8:18). Jesus quoted from Isaiah 6:9. On the face of it, it seems that he was saying that he used parables so that the people could not understand what he meant. But Jesus never deliberately tried to make the message of the gospel obscure, or difficult to understand. He was telling his disciples about secrets which had been hidden for generations because only those who follow Jesus can see and hear the message.

Jesus did not use parables so that people might not see and not understand. He used them so that those who have spiritual eyes and ears can grasp the message. Isaiah and Jesus are stating the truth that those who are not willing to receive the message of the kingdom will find the truth hidden from them.

Next Jesus went on to explain to his disciples (not to **'the others'** of verse 10) what this parable meant. He said that the seed is the Word of God — the message of the gospel. This message is what Jesus came to this earth to proclaim. It is the good news which all of God's servants proclaim today every time they preach the gospel of salvation, through grace alone.

There are only four kinds of hearers who listen to the message of Jesus. Each one needs to ask, 'What kind of hearer am I?' Our hearts, that means our spiritual natures, belong to one of four kinds when it comes to hearing the message of salvation.

Some people have hearts which are *hard*. They are just like the well-trodden paths of ancient Palestine. The message of God takes no root in them, and as soon as the message is given, Satan, like a bird, swoops down and takes it away. He is watching and waiting to snatch away the gospel message before it can take root in the hearts of those who are not willing to receive it.

Some people have hearts which are *shallow*. These are quick to respond to the message. They are easily driven to tears by the emotions aroused within them by the preaching of the cross. They are very quick to volunteer to dedicate their lives to following Jesus. Yet, when trouble comes into their lives their faith, such as it is, withers and dies. They fall away in the time of testing because they have never been firmly rooted in him in the first place.

Again, there are others who have hearts in which *the message of God has competition*. Just as soon as the good seed is sown, weeds quickly grow up and swamp the wholesome wheat. Likewise the worries, riches and pleasures of life take all nourishment away from the hearer, and he proves that he has never been born again at all.

But there are some people whose hearts are like good soil. They hear and retain the Word of God (that is, they think about it and make it their own), and they keep hold of it, come what may. It is people like these who go on to produce fruit for God's glory. We can see examples of good fruit in Romans 1:13; 15:25-28; Colossians 1:10; Galatians 5:22-23 and Hebrews 13:15.[2]

Light

Light spreads out, and darkness can never swamp it. If there was a power cut and you only had a small candle to give light, you would not hide the candle where it could not be seen, unless you wanted to cover up what you were doing. If you were in pitch darkness you would place the light in the highest position in the room so that its rays would shine out as far as possible.

Yet those who do not listen to the Word of God will never prosper. They do not let their 'light shine before men, that they may see [their] good deeds and praise [their] Father in heaven' (Matt. 5:16). In fact they have no light to give. They have been unwilling to hear the message of the cross and have never entered into the joy of sins forgiven and hope of heaven. They are blind to Christ and all that he stands for.

Jesus next said something which, on the face of it, seems very unjust. He said, **'Whoever has will be given more; whoever does not have, even what he thinks he has will be taken from him'** (8:18). Jesus is stating that salvation is free. The way to receive eternal life is to listen carefully to the message of the gospel and accept what Christ says. So, when Jesus said, 'Whoever has will be given more; whoever does not have, even what he thinks he has will be taken from him' (8:18) he means that 'The person who wants to understand God's message, and who listens to it sympathetically and reverently, will find his understanding increased.'[3] On the other hand, 'The man who thinks he has received the gospel, and keeps it hidden and never lets the facts be known, may find one of these days, when he comes to look for the reality of the gospel within him, that it is not in fact there — and never was.'[4]

The family of Jesus

Even the mother of Jesus and his brothers (or rather his younger half-brothers) were not able to get near to him because of the crowd (8:19). They had apparently come to tell him that he was overworking himself (see Mark 3:21). However, despite the large number of people around Jesus, someone got the message to the Lord that his family were outside waiting to see him. Then Jesus gave this strange reply: **'My mother and brothers are those who hear God's word and put it into practice'** (8:21). He did not mean that he cared nothing for his family. On the contrary, we know that he had great affection for them; while he was hanging on the cross he told John to look after his mother (John 19:25-27). He meant that all those who are true Christians are his family.

One day during my National Service in the army I was lying on my bunk reading my Bible. I discovered these words: 'Both the one who makes men holy [Jesus] and those who are made holy [God's people] are of the same family. So Jesus is not ashamed to call them brothers' (Heb. 2:11). I was so thrilled when I first read those words. It overwhelmed me to realize that not only was I a member of the family of God, but that Jesus was my brother. However, within a family there are not only privileges but responsibilities. This is what Jesus was speaking about in this passage. Living the Christian life today means that we must take care how we listen, and be careful what we listen to.

The power of Jesus (8:22-39)

By the time the Lord had finished teaching them, 'The disciples must have felt like postgraduate students in the School of Faith.'[5] Faith is always tested. Following all the teaching which the disciples received, Luke tells us about an incident which showed how Jesus taught them to trust him even with their lives.

A journey on the lake

Jesus said, **'Let's go over to the other side of the lake'** (8:22). Whenever Jesus proposes to do something it will certainly be completed. The disciples ought to have remembered this when they were scared out of their wits on the Sea of Galilee. When the Twelve got into a boat and set out there was obviously no sign that a dreadful storm would arise. But one came as unexpectedly and quickly as the storms of life can occur in our own experiences.

The storm that happened on that day was so bad that the boat was in great danger. Water began to be swept into it, and even these experienced fishermen saw that they were in a dangerous position, but there was one glimmer of hope for them. They had Jesus with them in the boat, and they knew that he could do miracles. The problem was that Jesus was utterly exhausted and had fallen asleep as they had sailed. (Even though Jesus is God himself, he is also perfectly human.) In fact Jesus was so tired that not only did the rocking of the boat not wake him up, but he even slept through all the roaring of the storm.

The only thing which did wake him was his disciples crying, **'Master, Master, we're going to drown'** (8:24). So **'He got up and rebuked the wind and the raging waters'** and, at his command, **'The storm subsided, and all was calm'** (8:24). One word from Jesus immediately brought about a great stillness and peace.

However, having rebuked the storm, he then turned and rebuked his disciples. He said to them, **'Where is your faith?'** (8:25). He meant, 'Didn't you realize that with me in the boat with you, you would be safe?' John Newton sums it up very beautifully in his hymn:

> Begone unbelief!
> My Saviour is near,
> And for my relief
> Will surely appear.
> By prayer let me wrestle,
> And he will perform;
> With Christ in the vessel,
> I smile at the storm.[6]

I believe they were afraid, not so much for themselves, but that Jesus would be killed before he could finish his work. They knew that he had more work to do and they wanted nothing to prevent the accomplishment of his great task.[7] Did they not realize that no one could harm him until his work was complete? He had said, 'Let's go over to the other side of the lake.' If that was his purpose, then nothing could prevent him from reaching his goal — not even a terrible storm (cf. 4:30). The psalmist, many years before, described such an event as this when he wrote,

> 'O Lord God Almighty, who is like you?
>   You are mighty, O Lord, and your faithfulness surrounds you.
> You rule over the surging sea;
>   when its waves mount up, you still them'

> (Ps. 89:8-9).

'In fear and amazement [the disciples] asked one another, "Who is this? He commands even the winds and the water, and they obey him"' (8:25). But their question was not answered at that point. They had to wait until the next incident to hear the right answer — and that was given by a demented man (see 8:28 and cf. 1:32; 4:34).

The value of a soul

When they resumed their sea crossing they came to the region of the Gerasenes. Matthew calls this 'the region of the Gadarenes' (Matt. 8:28). The Lord had gone all that distance just to deal with the needs of one person (cf.19:1-10). Luke tells us that as Jesus stepped ashore, he was met by a demon-possessed man from the town. The man had once lived in the town. He had once worn clothes and lived in a house; but now he was bereft of all of these things. Why? Because his behaviour had made him an outcast from society. His unsocial habits had caused the inhabitants of the town to put him in chains and mount a guard upon him. However, it seems that none of their efforts were of any use because we are told that many times he had broken his chains, and the demons which possessed him drove him into solitary places (8:29).

When this poor man saw Jesus, he reacted very violently. When evil comes face to face with the goodness and holiness of God there is a sharp conflict. This man **'cried out and fell at his feet, shouting at the top of his voice, "What do you want with me, Jesus, Son of the Most High God? I beg you, don't torture me!"'** (8:28). Why was the man in such a state? Jesus had commanded the spirit to come out of him. Many times it had seized him, and this was the reason why the man lived among the tombs, in a place where no one else would dare reside.

The Lord asked him what his name was and he replied, **'Legion'** (8:30). The reason he said this was because many demons had **'gone into him'**. A 'legion' was an army of some 6,000 soldiers. So this name spoke of a great number; a collection of evil spirits had ruined the man's life.

We can see the same kind of thing today, when we come across people who are possessed by today's evil spirits of alcohol, drugs, sex, sexual perversion and violence. These things can possess a person and then lead them to behave in a way which is totally unacceptable socially. As a result of their addiction, these people are often driven out of their homes to live in unnatural places like shop doorways, stairwells of flats and 'cardboard cities'.

Then the demons living within the man spoke to Jesus. **'They begged him repeatedly not to order them to go into the Abyss'** (the name given to the place of confinement for evil spirits and Satan). It is mentioned several times in Scripture: here, once in the letter to the Romans and several times in the book of Revelation (e.g. Rev. 9:1). It is the place of the final destruction of all evil and these demons knew that they would, one day, have to be destroyed, but they pleaded for a delay in their final destruction.

They asked that Jesus would give them permission to go into a large herd of pigs (there were about 2,000 of them — Mark 5:13). So Jesus gave them his permission. He did not order them to go into the pigs; he merely acceded to their request. They did not want to be left without a body to inhabit so they chose what, for the Jews, were unclean animals. But when the spirits entered the pigs the whole herd rushed down the steep bank into the lake and were drowned. It is always in the nature of evil to go down and drag the crowd with it. Destruction is always the end of those who persist in wandering away from the paths of God.

Naturally such an event caused the news of what Jesus had done to spread throughout all the locality; and everyone was afraid (8:34-35). These people had been keeping pigs, perhaps for many years. They may have been Gentiles. But what did they see? Did they comment upon the great miracle which had taken place? Did they notice **'the man from whom the demons had gone out, sitting at Jesus' feet, dressed and in his right mind'**? No, they only saw that their pigs were gone. And they were afraid and annoyed. Luke twice tells us about their fear (8:35,37).

So they asked Jesus to leave them. They placed more value upon their pigs than upon the salvation of one human being. Yet Jesus said, 'There will be more rejoicing in heaven over one sinner who repents than over ninety-nine righteous persons who do not need to repent' (15:7). In answer to their request Jesus did as they asked. **'He got into the boat and left'** (8:37). Just as he comes to us when we call upon him in faith, so he departs from us when we say we have no need of him — at least he seems to leave us when we turn our backs upon him.

Jesus only wanted to help this poor man. He did not drive the pigs into the lake. He had nothing to gain by taking away the livelihood of these farmers. He merely gave his permission for the spirits to enter the pigs. We too are often misunderstood when we try to help the needy and are scorned for our efforts.

But one person did not want to get rid of Jesus. The man who had been healed **'begged to go with him'** (8:38). This is one of the themes of these verses. In verse 24 we read of the disciples begging Jesus to stop the storm. We read of the demons in the man begging him not to torture them (8:28). We read of the demons begging Jesus to allow them to go into the pigs (8:32). We read of the inhabitants of the region begging Jesus to leave them (8:37) and now, in verse 38, we read of the cleansed man begging to go with Jesus.

It was natural that he wanted to go with the Saviour. Imagine how he felt. He had been healed. He had found a wonderful Saviour, and he wanted to be with him always. But Jesus said, **'Return home and tell how much God has done for you.'** That is what he did (8:39). He had not lived at home for a long time, but now he could return home. Sometimes Jesus told those whom he had healed to go and tell no one what had happened (e.g. the man healed from leprosy in 5:14), but here, in Gentile territory, there was little danger that people would try to stop the Lord's work. They knew and cared nothing for the Messiah. Yet the same Jesus who commanded the winds and waves to be still (8:24), and the evil spirits to come out of the man (8:29), still commands that sinners turn to him and be saved.

Not every storm that we read about in the Bible was calmed; Paul suffered terrible shipwreck. Not every person who was sick was healed; Paul still had his thorn in the flesh. But there is no force in all of creation which can destroy God's plan for our eternal salvation, or separate us from the love of God which is in Christ Jesus our Lord (see Rom. 8:38-39).[8] However strong the forces of evil are in this world, the power of Christ is stronger still. The powers of nature and the evil spirits all obey the commands of the Lord. We too should hear and obey what the Lord says.

Faith in Jesus only (8:40-56)

When Jesus returned to Capernaum he received a great welcome from a large number of people. In the crowd were two individuals:

a man and a woman. Both of them were humble enough to fall at the feet of Jesus (8:41,47), and both had only limited faith in the Lord. As Luke tells the story he focuses not on the crowd, but upon these two people and their great need.

A man

The man's name was Jairus and he was an important person, a ruler of the synagogue. He was not a priest or rabbi, but what some people would call a 'layman'. His religious duties 'were to make all the arrangements for the services. He would select for example, those who would lead in prayer, read the Scriptures and preach.'[9] However, despite his important position, he had a great need. His only daughter, who was about twelve years old, was dying (8:42). She was on the verge of womanhood (they married young in the time of Jesus) and had, no doubt, been the sunshine of her father's life. But now she was critically ill. Doctor Luke says she was 'dying'. All of Jairus' thoughts were solely taken up with the desperate plight of his daughter.

So Jairus abandoned all of his respectability and came to Jesus. It did not worry him that Jesus had been thrown out of the Nazareth synagogue (4:28-29). He must have realized that many religious people were beginning to be upset by the teaching of Jesus (see 5:21; 6:7), but he put all of those things to the back of his mind, and he came to Jesus just as he was — with all of his need. He fell at the feet of the Lord and pleaded with him to come to his house (8:41) without delay.

Jairus had a partial faith in Jesus. He believed that it was possible for him to heal his daughter, but he did not understand that Jesus could heal at a distance! How different from the centurion who said, 'Lord, don't trouble yourself, for I do not deserve to have you come under my roof... Say the word, and my servant will be healed'! (7:7). However, Jesus did not hold Jairus' deficient faith against him. He went with the man to his house, but as they walked along the busy streets of Capernaum they made very slow progress. There were so many people milling around that **'The crowds almost crushed him'** (8:42). This surely must have made Jairus feel very agitated — especially so when an interruption occurred.

A woman

The woman was very different from Jairus. We are not told her name. She may well have been wealthy at one time, because Mark tells us that she had 'spent all she had' (Mark 5:26). But now this woman was not only poor but, like the man on the other side of the lake (8:26-39), she was also a social outcast.

Her problem was that she had been subject to bleeding, and this had gone on for twelve years. She was like all women of childbearing age, but there had been no let-up in her flow of blood. Hardly a day went by without her having some discharge. No wonder she was weak! Naturally she had looked everywhere for a physician who could heal her. Luke, a doctor, did not want to let down his profession so he merely said, **'No one could heal her'** (8:43). However, Mark puts it more bluntly: 'She had suffered a great deal under the care of many doctors and had spent all she had, yet instead of getting better she grew worse' (Mark 5:26). We can imagine her frustration, and we can sense the anxiety of Jairus because of the delay. For twelve long years this woman had searched for someone who could heal her, and now she had heard that Jesus, the healer, was passing by.

But it was not only the bleeding itself which concerned the woman; it was the stigma which was attached to her disease that had caused her twelve years of heartache. Leviticus 15:19-30 taught that any woman with a flow of blood was unclean. Not only was she unclean herself, but anyone she touched was also unclean. Any bed on which she lay was defiled. Leviticus 15:22 says, 'Whoever touches anything she sits on must wash his clothes and bathe with water, and he will be unclean until evening.' This meant that she was very unlikely to receive any invitation to meals or parties. She could have no social contact with anyone. She was even barred from attending the temple and the synagogue worship, and she certainly would not be able to touch anybody.

Consider these two people. Jairus had a twelve-year-old daughter who was dying. During those same twelve years this poor woman had been forced to refrain from all religious ceremonial and social contact with anyone. Campbell Morgan says, 'In the house of Jairus [there had been] twelve years of sunshine and song and music and joy ... but for this woman there was, twelve years of darkness, and of shadow.'[10]

This is why she came up behind Jesus (8:44). She did not feel able to come face to face with him. She was a woman. She was unimportant. She was an outcast. She did not feel able to bother the Master, and perhaps she knew that he was on his way to the house of the important ruler of the synagogue — and in a hurry. So she said to herself, 'If I just touch the edge of his cloak I will be healed.' Jewish men wore robes with fringes on them. 'The fringes ended in four tassels of white thread with a blue thread woven through them. They were to remind the Jew every time he dressed that he was a man of God and committed to keeping God's laws.'[11] The robes were worn with one of the corners thrown over the left shoulder, and hanging down from the corner was a tassel. It was this tassel that the woman grasped, and immediately she touched it she felt renewed. The bleeding stopped and she began to regain her strength.

We can imagine her joy at this discovery. But that joy quickly turned to anxiety when Jesus asked, **'Who touched me?'** (8:45). We can imagine her cowering in the background trying to slink away without anyone seeing her. She had broken the law. She, in her bleeding condition, had touched someone. And the person she had touched was a rabbi! Surely she must have rendered him unclean.

But she had a temporary respite when Peter (it would be Peter!) said, **'Master, the people are crowding and pressing against you.'** He meant, 'Everyone is touching you; they can't help it.' But Jesus persisted, **'Someone touched me; I know that power has gone out from me'** (8:46). Of course, Jesus knew who had touched him, but he wanted her to come forward and testify to her healing. Did he do this to embarrass the woman? She had a nasty complaint which no woman would like to talk about in public. She had delayed Jesus, and by touching him (and doing it in public), she had defiled him.

However, **'Seeing that she could not go unnoticed, [she] came trembling and fell at his feet. In the presence of all the people she told why she had touched him and how she had been instantly healed'** (8:47). She declared that Jesus had made her well again. At last her deepest need had been met. The Lord did not make her come forward in order to embarrass her. He wanted everyone to know that this woman was now restored to society, and was now able to mix freely with everybody. She was no longer barred from public worship because the illness had been cured.

'Then [Jesus] **said to her, "Daughter, your faith has healed you. Go in peace"'** (8:48). She is the only person recorded in the Bible whom Jesus called by the intimate name of 'Daughter'. He wanted to put her at her ease so he said, 'Your faith has saved you.' He was not saying that her faith was perfect. She had thought that by touching his robe she would be healed, but he wanted to emphasize that it was not faith in robes or any religious relic which brought about salvation. It was faith in him alone which enables people to be be saved.

He said, 'Go in peace.' That was the very thing for which she had been searching during the past twelve years. Now she had found it; she had been given peace of heart, mind and body through faith in Jesus alone.

A messenger

At this point in the story a messenger arrived. '"**Your daughter is dead," he said. "Don't bother the teacher any more"'** (8:49). We can imagine how shattering this news must have been to Jairus. He must surely have thought, 'If only this woman in the crowd could have waited a little while longer, my daughter would still have been alive when Jesus got to her. But now it is too late.' Martha said a similar thing to Jesus when he arrived at the tomb of her brother Lazarus: 'Lord ... if you had been here, my brother would not have died' (John 11:21).

But one of the lessons that Jesus wanted to teach Jairus was that, with Jesus, it is never too late. '**Hearing this** [message from the servant], **Jesus said to Jairus, "Don't be afraid; just believe, and she will be healed"'** (8:50). What a tremendous thing to say to a newly bereaved father! We can imagine how he must have felt. Those of us who have lost children by death can remember how we felt when we received the dreadful news of the death of our son or daughter. When Jesus said to Jairus, 'Just believe,' he meant something similar to that which he said to the woman, 'Your faith has healed you.' It is faith in the Lord Jesus Christ that he was talking about. If we can but believe in him we will experience what the psalmist felt when he said,

'Even though I walk
through the valley of the shadow of death,
I will fear no evil,
for you are with me'

(Ps. 23:4).

As dazed as he was, Jairus allowed Jesus to lead him along the road to his house. When Jesus arrived he took charge of the situation. Luke tells us that **'He did not let anyone go in with him except Peter, John and James, and the child's father and mother'** (8:51). He stopped the people from **'wailing'** as well (8:52). It was considered respectful for the dead person to have a large number of people crying on behalf of the family (presumably they had cried so much that there were no more tears inside of them). Then the Lord said these amazing words: **'She is not dead but asleep.'** When the mourners heard this, **'They laughed at him, knowing that she was dead'** (8:53). 'Curiously these mourners are the only people in the New Testament expressly to have said to have laughed.'[12]

What did Jesus mean by saying, 'She is not dead but asleep'? No father would accept that his child was dead until he was absolutely certain of the fact. No mourners would gather at the home of someone who was merely in a coma; and the spirit cannot return to someone who has not been dead (see 8:55). When Jesus said that she was not dead he was calling death 'sleep'. This is an image which is often used in the New Testament to describe the death of believers (John 11:11-14; Acts 7:59-60; 1 Cor. 15:51; 1 Thess. 4:13-18). 'Sleep is a normal experience that we do not fear, neither should we fear death. It is the body that sleeps, not the spirit, for the spirit of the believer goes to be with Christ (Phil. 1:20-24; 2 Cor. 5:6-8). At the resurrection, the body will be "awakened" and glorified, and God's people will share the image of Christ (1 John 3:1-2).'[13]

Jesus then **'took [the girl] by the hand and said, "My child, get up!"' Her spirit returned, and at once she stood up. Then Jesus told [her parents] to give her something to eat.'** In the midst of all the spiritual activity Jesus was very practical. The child could not have eaten for days and she needed to be built up again so that she could be strong and well once more.

Quite naturally her parents were overwhelmed with joy and they wanted to go and tell everyone the marvellous news that their little girl had been restored to life again, but Jesus ordered them not to tell anyone what had happened. He did this because he did not want any unhealthy publicity to interfere with the normal life of this growing girl, and he did not want anyone to proclaim him as the great deliverer. His time had not yet come. People would get too excited if they had heard of yet another miracle and they might seize the opportunity to proclaim Christ as the one who had been sent to drive out the Romans and set up a Jewish kingdom once again. That would come later.

God still performs miracles

People are healed today. Often this is through normal medical means, but sometimes healing occurs by the unusual activity of God. Many times the healing which the Lord brings about today is a spiritual healing. I have a friend who has had many operations for cancer. She says that she has been healed, but she has not been cured. She still has the cancer but she has experienced the inner healing which the Lord alone can bring.

Does Jesus still raise the dead today? Yes he does. Anyone who is without Christ is described in the Bible as spiritually dead. Without his new life, the life of Christ, in our souls we cannot do anything of any spiritual good. Without the Saviour we are dead in our transgressions and sins (Eph. 2:1).

9.
What it means to be a disciple

Please read Luke 9

The task of the disciples (9:1-17)

Jesus' time in Galilee was fast coming to an end (see 9:51). From the point when he moved down to the south of the country (from verse 52 of this chapter) it becomes clear that his popularity was replaced by opposition. [1] From that point the Lord sent out his disciples to act on his behalf (9:1).

He gave them a twofold task. First of all, **'He sent them out to preach the kingdom of God'** (9:2), as John the Baptist had done (Matt. 3:2). They had to declare the fact that God's rule in this earth had begun in earnest, and they were to call men to turn from their sinful ways and turn to God in faith. So **'They set out and went from village to village, preaching the gospel and healing people everywhere'** (9:6). The word translated 'preaching' in verse 6 is different from the one in verse 2. There they were told to 'herald' the gospel (i.e., prepare the way for the Lord); but now in verse 6 they went everywhere 'evangelizing' (telling the good news of God).

Their other task was to heal the sick — a very practical ministry. They carried out both of these tasks **'from village to village ... everywhere'**, ministering to ordinary, poor folk.

The disciples were sent out in a hurry. The work of the gospel messenger is an urgent one. Just as John talked about the Pharisees as those who were '[fleeing] from the coming wrath' (3:7), so we should warn all those we meet to turn to Christ because the day of the 'wrath of the Lamb' is coming (see Rev. 6:15-17).

They were to take no staff; they would not need one because they should lean only upon God. They were to take no bag, because, unlike other preachers in those days, they would not need to carry a begging bowl; God would supply all of their needs through his people's generosity. They were to take no bread; just as the ravens fed Elijah in the Kerith Ravine (1 Kings 17:5), so the Lord would provide food for them by various means. They were to take no money; their needs would be few — luxurious living is not what they were to concern themselves with. They were to take no extra tunic; rich apparel was not what they should be taken up with — the whole of their time should be devoted to the proclamation of the message of God's love. Finally, they were to base themselves in the same house for the whole length of their stay (9:4). They were not to waste time looking for better lodgings; they should be content with what they had.

If anyone would not welcome them and the work they were doing, they were to **'shake the dust off [their] feet'** when they left the town (9:5). The strict Jews did that when they left Gentile territory. It was a sign that they did not wish to take any of the defilement of unholy people back into their own land. But Jesus told his disciples to do this for a different reason: he wanted to emphasize the message. The inhabitants of a village would probably be horrified to see the disciples shaking the dust off their feet. This act was designed to make them stop and consider the implications of their rejection of the gospel message.

The effect of the preaching

King Herod heard about **'all that was going on'** (9:7) and he was perplexed. Some people said that Jesus was John the Baptist come back from the dead, and John's death was evidently still disturbing Herod's mind. There were others who said that Jesus was Elijah; they knew that Malachi had prophesied that Elijah would return to the earth 'before that great and dreadful day of the Lord comes' (Mal. 4:5). Yet others said that Jesus was one of the prophets of long ago who had come back to life.

However, it seems that Herod was worried in case Jesus really was John come back to life. He said of John the Baptist, **'I beheaded John'** (9:9); he did not try to hide the fact or make excuses for it. But his reasons for seeing the Lord were the wrong ones. He wanted to know if John had come back as a ghost to haunt him. When he finally heard that he was going to set eyes upon Jesus, Luke tells us that he was greatly pleased, because 'for a long time he had been wanting to see him' (23:8). However, when the Lord refused to perform any miracles just to please the king, Herod ridiculed and mocked him and quickly sent him back to Pilate (23:11).

The feeding of the five thousand

Knowing that his disciples were exhausted, Jesus took them away to a remote place (9:12) on the north-eastern shores of Galilee, **'to a town called Bethsaida'** (9:10). There they would all be able to rest and relax with the Lord, but the crowds had other ideas. They had such an urge to see Jesus that they also hurried to this place and he **'welcomed them and spoke to them about the kingdom of God, and healed those who needed healing'** (9:11). We do not know what the disciples thought about the intrusion of these people, but we do know that a little later they said to Jesus, **'Send the crowd away so they can ... find food'** (9:12). Jesus, however, reacted rather surprisingly. He said to his disciples, **'You give them something to eat'** (9:13). But Philip said, 'Where shall we buy bread for these people to eat? ... Eight months' wages would not buy enough bread for each one to have a bite!' (John 6:5,7). All they had were five loaves of bread (they would have been very small loaves too) and two fish. However, when they handed over to Jesus all that they had, he took it, gave thanks to God for it, and then gave it to the disciples to feed the crowd. The amazing thing was that all 5,000 were fully satisfied. There were even **'twelve basketfuls of broken pieces that were left over'** (9:17).

Whenever we dedicate everything we have to Jesus, he can take it (however small it is) and use it in his service. These stories teach us the value of discipleship. If we truly follow the Lord, he will use even us for his glory.

Who is Jesus? (9:18-27)

Some time had passed since the feeding of the five thousand; that is why Luke starts this section with, **'Once when Jesus was praying**

...' In Mark 6:45 - 8:26 we read of some of the events which took place between the miracle of the loaves and the fishes and this incident. But Luke wants to concentrate on showing his readers that Jesus is the Saviour of the world. This is possibly why he left out some of the stories at this point; it was necessary (because of space) for Luke to be very selective in what he told his readers.

Eventually the disciples were able to spend some time on their own up in the northern city of Cæsarea Philippi (cf. Matt. 16:13; Mark 8:27). This city was built on the northern slopes of Mount Hermon. It was near the source of the Jordan river, and almost at the extremity of Jewish territory. It had been rebuilt by Herod's son, Philip, who named it after Tiberius Cæsar and himself.[2] It was originally called Paneas in honour of the Greek goat-god Pan and it was a thoroughly heathen place. Yet Jesus chose this place to speak to his disciples about the future. But first of all he prayed in private.

Jesus spoke about himself

The Lord asked his disciples, **'Who do the crowds say I am?'** (9:18). They answered, **'Some say** [that you are] **John the Baptist; others say Elijah; and still others, that one of the prophets of long ago has come back to life'** (9:19). We read of similar suggestions in Luke 9:7-8; but then Jesus asked his disciples the same question which was asked by Herod at that time: **'Who do you say I am?'** We can imagine that all of the disciples were puzzled. The crowds were 'thoroughly conscious that he was an exceptional, supernatural person; but because they had always pictured the Messiah as an earthly ruler, they were unable to see the true Christ in him.'[3] However, the question posed by Jesus to his disciples could not be avoided.

'What do you think about Christ?' That is a question which really puts anyone on the spot; an answer has to be given. Once again it is Peter who speaks up. He makes a bold declaration and says that Jesus is **'the Christ of God'** (9:20).

Hard sayings about Jesus

Because the disciples did not understand the full implications of his messiahship, the Lord **'strictly warned them not to tell this** [that

he was the Christ] **to anyone'** (9:21). 'The Jews detested their state
of subjection to the Romans and longed for deliverance. They were
ready to follow almost anyone who claimed to be Messiah... Had
Jesus been hailed widely as Messiah, people would have understood
it as a political and military claim. They would have completely
missed what he was teaching them.'[4] Jesus wanted his messiahship
to be kept quiet for the time being so that he could get on with his
real work. He never sought popular acclaim from the people. His
sole aim in life was to do his Father's will.

The Lord then told his disciples about four things which would
happen to him. He said, **'The Son of Man must suffer many
things'** (9:22). Jesus had been sent to do his Father's will and that
path of obedience was not an easy one. In the garden of Gethsemane,
just before his arrest, the Lord prayed in anguish saying, 'Father, if
you are willing, take this cup from me; yet not my will, but yours be
done' (22:39-46).

Not only was Jesus destined to suffer, but **'He must ... be
rejected by the elders, chief priests and teachers of the law'**
(9:22). These were the important religious rulers of the day. They
ought to have been perceptive enough to see who Jesus really was,
yet they rejected him. Isaiah 53:3 says, 'He was despised and
rejected by men, a man of sorrows and familiar with suffering.'
Jesus himself said that he must be rejected. And because of this he
can enter into the anguish of all those who have also faced the pain
of rejection (Heb. 4:15).

The third thing that he tells his disciples is the most painful one
of all for them to bear. He said that he must be killed. Think of what
that would have meant to his disciples. They knew Jesus to be good,
kind and gentle, a man who never did anyone any harm: so what did
he mean by saying that he must be killed? He meant that it was only
by dying as an atoning sacrifice that the Lord could take away any
of his people's sin. What great love there was (and still is) in the heart
of the Saviour, for him to suffer so much for his people — people
who are sinners!

But then the good news came. He said that the Son of Man **'on
the third day [must] be raised to life'**. The resurrection of Jesus is
the proof of our redemption. Jesus came back to life again. He was
raised up victorious over death, over sin and over Satan; and he will
remain alive for evermore. But before the disciples could begin to
ask him questions about this, he turned to speak to them again.

Hard sayings about the disciples

He said to them, **'If anyone would come after me, he must deny himself and take up his cross daily and follow me'** (9:23). Again he stresed the divine compulsion in this. He used the word 'must' once again. 'We all have our crosses to bear,' is something we often hear. Sometimes it is said to a person who has to look after an invalid, especially if the bedridden person is very ungrateful and demanding. Occasionally it is said to someone who has difficult people living in the house next door. The phrase is often used to speak of some annoyance which has to be borne through life without complaint. However, these disciples did not think of it in that way. They knew what crosses were for. A cross was a very cruel form of execution. It was something that the Romans had specially invented. People put to death by crucifixion suffered excruciating pain. But not only that: it took a long time for them to die; sometimes they endured tremendous pain for days before they expired. Crucifixion was one of the most cruel forms of death that has ever been invented by man. And it was specially reserved for 'traitors'; few people who saw someone dying in such torment would have the heart to disobey any Roman order.

The Lord went on to say that his disciples must **'take up [their] cross daily'**. There must be a continual (daily) denial of self, and a preparedness to suffer for the cause of Christ, whatever the circumstances, even death. In other words, anyone who wants to be a disciple (a learner, an apprentice) of Christ must be completely dedicated to the Lord and willing to obey him in all things. The whole of the person's life would be turned upside down. The only way for any of his followers to save their lives was to give them away to the Lord. 'If a person owned the whole world, he would still be too poor to buy back a lost life.'[5] Anyone who is ashamed of Christ will never take up his cross and follow him; it will be much too painful a business. To be a follower of Jesus takes a lot of courage. It is not for the faint-hearted. Paul was not ashamed to be known as a follower of the Lord. He said, 'I am not ashamed of the gospel, because it is the power of God for the salvation of everyone who believes' (Rom. 1:16).

There is a judgement day coming. If we act as though we are ashamed of Jesus now, then the Lord tells us that **'The Son of Man will be ashamed of [us] when he comes in his glory and in the**

glory of the Father and of his holy angels' (9:26). Jesus told his
disciples that some of them would see the kingdom of God before
they died. He may have been referring to the outpouring of the Holy
Spirit at Pentecost, but he may have meant that some of them would
still be alive when Rome destroyed Jerusalem, the temple and all the
old sacrificial ritual of Judaism; this happened in A.D. 70 when
Titus and the Roman army overthrew all the holy places. We should
live our lives in a way that shows we are unashamed of Jesus and
seeking to witness to his grace with a great and holy boldness.
Joseph Grigg sums all this up so well in his hymn:

> Jesus, and shall it ever be,
> A mortal man ashamed of thee?
> Ashamed of thee, whom angels praise,
> Whose glories shine through endless days!
>
> Ashamed of Jesus, that dear Friend,
> On whom my hopes of heaven depend!
> No! When I blush, be this my shame,
> That I no more revere his name.[6]

The transfiguration (9:28-36)

During the eight days following Peter's declaration (9:20), the
disciples were alone with their Lord, thinking over the things that he
had said. Jesus then went up into the mountain so that he could be
alone with his Father. We are not told the name of the mountain.
Traditionally it is said to be Mount Tabor, but most conservative
commentators think that it was more likely to be Mount Hermon,
which is near Cæsarea Philippi.

Something important was going to happen, so the Lord needed
to spend time alone with his Father. Jesus took with him Peter, John
and James. These were the same three disciples who accompanied
him when he raised Jairus' daughter from death (8:51), and he
would take these same three with him while he prayed in the Garden
of Gethsemane (Mark 14:33). They were representatives of the rest
of the Twelve and also of the whole redeemed people of God.

As Jesus was praying, **'The appearance of his face changed,** and his clothes became as bright as a flash of lightning' (9:29). Matt. 17:1 and Mark 9:2 tell us that Jesus was transformed before them. The Greek word used here is transliterated into English as a 'metamorphosis'. We think of that word as the process undergone by the chrysalis of a caterpillar when it changes into a beautiful butterfly. That radical and compete change is an illustration of the transfiguration of Jesus from a perfect man to the God-man shining with the glory of the Lord.

However, it appears that Peter, John and James were unaware of this change because it seems that they had gone to sleep while Jesus was praying. After all, it was probably night-time. They had climbed up the mountain and, with the benefit of hindsight, we know that they were to do the same thing later on while Jesus was praying in the Garden of Gethsemane, even though on that occasion he had instructed them to 'stay ... and keep watch' (Mark 14:34). So the disciples who had been specially selected by the Lord to go with him missed the beginning of this marvellous event. How we all need to obey the injunction of the Lord to 'Watch'!

The companions of Jesus

'Two men, Moses and Elijah, appeared in glorious splendour, talking with Jesus' (9:30-31). Moses and Elijah appeared on the mount because they were symbolic of the Law and the Prophets. Moses was the lawgiver and Elijah was a very great prophet. 'The Law and the Prophets' was a description given to the whole of the Jewish Bible — the part that we call the Old Testament. Jesus said that he had come to fulfil the Law and the Prophets. On the road to Emmaus he would say to the two disciples, 'Everything must be fulfilled that is written about me in the Law of Moses, the Prophets and the Psalms' (24:44).

They spoke about the departure of Jesus (9:31). The word that is used for **'departure'** is 'exodus'. It means 'to go out'. The book of Exodus records the wonderful deliverance accomplished for the Israelites who were held in the slavery of Egypt. That deliverance was achieved through the sacrifice of the Passover lamb (Exod. 12). Moses, Elijah and Jesus all spoke of sacrifice. The sacrifice which was offered in the time of Moses was a lamb; at the time of Elijah it was a bull (1 Kings 18); but the sacrifice offered by the Lord Jesus

Christ on the hill of Calvary would be the one sacrifice made once for all for the cleansing of sin for all who will believe on him alone for salvation.

The departure, or exodus, of Jesus was to be something which **'he was about to bring to fulfilment at Jerusalem'** (9:31). This was the turning-point in the life of Jesus on earth. From that time onwards he was prepared for the end and shortly he would 'steadfastly set his face to go to Jerusalem' (9:51, AV).

Wicked men would put Jesus to death on the cross, in Jerusalem. But Peter later told the crowd in the same city of Jerusalem, on the Day of Pentecost, that the death of Jesus was 'by God's set purpose and foreknowledge' (Acts 2:23). The cross was not something which happened because God's plan went wrong, or Jesus ovestepped the mark. God planned the cross from before the creation of the world so that his elect could be saved for all eternity (see e.g. Eph. 1:4). That is what Moses, Elijah and the Lord were talking about on the mountain. They were discussing this, the greatest event in the world, which Jesus was to bring to fulfilment at Jerusalem a few months later. The whole of the Old Testament (the Law and the Prophets) spoke of Christ and his atoning death.

The disciples woke up

At this point Peter, John and James were all suddenly wide awake. It seems that they woke up in time to overhear part of the conversation which was taking place (otherwise we would not have known about it). But the thing that gripped their attention was the glory of Jesus, and the two men standing with him (9:32). Somehow they knew that they were Moses and Elijah. However, what arrested them even more than the wonder of seeing these two great men from the past was the glory of Christ.

Peter had seen something of the wonder of Jesus on that day when he had caught a great number of fish. Then he had fallen on his knees and said, 'Go away from me, Lord; I am sinful man' (5:8); but now he was overwhelmed by the sight of the glory of the Lord. He was so struck with it all that he made numerous references to it when he wrote his epistles (1 Peter 1:11; 4:13; 5:1,4; 2 Peter 1:17-18).

Once again we see that Peter was not slow to speak up. He said, **'Master, it is good for us to be here. Let us put up three shelters — one for you, one for Moses and one for Elijah'** (9:33). He does not say, 'Let us make six shelters, one for each of us who are here on the mount.' He did not consider that he and his friends were on the same footing as Jesus, Moses and Elijah. But, even so, Luke tells us that **'He did not know what he was saying'** (9:33). Moses and Elijah did not need earthly dwelling-places (as the children of Israel had needed them during their wilderness wanderings). The house of these two great saints was in heaven. But it must also have been a comfort for the disciples to have seen Moses and Elijah. This was, for them, living proof that there is a life after death. Moses had died nearly 1,500 years before, and Elijah had been taken up to heaven in a whirlwind more than 900 years before that time.[7]

Neither could Peter delay the departure of Moses and Elijah. They had to return to heaven because that was their home; their visit had accomplished what it set out to do. Just as it was wrong for Peter to try to delay their return to glory, so it is wrong for any of us to try to call spirits away from their eternal rest (see 1 Sam. 28:7-19).

Next Luke tells us, **'While [Peter] was speaking, a cloud appeared and enveloped them, and they were afraid as they entered the cloud'** (9:34). We do not know whether the cloud encompassed all six, or only Jesus, Moses and Elijah, but it seems more likely that the disciples were left outside of it. The cloud symbolized the glory of the Lord. We read in Scripture of a bright, white, or luminous cloud indicating the presence of God (see Exod. 13:21; 16:10; 40:35; 1 Kings 8:10-11; Neh. 9:19; Ps. 78:14; Rev. 14:14-16). Out of this cloud the voice of God said, **'This is my Son, whom I have chosen; listen to him'** (9:35). Similar words were heard at the baptism of Jesus as God himself authenticated the person and work of Jesus as the Christ.

The voice was not only a confirmation to Jesus of his role as the Messiah, but it was an encouragement to the disciples to press on in faith with the confession which Peter had made at Cæsarea Philippi (9:20). The phrase, 'Listen to him' was something which indicated that Jesus was that great prophet whose advent had been predicted many years before. In Deuteronomy 18:15 we read, 'The Lord your God will raise up for you a prophet like me from among your own brothers. You must listen to him.' Matthew tells us that 'When the disciples heard this, they fell face down to the ground, terrified. But Jesus came and touched them. "Get up," he said. "Don't be afraid"' (Matt.17:6-7). **'When the voice had spoken, they found that Jesus was alone'** (9:36). 'They saw no one except Jesus' (Matt.

17:8). David Gooding says, 'The Lawgiver and the prophet were gone. For all their eminence they were but men. Their role in history had been preparatory to the incarnation, death and resurrection of Christ. Now that he had come, they retired. The actual redemption of the world would depend on Christ and on Christ alone.'[8]

Luke ends this story by saying that **'The disciples kept this to themselves, and told no one at that time what they had seen'** (9:36).

Our response

We should not always be looking for excitement and startling experiences; they come but seldom. We cannot depend for our strength upon wonderful happenings. 'They are not the basis for a consistent Christian life. That can come only through the word of God. Experiences come and go, but the Word remains.'[9]

Also we should be conscious of the need in our own lives of a spiritual 'transfiguration' experience every day as we 'walk with the Lord'. In Romans 12:1-2 Paul tells his readers, 'I urge you brothers, in view of God's mercy, to offer your bodies as living sacrifices, holy and pleasing to God — this is your spiritual act of worship. Do not conform any longer to the pattern of this world, but be transformed by the renewing of your minds. Then you will be able to approve what God's will is — his good, pleasing and perfect will.' 2 Corinthians 3:18 says that all true believers should reflect the Lord's glory as they are 'being transformed into his likeness with ever-increasing glory, which comes from the Lord, who is the Spirit'.

Some graphic contrasts (9:37-50)

We now come to the end of the first part of Luke's Gospel and we notice some sharp contrasts. Jesus and his disciples are now going to start on their final journey to Jerusalem.

The mountain and the plain

When they came down from the glories of the mountain they were confronted with the confusion of men. There was a man in the crowd who called out, **'Teacher, I beg you to look at my son, for he is my only child. A spirit seizes him and he suddenly screams; it throws him into convulsions so that he foams at the mouth. It scarcely ever leaves him and is destroying him'** (9:38-39). Then he added something which must have made Peter, John and James feel somewhat ashamed. The man said, **'I begged your disciples to drive it out, but they could not'** (9:40).

Many times in this Gospel we have seen the love which the Lord extends to those who are especially vulnerable. Outside of the town of Nain he brought back to life the only son of a poor widow (7:12). In Capernaum Jesus granted new life to the only daughter of a ruler of the synagogue (8:42), and now we see a man whose only child was grievously ill. The evil spirit attacked the lad almost continuously and when this happened he screamed in fright and rage as the spirit threw him to the ground. (The word is 'a wrestling term in the Greek'.)[10] The boy had convulsions and foamed at the mouth. The effect on the lad was that he was being destroyed!

Why were the disciples so powerless to help this lad, especially after their experiences in 9:6? One reason may have been their pride. Perhaps they had become complacent or they had failed to pray. The Lord said, 'This kind can come out only by prayer' (Mark 9:29). But they may also have lacked the power to perform this healing because they were jealous because they had not been chosen to accompany the Lord up to the mount. Whatever the reason, these disciples (the nine who had remained on the plain, plus all of the other followers of Jesus), were rebuked by the Lord.

Luke tells us that Jesus said, **'O unbelieving and perverse generation ... how long shall I stay with you and put up with you?'** (9:41). The Lord sounds very exasperated with his followers. God had said something similar to Moses and Aaron when he heard about the complaints of the ungrateful Israelites. He had asked, 'How long will this wicked community grumble against me?' (Num 14:27).

Then the Lord said to the man, **'Bring your son here.'** But even while the man was in the process of doing so the demon threw the boy to the ground in a convulsion (9:42). Satan never gives up. Even when he sees that he is defeated and there is no hope for him to succeed in his evil plans, he still insists on having one final fling. Yet Jesus was not put off by this action of the Evil One. He might seem to hesitate to help us when we are disobedient, but he never leaves it too late to deal with Satan or any of his evil hosts. **'Jesus rebuked the evil spirit [and] healed the boy'** (9:42) and it was all done by one word from the Lord. Just as Jesus rebuked the raging waters on Galilee with a word, and all was then calm (8:24), so he rebuked this evil spirit, and the lad was healed.

Finally Jesus did something which was very tender. He gave the boy back to his father. The father had not had his son for a good long time, because the lad had seldom been in his right mind. But now the father had him back in the fullest sense of those words; the right relationship between them was restored once more because of the intervention of Jesus.

The crowds and Jesus

The crowds **'were all amazed at the greatness of God'** (9:43). They gave the glory to the one from whom all good things come, but still they did not show that they had grasped who Jesus really was. They had not understood that he was God's chosen one (9:35) or, as Peter put it, 'the Christ of God' (9:20).

But what a contrast there was between the words of the people and those which Jesus spoke to his disciples at that time! He said, **'Listen carefully to what I am about to tell you'** (9:44). He had already spoken about his death (9:21-22) and he was going to carry on telling them about these momentous coming events, but they would not begin fully to understand the implications of his departure until after his death (24:24-25).

He continued, **'The Son of Man is going to be betrayed into the hands of men'** (9:44). He had spoken of his coming suffering, rejection, death and resurrection (9:21-22), but now he tells them that he is going to be betrayed, although he did not explain that the betrayer was to be one of their number. He further adds that he is going to be betrayed into the hands of wicked men — men who ought to have known better. We know what happened in that final week of his life on earth, but these disciples, at that time, were kept from understanding what this meant (9:45). Luke tells us that **'It was hidden from them.'** It was not only hidden from them because they did not need to know at that time (see John 12:37-40; 2 Cor. 3:14). It was hidden because they were bewildered. They were so confused that **'They were afraid to ask him about it'** (9:45).

Childishness and childlikeness

After the dismal failure on the part of the disciples to heal the boy we might have thought that the Twelve would have been rather crestfallen, but they were not. As we read about them in verse 46 we discover that they were arguing. It seems that they had now journeyed back to Capernaum (so Mark tells us in 9:33) and as they entered the house where they were staying an argument started among them about who was going to be greatest among them. Selfishness had raised its ugly head. Jealousy breeds all kinds of evil attitudes.

Why are Christians so concerned about status? There are various tasks to be fulfilled in the church of Jesus Christ. Those in leadership have very great responsibility, but they are no more important than the humblest believer in the Lord Jesus Christ. I am always very wary of those who aspire to office in a church if I suspect that it is merely so that they can be thought of highly. Sometimes it is a man's wife who is pushing him to do an 'important' job in church life so that she can say something like, 'My husband is a deacon, you know.' No Christian should be over-concerned about his status and position; rather he should seek only to live near to the Lord. That is the greatest position any of us can ever have.

To deal with their argument, Jesus **'took a little child and made him stand beside him. Then he said to [his disciples], "Whoever welcomes this little child in my name welcomes me; and whoever welcomes me welcomes the one who sent me. For he who is least among you all — he is the greatest"'** (9:47-48). By using one simple object lesson, Jesus silenced all of the arguments of the disciples. He did not take a teenager — perhaps because they tend to act as though they know everything that is worth knowing! A friend of mine has a yellow diamond hanging in the back of his car with this notice on it: 'Hire a teenager while they still know everything.'

But Jesus **'took a little child and made him stand beside him'** (9:47) — not behind or in front of him. Jesus frequently had children around him and he showed his love for them. Why did the Lord place a child in the midst? He did it because children are characterized by such traits as unpretentiousness and humble trustfulness. Jesus is teaching his disciples that they should be the same. This is how Hendriksen puts it: 'Jesus is telling his disciples to forget all about

themselves, their rank and importance; and instead, to concentrate
their attention on this child standing by the Master's side. They
should not only "become like" this child (cf. Matt. 18:1-4) , but
should "welcome" it (cf. Matt. 18:5), and others like it.'[11]

The attitudes of John and Jesus

**"'Master," said John, "we saw a man driving out demons in
your name and we tried to stop him, because he is not one of
us'"(9:49).** We know nothing about this other healer except that he
was not one of the number who followed Jesus, and he was actually
casting out demons in the name of Jesus. Was he a genuine believer
in the Lord Jesus Christ or not? Luke does not tell us. All we do know
is the reaction of John, and the reaction of Jesus to what John said.
John said, 'We tried to stop him.' He was incensed that someone
who was not of their company was doing healing work. He said,
'This is not right because he is not one of us.'

But Jesus said, **'Do not stop him ... for whoever is not against
you is for you.'** He did not say, 'Whoever is not against *me*'. He said,
'Whoever is not against *you* is for you.' In effect the Lord was telling
them, 'If he is not interfering with your work, then leave him alone.'
Jesus said a similar thing to Peter when that apostle asked the Lord
what would happen to John at his death. Jesus just turned to Peter
and said, 'What is that to you? You must follow me' (John 21:22).
Gamaliel takes the same line with those who wanted to put some of
the apostles to death. He said, 'Leave these men [the apostles] alone!
Let them go! For if their purpose or activity is of human origin, it will
fail... But if it is from God, you will not be able to stop these men;
you will only find yourselves fighting against God' (Acts 5:38-39).

It seems to me that there are far too many people in the Christian
world today who are being over-critical of those with whom they do
not see eye-to-eye in every particular — perhaps because these
others do not run their churches in the same way as themselves. In
this section Jesus is saying something like this: 'Don't try to stop
them if they are not trying to interfere with your work. What really
matters is that you follow me and get on with the work which I have
given you to do.'

And so with verse 50 we come to the end of Luke's account of
the Galilean ministry of the Lord Jesus Christ. Jesus was now
proceeding to Jerusalem. He was going there in order to accomplish

his great work of redemption, by dying on the cross of Calvary to save lost men, women and children from their sin. As he resolutely set out to go to his death because it was his Father's will, so let us always seek to be determined to do that which is right and pleasing in God's sight.

The journey of life (9:51-62)

Jesus had turned his back on Galilee and began to travel to Jerusalem. Verse 51 is a kind of text for the whole of the second half of Luke's Gospel. Up until this point the Lord had been busy, mainly performing marvellous deeds, but from this point onwards he concentrated much more on his work of teaching his followers about the kingdom of God, rather than on performing miracles. Hardly any of the teaching in the second half of Luke's account of the gospel (some of it very well known indeed) is recorded elsewhere in the Scriptures.

Luke tells us that **'The time approached for [Jesus] to be taken up to heaven'** (9:51). In Luke 9:31 Jesus had spoken with Elijah and Moses about his departure, or exodus. Now Luke speaks of the ascension of the Lord. The ascension comes after the pain of the cross. Jerusalem meant joy and celebration for the Jews. It was the holy city. It was the location of the temple (where God's presence dwelt in power). It was the place where many joyous festivals were held. Yet, for the Lord, Jerusalem spoke of the pain of betrayal, suffering and death. However, the culmination of our Lord's journey through life was his ascension, the time when Jesus was taken up into heaven. Because of the 'joy set before him [Jesus] endured the cross, scorning its shame, and sat down at the right hand of the throne of God' (Heb. 12:2). We sing about it in the hymn, 'Look, ye saints, the sight is glorious!' The fourth verse goes like this:

Hark, those bursts of acclamation!
Hark, those loud triumphant chords!
Jesus takes the highest station:
Oh, what joy the sight affords!
Crown him! Crown him!
King of kings, and Lord of lords.[12]

But before that glorious coronation day much suffering lay ahead for the Lord.

So, with only about six months left of his earthly life, Jesus resolutely set out for Jerusalem. A number of times Luke specifically speaks of Jesus travelling to Jerusalem for the last time (9:51,53; 13:22,33; 17:11; 18:31; 19:11,28). That was the purpose of his life at that time.

Rejection

Jesus sent messengers ahead of him **'into a Samaritan village to get things ready for him'** (9:52). Samaria was a province which lay between Galilee in the north and Judea in the south. For centuries there had been bitterness between the Samaritans and the Jews, so much so that the Jews did not associate with Samaritans (John 4:9). But, despite this, Jesus deliberately made contact with them. He did not treat them as outcasts and he even told stories which had Samaritans as their heroes. The most well-known of these is that of 'the Good Samaritan', which is recorded in Luke 10:25-37.

However, **'The people there did not welcome him, because he was heading for Jerusalem'** (9:53). He was going to celebrate in the temple and the Samaritans resented the Jewish temple. Many centuries earlier they had built their own holy building on Mount Gerizim, but the Jews had destroyed it some hundreds of years previously. It was not surprising that there was such great hostility between these two groups of people.

James and John said to Jesus, **'Lord, do you want us to call fire down from heaven to destroy them?'** (9:54). Perhaps their recent meeting with Elijah had reminded them of what the great prophet had done on one occasion (2 Kings 1:9-16). But Jesus **'turned and rebuked them'** (9:55). Earlier he had instructed his disciples, 'If people do not welcome you, shake the dust off your feet when you leave their town' (9:5) but he had said nothing about destroying them. Their own rejection of the Saviour would be bad enough punishment for any of them to bear, so Jesus and his disciples **'went to another village'** (9:56). He turned his back on them.

The cost of following Jesus

Following Jesus requires a great deal of determination. Luke picked out three examples of people who aspired to being followers of

Jesus. He tells us that this first incident, at least, occurred **'as they were walking along the road'** (9:57). **'A man said to [the Lord] "I will follow you wherever you go"'** (9:57). Perhaps this man had often heard Jesus preach and seen him heal the sick, and he was caught up with the romantic idea of following him. But Jesus knew his heart, so he threw out this challenge to him: 'Foxes have holes and birds of the air have nests, but the Son of Man has nowhere to lay his head' (9:58). Jesus was saying to him, 'If you follow me you have to forget all ideas about living in a beautiful and comfortable home.' Jesus had nothing on this earth that he could call his own possession — except his seamless robe — and he sometimes requires his followers to have the same loose grip on the comforts of life as he did.

The second man Luke spoke about is one whom Jesus approached and said, **'Follow me.'** He used the same word, 'Follow,' but now Jesus issued the challenge to follow him. The man replied, **'Lord, first let me go and bury my father'** (9:59). That sounds a very reasonable request because Jesus was very concerned that people should show proper respect for their families (Matt. 15:3-9). So why did Jesus reply to the man, **'Let the dead bury their own dead, but you go and proclaim the kingdom of God'**? (9:60). How can dead people carry out a funeral? Jesus was not talking about those who are physically dead, but about those who are spiritually dead. He meant that unbelievers are totally dead to the things of God; they have no spiritual life about them at all (Eph. 2:1). Those are the men who should deal with the ceremonies concerning the physically dead.

Jesus was harsh with this man because he was making the point that the work of the kingdom will not wait; it is an urgent task. It may well have been that the man's father had not even died yet; in fact he might live for another ten years or more. The Lord's work demands a hasty obedience. If this man was not prepared to put following the Lord even before family cares, then he would not make a suitable follower of the Master. Many a person called to overseas missionary work has had to wrestle with this problem.

Finally we read about another person (presumably a man) who said, **'I will follow you, Lord; but first let me go back and say goodbye to my family'** (9:61). On the face of it, this seems a reasonable request to make. But Jesus replied, **'No one who puts his hand to the plough and looks back is fit for service in the kingdom of God'** (9:62). Twice we have the word 'back' mentioned.

The man said, 'Let me go back and say goodbye,' and Jesus talks about the folly of a man ploughing who looks back.

Those who follow Christ must be people who are determined to look forward. If the man had gone back to say goodbye he might easily have been persuaded to stay back with his friends and family and, in any case, the farewell parties would have gone on for a week or more. The man who takes his eyes off the mark towards which he is steering, and looks back, is bound to drill a crooked furrow.

All who follow him must be single-minded in their task. They must have their eyes looking ahead to the goal which is before them. They must not constantly be hankering back to their old way of life. Lot's wife was very reluctant to leave the sinful pleasures of Sodom and Gomorrah. We know what happened to her. She 'looked back, and she became a pillar of salt' (Gen. 19:26).

10.
Ambassadors for Christ

Please read Luke 10

The work of ambassadors (10:1-24)

Christ's team of workers widens out further at the beginning of chapter 10. We read that Jesus appointed seventy-two others to go ahead of him to prepare for his arrival (10:1). There is some dispute about whether the text says seventy or seventy-two were sent out at this time,[1] but the number makes little difference to their work and its significance. It seems that the twelve apostles were representatives of Israel (with its twelve tribes) and the seventy-two disciples were representative of the rest of the nations of the world (there are seventy nations listed in Genesis 10 — the Septuaguint version details seventy-two).[2] If this is the meaning then it is in line with one of the major themes of Luke's Gospel: Jesus is the Saviour of the world.

Jesus sent this new group of ambassadors out in pairs. He had done the same with the twelve in 9:1-6 (the parallel passage in Mark 6:7 states that they went out two by two). A careful reading of Luke's second volume tells us that in the early church the same practice prevailed. Barnabas and Saul went out together (Acts 13:2), Judas and Silas were sent out in Acts 15:32 and Paul chose Silas to accompany him on his missionary journeys (Acts 15:40). Later on, we read that Silas and Timothy stayed in Berea (Acts 17:14) and in Acts 19:22 Luke tells us that Timothy and Erastus were sent to Macedonia. Modern missions that have sent out teams to pioneer

situations have tended to achieve much more than those which have
sent out solitary missionaries.

The Lord sent these unnamed seventy-two with clear instructions. He told them that **'The harvest is plentiful'** and encouraged
them to pray for more workers (10:2). If extra workers were needed
in those days, when they had the Lord with them, then it is certain
that we need a great increase today in those who are willing to go out
into all the world and preach the gospel to every creature.

The Lord also warned them of the dangers of their mission. He
said, 'Go! I am sending you out like lambs among wolves' (10:3).
He emphasized the seriousness of the situation. He said that these
disciples were as helpless as lambs among hungry wolves, but
nevertheless he still said to them, 'Go.' They were to go on their
mission remembering that Jesus had sent them. However, they were
not only going out with his authority; they were sent forth in his
strength and power, and with the knowledge that he would protect
them. During the whole of their mission they were to be faithful in
doing the work that Jesus had sent them to do; they would then
discover that nothing could prevent them from carrying out the
Master's task.

Centuries later Hudson Taylor, the great missionary to China,
said that 'The Lord's work, done in the Lord's way, will be
successful.' This is as true for us now as it was for Taylor in the last
century. When we go out to work for the Lord, let Scripture be our
guide as we seek to reach the lost for Christ. It is the Lord, and not
societies, who sends out his workers on to the mission-field!

Following these injunctions Jesus gave them clear instructions
regarding their provisions. They were to take no purse or bag or
sandals (10:4). They were to go as they were, because the Lord
would provide for all their needs. They were not to be hesitant about
accepting food and shelter from others, and they were to allow
nothing to delay them. He said, **'Do not greet anyone on the road'**
(10:4). This did not mean that they should treat people rudely and
refuse to say, 'Good morning,' to anyone. Jesus meant that they
should not stop along the road and exchange the customary lengthy
greetings and salutations; this was a process which could take many
days. Their mission was urgent, and they should get on with it. The
same haste is required of us in our proclamation of the gospel.

How should they behave when they arrived at their destination?
They should act in the same way as the Twelve were told to do when

Jesus sent them out in Luke 9:1-6. His principles for work do not change. They were to give the customary greeting, **'Peace to this house'**, whenever they arrived at a new location.

Another principle that Jesus laid down was that they should stay based in the same house for the whole of their visit to a particular town. But what should they do if they discovered that they had chosen to lodge in a very poor house? Jesus said, in effect, 'Never mind. You must remain there.' They had to remember that they were not tourists seeking the best accommodation they could find. Nor were they to be 'spongers', seeking to make money out of their preaching, as some travelling 'evangelists' in the early church apparently did. Their task was to preach the gospel to all who would hear. Their bodily comforts should count for very little. The work of preaching the kingdom was far too important for them to worry about luxuries. This is a lesson which all preachers of the gospel should remember today — especially those who live in affluent countries.

Next we are told that they were to eat whatever was put before them (10:8). But what should they do if they found themselves staying in a Gentile household — as they might well do across the Jordan in Perea? If the food they were given was not strictly 'kosher', then Jesus said they were not to worry. When he said to them, 'Eat whatever food you are given,' he meant that preaching the gospel is much more important than any dietary laws. Peter learned this lesson in the house of Cornelius in Acts 10 and Paul was to say a similar thing in 1 Corinthians 10:23-33.

The Lord was telling the disciples to get on with the work of the kingdom, regardless of any obstacles which might be put in their way. They were to heal the sick by meeting the social and medical needs of the people. But, above all else, they were to say to the people, **'The kingdom of God is near you'** (10:9). They were to call people to repent of their sin and turn to God in faith. The people to whom these seventy-two were being sent had a much greater privilege than the inhabitants of Sodom; the inhabitants of that wicked city heard no call to repentance.

The rejection of the gospel

It is an awful thing for anyone to reject the gospel of salvation. These gospel messengers were to give a solemn warning to those who turned their backs on the message of the kingdom. If they were not welcomed in any place then they were to go into the streets of that particular town and shake the dust off their sandals as a sign against them. This is something which the strict Pharisees did whenever they re-entered Israel after they had been in Gentile territory. Jesus probably told the seventy-two to do this so that the inhabitants of a town which refused to welcome his messengers would be shocked and perhaps brought to consider their ways and come to repentance.

Jesus told his disciples about specific towns which had taken no notice of the gospel (10:13,15). Korazin, Bethsaida and Capernaum were all around the Sea of Galilee. Their inhabitants had all had the privilege of hearing Jesus preach in their streets and seen him performing wonderful miracles. Yet they had refused to recognize that Jesus was the Lord Christ. They had declined to repent of their sinfulness and turn to him for cleansing from their sin. So Jesus points out that the punishment of Sodom, Tyre and Sidon will be a little less on the Judgement Day than that which awaits those towns who had the opportunity of responding to Jesus. Every Jew would have known of the terrible destruction which had come upon Sodom in the time of Lot (Gen. 19:24-28). They would also have known of the prophecies against the proud Phœnician city of Tyre (Amos 1:9). Yet, said Jesus, the inhabitants of those wicked cities would surely have repented and sat in sackcloth and ashes if they had seen the miraculous acts which these Galilean towns had witnessed.

The Lord then singles out Capernaum, where he seems to have had his headquarters, 'You think that you will be lifted up to the skies; but no, you will go down to the depths' (10:15). How sad it is that many people are like the citizens of Capernaum; they refuse to seek the Lord in humility. They think that everything is going to be all right for them at the end of time. They think that they will be lifted up to heaven, but, said Jesus of all those who refused to welcome him and repent of their sins, they will go down to hell. Anyone who visits Israel now will not find a town where Capernaum once stood; all that can be seen is a few old ruins.

At this point Jesus reinforced the authority of these seventy-two. He said, **'He who listens to you listens to me; he who rejects you rejects me; but he who rejects me rejects him who sent me'** (10:16). What solemn words these are! These unnamed disciples represented Jesus and Jesus represented God the Father. We should take care that we never turn our backs upon any servant of God who faithfully preaches his Word.

The return of the seventy-two

We are not told how long these disciples were away on their journey, but when they returned, they came back with joy. They told Jesus, **'Lord, even the demons submit to us in your name'** (10:17). Jesus had sent them to heal and preach the gospel. He never said that they would be able to make demons obey them. But this, in fact, is what happened.

Then Jesus told them, **'I saw Satan fall like lightning from heaven'** (10:18). Isaiah tells us how Satan was originally one of God's angels, but he became much too proud and, as a consequence, he was cast out (Isa. 14:12-15). What did Jesus mean when he said to the seventy-two, 'I've seen him fall'? I believe that he was telling them that, although Satan is very powerful and he is always trying his best to disrupt the work of the gospel, we should not despair. He has fallen; he has had his wings clipped. Christ did that when he was on the cross of Calvary. Satan is powerful still; but his power, none the less, is limited.

The Lord said this to encourage them. Furthermore he declared, **'I have given you authority to trample on snakes and scorpions and to overcome all the power of the enemy; nothing will harm you'** (10:19). We can imagine their joy. They had not only been able to cast out demons from the demented, but they were given this further sign of Christ's approval of their work.

But, then, to get things in their true perspective, Jesus said, **'However, do not rejoice that the spirits submit to you, but rejoice that your names are written in heaven'** (10:20). When a person is saved the angels in heaven rejoice greatly. The new believer's name is written in the Lamb's book of life (Rev. 21:27); and God uses indelible ink; once a person's name is written in God's book it cannot be erased! John tells us that no one can pluck any believer from God's hand (see John 10:28).

Jesus rejoices

This is the only time in the Bible that we actually read that Jesus was full of joy. What made him joyful? It was because the secret of the kingdom had been revealed to his children. **'At that time Jesus, full of joy through the Holy Spirit, said, "I praise you, Father, Lord of heaven and earth, because you have hidden these things from**

the wise and learned, and revealed them to little children. Yes,
Father, for this was your good pleasure"' (10:21).

There is no philosopher on earth who can discover by his own
reasoning who Jesus really is, or who God is. These things are only
unfolded to those who are humble enough to come to Jesus as little
children, those to whom God chooses to reveal himself. **'All things
have been committed to me by my Father. No one knows who the
Son is except the Father, and no one knows who the Father is
except the Son and those to whom the Son chooses to reveal him'**
(10:22).

Jesus then turned to his disciples and told them of the great
privilege which was theirs. They had seen Jesus. The prophets and
the kings of the Old Testament had all wanted to see Christ. They
had seen him in a shadowy form. They had seen him afar off. But
these disciples had actually seen the Lord; they had seen what Jesus
did and they had heard what he had said.

Do we value the privilege which is ours, those of us who have
seen Jesus with the eyes of faith? Do we recognize Jesus for who he
is? And are we obeying his Word and honouring him as we ought?
To us he has committed the task of passing on the glorious message
of salvation. The question that we need to ask ourselves is: 'Are we
falling down in the task?'

The Good Samaritan (10:25-37)

There follows one of the most well-known stories in the whole of the
Bible. When a young lad helps a sweet old lady over a busy road she
sometimes thanks him by saying, 'You are a Good Samaritan.' Even
the anonymous telephone service which helps to prevent many
suicides has taken its name from this parable; there are many
branches of 'the Samaritans' all over the world. But if we think of
Good Samaritans merely as people who lend a helping hand to
others, then we are completely misunderstanding the meaning of
this story.

The setting

Jesus was evidently teaching a group of people and he had their rapt
attention. But suddenly a religious teacher stood up for the sole

purpose of testing Jesus. This man took the opportunity to assess how knowledgeable Jesus was. He wanted to see if he fitted in with the standards which were acceptable to the religious experts of the day.

Yet the question which he asked Jesus was a very good one. He said, **'What must I do to inherit eternal life?'** (10:25). What is eternal life? It is is not merely life which goes on and on. When the Bible speaks about eternal life it is talking about the quality of life in the hereafter. It is telling us about life which is lived to the full (see John 10:10).

This is a question which everyone ought to ask, but people do not want to think about what lies beyond the grave. We behave as though this life will go on and on for ever. But, if we try to ignore thinking about what happens to us when we die, we are behaving very foolishly.

However, although the religious expert asked a good question, he put the emphasis in the wrong place. He was concerned about what he had to do. He asked, 'What must I do to inherit eternal life?' He assumed that eternal life is a reward for some action taken by us on earth.

That is how we often think of it today. We like to think that God will look upon us kindly if we act in right ways. We behave as though our salvation depends upon the amount of good works that we perform and the number of religious services we attend.

But despite the scribe's wrong attitude, Jesus did not confront him with the error of trusting in good works for his salvation; in fact all the way through this passage the Lord keeps up this emphasis on 'doing'. Jesus asked the religious expert a question: **'What is written in the Law? ... How do you read it?'** In other words, he asked him what he thought the Bible taught in regard to this question of eternal life. He directed this man, who was an expert in the Bible, to the Bible itself. He did not say, 'What do the philosophers say about how we inherit eternal life?' He did not even say, 'What do the religious teachers say?' He took the man directly to the sacred Scriptures. In the same way we should always go to the same source to find the answers to our questions about life and eternity. Everything that we need to know about real life and the future is contained in this sacred book.

We do not know whether the man was taken aback or not but he gave the correct answer to the question that Jesus asked him. He

said, '"Love the Lord your God with all your heart and with all
your soul and with all your strength and with all your mind";
and, "Love your neighbour as yourself."' He gave Jesus a straight
quotation from Deuteronomy 6:5 and Leviticus 19:18 and Jesus
replied, 'You have answered correctly... Do this and you will live'
(10:28). The Lord emphasized what the man should do.

In saying this, the Lord was telling the man nothing new. The
scribe must have felt a bit of a fool because he found it necessary to
try to justify himself. He asked Jesus, **'Who is my neighbour?'** But
before we look at the story Jesus told, we need to stop and consider
these words of the Lord: **'Do this and you shall live.'**

Evangelicals say, 'No one inherits eternal life by performing
good works.' How does that tie in with these words of Jesus: 'Do this
and you will live'?Jesus, of course, was correct. It is true that if
anyone loves the Lord his God with all his heart and with all his soul
and with all his strength and with all his mind; and if he loves his
neighbour as himself, then he will inherit eternal life. The problem
is that no human being, except the Lord Jesus Christ himself, has
ever been able to love God with all his heart, all of the time. We all
know that Paul was correct when he wrote to the Romans, 'No one
will be declared righteous in [God's] sight by observing the law;
rather, through the law we became conscious of sin' (Rom. 3:20).
We have all failed when it comes to loving God with all our heart,
all the time. We all sin. Time and time again we read this, both in
the Old Testament and in the New. Also our own experience tells us
that this is true.

But the religious expert did not want to think about this failure.
He wanted to avoid thinking about this knowledge concerning
himself. So he asked Jesus, 'Who is my neighbour?' (10:29). To
answer him Jesus told this story.

The story

Jesus does not tell us that it is a parable. It may have been something
which had actually happened. This would then explain why the man
did not say, when Jesus had finished the story, 'But no Samaritan
would do that for a Jew.' Whatever the case, the story is as
instructive for us as it must have been for the people who heard Jesus
tell it on that day.

Jerusalem was about 3,000 feet above sea level and Jericho was some 1,000 feet below sea level. This means that the seventeen-mile journey from Jerusalem to Jericho was downhill. That is why Jesus said that **'A man was going down from Jerusalem to Jericho.'** The road was full of twists and turns and the countryside was very hilly. It was just the kind of place where robbers could hide, and then pounce out on unsuspecting travellers as they passed by.

The story concerns a man who was, presumably, a Jew. He was travelling alone down this dangerous road when he fell into the hands of robbers. The word 'fell' is a very violent one, and it shows that force was used for this mugging. The man lost everything, even his clothes (which could be sold by the thieves). On top of this they beat him about so badly that he was left half dead.

We can imagine the plight of the man. We could speculate about the foolishness of his actions. We could say, 'He deserved all that he got, travelling alone like that on such a notorious road.' But however much we might say that the man's misfortune was caused by his own folly, it does not alter the fact that as he lay by the roadside, he was in a desperate situation. He was in great need of help.

As Jesus continued with his story, he told of three people who happened to be travelling upon the same road. First of all, a priest came along. The listening crowd would have said to themselves, 'Surely here is help at hand for the man.' But, Jesus told his audience, when the priest saw the man, he passed by on the other side (10:23). He had no excuse for his negligence; he saw the man. So why did he not help him? Perhaps this priest had been taking services at the temple and he was in a hurry to get home. He would certainly have known that if the man was dead, and he touched him, then he would be defiled for some while (see Lev. 21:1-4). So, like so many people of today, he preferred not to get involved with this case. 'It's not my problem', he would have said to himself. Some of the crowds may have raised their eyebrows at this, because the priest had refused to help the man who was in need.

Jesus continued with the story by saying that a Levite came along. Levites were helpers of the priests. They, too, worked in the temple. Just like the priest, they would fear to be defiled through touching a dead body. It may be that the Levite was also thinking that the man had been left there by the robbers as bait. Perhaps the thieves were still hiding among the rocks, waiting to pounce out on anyone who was foolish enough to stop and examine the body. But, whatever was going through the Levite's mind, he too passed by on the other side.

By that time I wonder if the religious expert was saying to himself, 'Ah, now Jesus is going to tell us about an ordinary Jew who came along and helped the man! He's had a go at complaining about the inhumanity of the priests. He's shown up the lack of compassion in Levites; now he's going to tell us how someone who did not hold a particular religious office helped the man, while religious experts failed.' But, if that is what the scribe was thinking, he was wrong.

We can imagine everyone gasping when Jesus said, **'But a Samaritan, as he travelled, came to where the man was'** (10:33). What makes this story remarkable was the fact that the Samaritans were hated by the Jews, and the feeling was mutual! John tells us that Jews do not associate with Samaritans (John 4:9). But, despite all of the long history of enmity between these two groups, this particular Samaritan in the story that Jesus told took pity on the Jewish man who had been beaten up and left to die (10:33).

He went to him, despite the possible danger to himself. He bandaged his wounds, pouring in oil and wine — the oil to cleanse and the wine to disinfect. He put the man on his own donkey; he was not too proud to give him a lift. He brought him to an inn; he did not just patch him up and then send him on his way. He took care of him, even though the man was one of the hated Jews. He stayed the night (see 10:35), presumably to see that he was making suitable progress. He gave two silver coins to the innkeeper. This was the equivalent of two days' wages — enough for many days' stay at the inn. And he said to the innkeeper, **'When I return, I will reimburse you for any extra expense you may have'** (10:35). He took the whole cost of caring for the man upon himself. The Samaritan owed the Jew nothing. He just saw that the man was helpless and in great need, and he did everything he could to help him.

Chuck Swindoll told (in a radio service) of students at a Bible Seminary who had to hand in one of their assignments at 9 a.m. on a certain morning. All of them had been up most of the night working on their essays, having left it until the last minute. As they rushed through the campus grounds to the lecture room they passed another student lying beside the pathway; he had what looked like blood pouring from his head. Because the essay had to be handed in, no one stopped to look at the lad; their assignment was all-important. As it happened the other student was not hurt; he had just engineered this 'accident' to see if anyone would stop to help him. The title of the assignment, by the way, was, 'Explain the real meaning of the Good Samaritan!'

The final question

Jesus asked the expert in the law, **'Which of these three do you think was a neighbour to the man who fell into the hands of the robbers?'** (10:36). The scribe was in a bit of a quandary about this. The answer was obvious. It was the Samaritan. But the religious expert did not want to take that hated name on his lips — even after hearing this story! So he said, **'The one who had mercy on him.'** Initially the religious man had been wanting to know what he had to do to inherit eternal life. Jesus keeps this theme running right until the end of this incident. The Lord told him to **'Go and do likewise.'**

But this is not something that the religious person wanted to hear. He wanted to build his religion, his hope of eternal life, upon doing pious deeds. He was shocked when Jesus said, 'Helping your neighbour, even when you hate him, is obeying God.' He wanted to choose which good works he would perform. But Jesus said, 'Copy what the Samaritan did in loving your neighbour.' The Lord said, 'You have heard that it was said, "Love your neighbour and hate your enemy." But I tell you: Love your enemies and pray for those who persecute you, that you may be sons of your Father in heaven. He causes his sun to rise on the evil and the good, and sends rain on the righteous and the unrighteous. If you love those who love you, what reward will you get? Are not even the tax collectors doing that? And if you greet only your brothers, what are you doing more than others? Do not even pagans do that? Be perfect, therefore, as your heavenly Father is perfect' (Matt. 5:43-48).

The religious expert introduced the theme of showing mercy to the needy. In saying, 'Go and do likewise,' Jesus was telling the scribe to go and live a life of showing merciful compassion to all who are in need. The law demands that we obey God perfectly. If we can do this for all of our lives then we will inherit eternal life. But, as we have seen, every one of us has failed in our attempts to keep all of the commandments. It is not our obedience which will gain us eternal life, because we have failed in that respect. It is the obedience of Christ which provides the only hope for us. Just as Jesus taught that everyone is our neighbour, so he died for all sorts and conditions of men. And God will have mercy upon all those who come to him acknowledging their own inability to keep the law, and putting their reliance upon the atoning merits of the Lord Jesus Christ alone for salvation.

Work or worship? (10:38-46)

Christian service is very vital work. At the begining of this chapter we saw that Jesus had sent out the seventy-two as his ambassadors. They were very busy going from village to village with the message of the gospel, and Jesus was full of joy because of all the things they had done to further the work of the kingdom. Then from the story of 'the Good Samaritan' we learnt that we should all be good neighbours, showing Christian love and concern for all who are in need.

However, in this incident in the home of Martha and Mary, we see a diferent side of the picture. Luke does not wish to give his readers the impression that following Christ is something which demands only hectic activity; he wants to emphasize the need for Christians to rest at the feet of the Lord on occasions. His concern is to show us the importance of true Christian worship.

Jesus arived at Bethany

John tells us that Martha, her sister Mary and her brother Lazarus all lived in the town of Bethany, just outside of Jerusalem (John 11:1). Jesus and the Twelve were on a journey through Judea and they came to this village where these friends of the Lord lived (10:38). It is likely that Jesus had sent word on ahead to say that he would be arriving shortly. We know that this was his normal practice (see 9:52) and we can picture the busy activity going on in the house as everyone prepared for his visit. Luke tells us that Martha opened her home to him. She was evidently the oldest sister; otherwise it would not have been called *her* home. Perhaps she was a widow who had her younger sister and brother living with her. Anyway, it would seem that she was an excellent hostess who had organized everything in advance of the Lord's visit.

We can imagine how we would behave if we were told that a well-known and well-loved preacher was going to visit our house.

Nor was it only Jesus who had to be entertained: his twelve disciples had to be fed too!

None the less, despite all of this activity, Luke does not tell us about the actual arrival of the Lord; that is not the lesson which he is seeking to teach at this point. He merely sets the scene by saying that Jesus came to the village where Mary and Martha lived, and Martha opened up her home to him.

Mary sat at the feet of Jesus

Mary is mentioned three times in the Gospel records and on each occasion she is at the feet of the Lord. The other two places are in John 11:32 and John 12:3.

In those days, when people wished to learn from a great teacher they sat at his feet. We are told that Paul sat at the feet of Gamaliel, one of the most respected of the Jewish teachers (see Acts 22:3, AV). To be in that position showed honour and respect for the teacher. Anyone learning in such a way would literally be forced to 'look up' to the instructor. We do not know how soon after the arrival of Jesus Mary assumed this position, but it may well have been not long after the Lord entered the house.

What a homely picture this is! We do not know whether Lazarus was absent at this time, or whether he is simply not mentioned because he plays no part in the story. It is on Mary that our attention is focused.

Martha had other things to do

Mary's sister had the responsibility of making all the preparations for the Lord's visit. Luke emphasizes her work in such a way that we can almost hear her banging about in the kitchen, slightly annoyed that everything had been left to her. We are told about **'all the preparations that had to be made'**.

We can imagine Martha's frantic activity as she thought about all there was to do to make the Lord comfortable for his stay. A hundred and one questions must have been hurrying around in her mind. To express it in terms of modern Western culture, she would have been wondering, was the best tablecloth clean, and did it need ironing? Had dreamy Mary prepared the vegetables properly, and were they soaking in water to stop them going brown? At what time should she start to cook each different dish? How was she going to fit all the disciples into their places for the meal? Had the living room been thoroughly swept and cleaned? And what was she going to do if the food ran out before everyone had eaten their fill?

We are told that all these things distracted her. What was she distracted from? She was diverted from the Lord. Martha was like the Pussy Cat in the nursery rhyme which had been up to London to visit the queen, but when she entered the room where Her Majesty was, all she saw was a little mouse under a chair.

Martha had the Lord of glory in her own home, but she was so busy working, trying to make him comfortable, that she never had time to stop and listen to what he had to say to her.

Martha became angry

Martha was very conscious of all the things she had to do. Her activity wore her out. She was busy preparing her home for the Lord, but she worked so hard that she could not enjoy the Lord's presence when he was there. All she could think about was her 'lazy sister'.

When we become overworked and overtired we can easily act irrationally. We are so busy with all the things that we have to do that we start noticing how little others appear to be doing. The devil can cause a bad spirit to enter the minds of those who are over-active in the work of the Lord. Think of those times when Christians fall out with one another. It is often because a root of bitterness or jealousy comes into the hearts or minds of those who are spending too much time working rather than sitting quietly in adoration at the feet of Jesus.

Things became so bad that in the end Martha turned on Jesus and complained, **'Lord, don't you care that my sister has left me to do the work by myself? Tell her to help me!'** (10:41). How awful for anyone to speak to the Lord like that! Martha was so cross with Mary that she blamed Jesus. She accused Jesus, of all people, of being uncaring! All of this happened because Martha was over-anxious, overworked, overtired and over-worried. She was worried inside and busy outside. As a result, she ordered Jesus to 'tell [Mary] to help me'.

Even so, the Lord was not hard on Martha. He could have said, 'Why are you only concerned about yourself, Martha? Why do you say, "*My sister* has left *me* to do the work *by myself*. Tell her to *help me*"? You are only taken up with yourself, Martha. How *you* feel is all that concerns you.'

A gracious rebuke

Instead the Lord said, very gently, **'Martha, Martha … you are worried and upset about many things, but only one thing is needed'** (10:41). Jesus did not mean that food was unnecessary. He meant that he would much rather have Martha's attention than enjoy her most delicious cooking. Food, furniture and tablecloths will all pass away one day, but the presence of Jesus remains with his people for ever.

Jesus said, 'Only one thing is needed' (10:42). What is that one thing? It is what Mary chose. She sat at the Lord's feet, listening to what he said (10:39). 'We can become so involved with the work of the Lord that we neglect the Lord of the work.' [3] Naturally, service is essential, but we must not ignore our private devotions.

Mary and Martha were both true believers, but they were different from each other. They both emphasized different aspects of the Christian life. The work of the Lord would not go forward if everyone spent all day on their knees and never lifted a finger even to peel a potato. However, we also must take great care to spend time about our own personal devotions, listening to what the Lord has to say to us. In the home of Martha and Mary Jesus was teaching about the need for balance in the Christian life.

Those of us who are always doing things for the Lord, and for others, must also remember that we need to spend sufficient time quietly waiting before the Lord. We need to ask ourselves questions like, 'How important to me is my daily prayer time? Do I find reading and studying the Bible a chore? And how much time do I spend getting into a receptive frame of mind waiting to hear what the Lord is going to teach me each day?'

Martha, like the lawyer in the previous story, was trying to justify herself. 'Discipleship is about knowing what is important and putting first things first.' [4] Paul said, 'Physical training is of some value, but godliness has value for all things, holding promise for both the present life and the life to come' (1 Tim. 4:8). The Lord said, **'Mary has chosen what is better, and it will not be taken away from her'** (10:42). So the next time that we find that we are overworked and irritable with the Lord's people, let us seek first our heavenly Father's kingdom and his righteousness. If we do, we shall discover that everything else will fall into its proper place (see Matt. 6:33).

Charles Wesley summed up this story beautifully in his verse:

Oh, that I could for ever sit
With Mary at the Master's feet!
Be this my happy choice.
My only care, delight, and bliss,
My joy, my heaven on earth, be this,
To hear the Bridegroom's voice.[5]

11.
True religion and false

Please read Luke 11

Persistent prayer (11:1-13)

With all of the pressures of today's family and business commitments many children find it very difficult to keep in touch with their parents; fathers especially seem to be neglected. But Jesus never found it difficult to keep in touch with his Father. We often read of him praying. We read here, **'One day Jesus was praying in a certain place'** (11:1). It was his daily habit to pray regularly to his Father.

Some Christians are concerned lest forming a routine of prayer develops into sheer legalism. But, none the less, regular times of prayer are very good habits to cultivate. If we do not pray at the same time and place each day, then we might find that we lose the appetite for communion with our Father altogether. We should never pray only when we feel 'in the mood'.

The Lord's Prayer

One of the disciples had been watching Jesus very closely. It may have been one of the Twelve, or one of the seventy-two, or it may have been any of those who followed the Lord from place to place. Whoever it was did not interrupt the Lord's prayer-time. The disciple knew that prayer-time was a precious thing for the Lord. Even so, the disciple had a burning desire to ask the Lord something, but he waited until Jesus had stopped praying. Then he said, **'Lord,**

teach us to pray, just as John taught his disciples' (11:1). Not only did John the Baptist pray himself, but he taught his disciples to pray also.

Jesus said, **'When you pray, say: "Father ..."'** The words which we read in verses 2-4 are largely a repetition of what he had said much earlier (in Matt. 6:9-13). So why did the Lord repeat the prayer? He said it again because it is a pattern for prayer. While it is not wrong to repeat the same words in prayer, Jesus is surely saying that these are the kind of things we should pray for. Jesus never called it 'the Lord's Prayer'. In fact it is more helpful for us to think of it as 'the Disciples' Prayer'. After all, Jesus could never pray, 'Forgive us our sins,' because he never committed any wrong.

However, it is a good prayer for anyone to learn and to pray. It starts with 'God' and it describes him as 'Father'. He is the ideal Father, the one who truly cares for his children all of the time. This is one of the themes of this section (see 11:7,11,13).

Next, the glories of God are spoken about. **'Hallowed be your name.'** The name stands for the person. We should therefore make sure that God's name is always hallowed; we can do that by seeing that the Lord is set apart and occupies a special place in our affections and receives special honour.

'Your kingdom come.' The reign of God is a major theme in the Bible. The kingdom of God must soon come in all its fulness, and when that day arrives every knee shall bow at the name of Jesus and every tongue will confess that he is Lord (Phil. 2:10-11). In our prayers we should be pleading for that time when God will fully reign in the hearts and lives of his willing people.

In the second half of the prayer the needs of God's people are asked for. **'Give us each day our daily bread'** (11:3). This speaks not only of food and drink, but also of every bodily need. **'Forgive us our sins, for we also forgive everyone who sins against us.'** God does not forgive us just because we forgive others. He does not forgive us, with the same generosity, or otherwise, that we forgive other people. But he does demand that we, if we want to be forgiven ourselves, should also be prepared to forgive others.

'And lead us not into temptation.' God does not lead us astray (James 1:13). But he does know what kind of evil is waiting to ensnare us. This is why we need to pray for his protection and for his hand to stop us from going astray into temptation.

A story illustrating prayer

The setting is a village. In small villages everyone knows everyone else. If anyone refused hospitality to a visitor it would bring shame upon the whole community.

This parable concerns three men; at least one of them is a father (probably all three are; all decent men were married in those days). The first man had been travelling and at midnight he arrived at the home of his friend. Probably he had been travelling at night because the heat of the day would have made the journey too difficult.

The second man was thrilled to see his friend and welcomed him into his humble home. This meant that he would have immediately prepared a simple meal (usually bread and wine). But the cupboard was bare! So he straight away thought of his other friend who lived nearby and he went and called out to him for help. (During the daytime the third friend's door would have stood open, ready to welcome anyone who wished to go in, but now the door was not only shut but locked because it was midnight!) The house would probably have consisted of just one room. The family would have been sleeping on a raised part, very likely all in one bed for warmth, and the animals would have been brought inside to sleep in the part of the room which was used for living quarters during the day.

The third friend would have found it difficult to get up — not because he had no spare bread, nor because he did not want to help his friend, but because he did not want to disturb the children and set all the chickens clucking and the other animals making a dreadful noise. This is where Jesus ended the story.

Then the Lord brought out the teaching. He said, **'I tell you, though he will not get up and give him the bread because he is his friend, yet because of the man's boldness he will get up and give him as much as he needs. So I say to you: Ask and it will be given you; seek and you will find; knock and the door will be opened to you. For everyone who asks receives; and he who seeks finds; and to him who knocks, the door will be opened'** (11:8-10).

The progression in persistence went: 'Ask', 'seek' and 'knock'; each demanded a little more than the former. Jesus is teaching us that in prayer we must be persistent. God, our heavenly Father, delights to hear his children's prayers. But he does not keep us in suspense for long. He does not desire that we keep on asking just to tease us. The Lord tells his disciples that God is good to his children. **'Which of you fathers, if your son asks for a fish, will give him a snake instead? Or if he asks for an egg, will give him a scorpion?'**

No father who truly loves his children will ever give them anything which is harmful for them (even if they ask for it); no loving mother will let her small child have a sharp knife to play with, just because he asks for it. 'So', says the Lord, **'if you then, though you are evil [sinful], know how to give good gifts to your children, how much more will your Father in heaven give the Holy Spirit to them who ask him?'** (11:13).

The moment anyone becomes a true, born-again Christian, he receives the Holy Spirit. No one can believe in the Lord Jesus Christ for salvation without the power of the Holy Spirit. And God continues to give the Holy Spirit to those of his children who are obedient to him and who ask him for good, spiritual gifts. God is our Father and he desires what is best for us because he loves us. He delights to hear us pray.

This parable does not teach us that God is like the friend who is tucked up in bed and does not want to be disturbed at midnight. The whole point of it is that God is not like that. This is a story to show the contrast between a human father and our heavenly Father. That is why the Lord said, 'If you, though you are evil, ... how much more will your Father in heaven give ...' (11:13). Warren Wiersbe says, 'Persistence in prayer does not mean that we must twist God's arm to get what we want. It means keeping in close communion with the Father, knowing his will and asking him to perform it.'[1]

Darkness or light (11:14-36)

Some people say that there is no personal devil. They speak vaguely about a sense of evil being present, but they get very cross when the source of that evil is named as the devil or Satan. Yet Jesus had no doubt about the reality of a personal devil. He talked about the absurdity of 'Satan being divided against himself' (11:18) and he pictured Satan as a **'strong man, fully armed, [guarding] his own house'** (11:21). Indeed some of the crowds said that Jesus drove out demons by Satan; they gave him the name **'Beelzebub, the prince of demons'** (11:15). Today we need to recognize Satan for who he is — the Evil One (1 John 2:13), the deceitful one (2 Cor. 11:3) and the fierce and cruel one (1 Peter 5:8).

A partnership?

Jesus was accused of being in league with the devil. As he journeyed towards Jerusalem there were many more of the religious people who were opposed to him. At first they did their evil work surreptitiously. They mixed in with the crowds and started complaining. Jesus had healed a man who could not speak. He could not repeat the Lord's Prayer, sing praises to God or even ask anyone for bread. But Jesus drove the demon out of him; and, as a result, he was able to speak (11:14). No wonder the crowds were amazed at this. They had probably known the poor man all his life. He was also blind (Matt. 12:22) but after Jesus had dealt with him, he could both see and speak.

When the crowd showed their amazement at this miracle, some said that Jesus performed such miracles through the devil, and others muttered that they wanted to see a sign from heaven before they would believe in him. However, Jesus was aware of their murmuring. He **'knew their thoughts'** (11:17) and he refuted their charges. He said that their accusation was illogical. Everyone knew that the devil was responsible for these evil spirits which were afflicting so many people. If Jesus was driving out the evil spirits by the power of Satan then that did not make sense. No kingdom or house which is divided against itself can hope to succeed. And certainly Satan would not work against himself in driving out demons.

Next Jesus said that they were condemning themselves by their accusations. There were Jewish exorcists, who were going around the countryside at that time claiming to cast out demons (as Jesus actually did). **'Now'** said the Lord, **'by whom do your followers drive them out?'** He was asking how their works were different from his. 'Christ's miracles show that the kingdom of God is present, not the kingdom of Satan.'[2]

Also their accusations were really an admission of Christ's power. Jesus could not defeat Satan unless he was stronger than the Evil One. Our Lord is the one who has outpowered the devil. When Jesus spoke about the finger of God he was speaking of something which is very strong. When the magicians of Pharaoh saw the plagues which had come through Moses they declared, 'This is the finger of God' (Exod. 8:19). One description of the Holy Spirit is 'the power of God' and in Matthew's account of this incident Jesus said, 'If I drive out demons by the Spirit of God, then the kingdom of God has come upon you' (Matt. 12:28). In answering these accusations Jesus was saying, 'I am not in league with the devil. I am in league with the Holy Spirit.'

No room for compromise

Jesus demands complete obedience from his disciples. He says, **'He who is not with me is against me, and he who does not gather with me, scatters'** (11:23). The Lord was saying that there is no middle way. There is no room for compromise in regard to following him. He illustrates this by painting a picture of a moral man.

He speaks about the condition of a man from whom the evil spirit has departed. When we think of such a person we congratulate him. He has given up smoking. He no longer drinks alcohol to excess. He is living a clean, upright moral life. He not only attends church, but he goes to prayer meetings as well! But the problem is that this man has done nothing more than 'turn over a new leaf'. He is not 'with Jesus'. He does not gather 'with the Lord'. He is merely seeking to live a good life in his own strength. He has got rid of all the evil within him, but he has put nothing in its place. He has not got right with God. He is just an empty body, so far as spiritual life is concerned.

There are many people trying to earn their way to heaven by seeking to live like this. But one day, said the Lord, the evil spirit will return (because it can find nowhere else to rest) and it will discover that this man's life is swept, clean and in order. It will be delighted and will go and find seven other spirits more wicked than itself. And it will say, 'Come and join me. There is plenty of room in this man's life, and there is nothing within him to drive us away.'

A life refined, but lacking God's presence, is open to occupancy by evil. **'And the final condition of that man is worse than the first'** (11:26).

An interjection

At that point **'A woman in the crowd called out, "Blessed is the mother who gave you birth and nursed you"'** (11:27). Again it is only Luke who tells us of this unnamed woman. The words which she called out were an Eastern way of blessing. Mary, the mother of Jesus, was a very godly woman. She often listened to the words of Jesus and thought deeply about them. So in replying to the woman Jesus did not detract from what she said. But he added to it. He said, **'Blessed rather are those who hear the words of God and obey it.'** 'Mary is not blessed by virtue of her motherhood but by her ability to recognize God's word.'[3]

Jesus had earlier said that the one who 'hears my words and puts them into practice' is like a wise builder (6:47-48), and a little later, Jesus said, 'My mother and brothers are those who hear God's word and put it into practice' (8:21). The Lord constantly emphasizes the importance of obeying God's Word. There must be no compromise when it comes to the Scriptures. The Ven. George Austin, of York Minster, said that he walked out of a particular session of the World Council of Churches in Canberra in 1991 because the chairman ruled that the Bible must not be taken into consideration at that point.[4]

Signs given already

Some of the crowd tested Jesus by asking for a sign (11:16). What kind of sign did they want? Did they want him to show that he was the Messiah by moving the planets around the sky? Did they want him to bring about a great earthquake and wreak destruction on the earth? Or did they want him to call down from heaven the great thunderous voice of God to speak to them?

But if Jesus had done something like that, what good would it have done? Many signs had already been given to show that Jesus was the Son of God. He had performed numerous miracles (called 'signs' in John's Gospel) and many signs of the power of God had been given in the past. So, eventually in verse 29, Jesus selected two signs — both of them recorded in the Old Testament and both of them given to Gentiles.

Jesus told them, 'No sign will be given you except the sign of Jonah.' Most people know the story of Jonah and the great fish. It is a sign of death, burial for three days and resurrection to life again. That was a picture of the Lord Jesus Christ. His resurrection is the proof that he is the Messiah, the Son of God. That sign had already been given through the prophet Jonah.

Then Jesus reminds them of another person: **'the Queen of the**

South' (11:31), that is, the Queen of Sheba (which was probably situated in Southern Arabia). **'She came from the ends of the earth to listen to Solomon's wisdom.'** That was the second sign.

If the people wanted a sign then they had to give heed to these clear indications which had already been given in the Scriptures. They would have to humble themselves, though. Gentiles were 'outside of the pale' so far as Jews were concerned. They were so proud of being sons of Abraham that they were not prepared to admit that there was anything wrong in their lives. They were trusting that all Jews would be saved. But that is not what the Lord taught.

In this passage he speaks very strongly about the need for personal repentance. He said, **'The men of Nineveh** [evil, heathen men] **will stand up at the judgement with this generation** [the people to whom Jesus was speaking] **and condemn it; for they repented at the preaching of Jonah'** (11:32). The need for everyone, whoever they are, to repent of their sins is thundered out throughout the whole Bible.

The second thing that they needed to do was to listen carefully to God's Word, through Jesus. Jesus is stronger than Satan (11:21-22). Jesus is greater than Jonah (11:32); and Jesus is more glorious than Solomon (11:31).

The need for light

Jesus had already used the figure of a lamp in the Sermon on the Mount. Now he takes up the same theme again. He speaks of the light shining out into the darkness of the world. He says that the light of the glories of Christ must be placed in a high place so that its rays will shine out into the darkness round about.

Then the Lord talks about our eyes. He says that **'Your eye is the lamp of your body'** (11:32). He means that God's light is shining very brightly. But that light needs to be let into our hearts. The psalmist said, 'The entrance of thy words giveth light' (Ps. 119:130, AV). We all need to examine whether we have the light of God's Word in our hearts, because Jesus gives us all a warning. He says, **'See to it, then, that the light within you is not darkness'** (11:35). He means that it is so easy to deceive ourselves into thinking that we have the light of God within us, when all the while it is not the true light of God which is shining in our hearts but the 'light' of Satan, which is, in reality, darkness.

How can we test whether we have the true light within us? We can make sure that we have taken due notice of the signs which have been given to us. We must recognize that Jesus is God's Son and that he has come into the world to save sinners. We must come in repentance before him, just as the citizens of wicked Nineveh did long ago, when they saw and heard Jonah, who had died, had been buried and had risen again from the dead. And, above all, we must be like the Queen of Sheba and take great pains to listen to the one who is greater than Solomon.

If we sincerely do these things then our whole bodies will be full of light. No part will be dark: **'It will be completely lighted, as when the light of a lamp shines on you'** (11:36). Then we shall be those who hear the Word of God and obey it' (11:28).

Religious people beware! (11:37-54)

In these verses Jesus says 'Woe' six times. The first three times he speaks particularly to the Pharisees and the second three woes are addressed to the scribes, the experts in the law. A 'woe' is a saying that should cause people to stop short in their tracks. This was the intention of Jesus when he spoke to these religious people.

An encounter with the Pharisees

'When Jesus had finished speaking, a Pharisee invited him to eat with him; so he went in and reclined at the table' (11:37). Why did the Pharisee invite Jesus to a meal? Almost certainly it was not because he wanted to know about his teaching; rather he wanted to catch him out, and felt that he had more chance of doing this if he and his friends could observe him in his own home at close quarters.

The Lord obviously knew the reason why the Pharisee had invited him, so why did he go? He went because he wanted to give even these religious people an opportunity to repent, as the people of Nineveh had done when they heard the preaching of Jonah.

We, too, must take every opportunity put before us to preach the gospel. We should not shun to enter any building or any community, provided our faith and our teaching are not compromised and we ourselves are not contaminated. The Salvation Army often go into public houses, not to join in with the social jocularity, but to spread the Word of God.

When the meal commenced, the Pharisee noticed that Jesus did not first wash before he started eating (11:38). This was the custom; it had nothing to do with hygiene. It was a ceremonial washing which was required by the religious conventions of the day. Luke tells us that the Pharisee was surprised at Jesus' failure to conform to the accepted ritual. But Jesus obviously knew what his host was thinking (cf. 11:17) so he immediately compared the Pharisees to cups and dishes which were meticulously washed on the outside. He meant that these religious people looked clean and holy outwardly, but on the inside they were full of greed and wickedness. They were busy making a great deal of money (perhaps by underhand methods) filling their cups and dishes with their ill-gotten gains. But they were keeping these riches for themselves instead of giving what was inside their dishes to the poor (11:41).

Then Jesus pronounced three 'woes' upon the Pharisees (presumably there were also a number of other guests, mainly Pharisees). He spoke about their wrong priorities. They were most meticulous to give a tenth to God. That was the law. They went so far as to make sure that everyone knew that they even gave a tenth of their garden herbs to the Lord. But, despite these actions, of which they were so proud, they neglected justice and the love of God. Micah, one of the prophets they supposedly admired, had said,

> 'What does the Lord require of you?
> To act justly and to love mercy
>   and to walk humbly with your God'
>
> (Micah 6:8).

Their problem was that 'They were laying emphasis on the trivial, and neglecting the essential.'[5]

Jesus then spoke about the unwarranted pride of these people. He said, **'Woe to you Pharisees, because you love the most important seats in the synagogues and greetings in the market-places'** (11:43). The seats at the front of the synagogues were nearest to the Torah scrolls and they faced the rest of the congregation. Anyone who sat on such seats could not only see everything that was going on, but could be noticed and identified as 'someone important'. The further the seats were away from the front, the less important the people were — or the more humble they were!

The Lord spoke about the way in which these religious people misled others: **'Woe to you, because you are like unmarked graves, which men walk over without knowing it'** (11:44). Graves were whitewashed to mark them out so that pilgrims to Jerusalem could avoid walking on them. Numbers 19:16 teaches that anyone stepping on a grave became defiled for seven days; he could not enter the temple until the days of his purification had taken place. Jesus compared the Pharisees to unmarked graves. He meant that anyone who had contact with the Pharisees was, in fact, being defiled because these religious people were not teaching the true Word of God.

An encounter with the scribes

'One of the experts in the law answered him, "Teacher, when you say these things, you insult us also"' (11:45). In answer, Jesus pronounced three 'woes' on the scribes — which was not a very diplomatic thing to do! He said, **'And you experts in the law, woe to you, because you load people down with burdens they can hardly carry, and you yourselves will not lift one finger to help them'** (11:46). They had loaded the people down with such a multiplicity of religious rules and regulations that they just felt weighed down with all the effort of trying to keep these rules. And all the while, these religious people were no help to the ordinary man in the street; they would not lift a finger to help him (this passage is where that phrase comes from).

We, too, must make sure that we do not give the impression that to follow Christ requires a great emphasis on legalism. To know God is not a heavy weight; it is freedom — perfect freedom.

Then the Lord pronounced his second 'woe' to the scribes (the fifth one in all): **'Woe to you, because you build tombs for the prophets, and it was your forefathers who killed them'** (11:47). These people were busy building tombs, monuments to the prophets, when all the while they were approving what their forefathers had done in putting them to death. However, Jesus told them that God was going to send more prophets and apostles and these same people, and their like, would one day kill and persecute them

(11:49). He meant that these current religious teachers were no better than their forefathers who killed Abel, the first martyr (Gen. 4:8) and Zechariah, the last one according the Jewish Bible (2 Chron. 24:20-21) — and many more in between!

Here they were, building lovely monuments to the memory of past prophets, and yet they were opposing Jesus and his followers who would come after them. William Barclay says, 'The only prophets they admired were dead.'⁶ And Bishop Ryle comments, 'When a man can see no beauty in living saints, but much in dead ones, his soul is in a very rotten state.'⁷

Lastly Jesus said, **'Woe to you experts in the law, because you have taken away the key to knowledge. You yourselves have not entered, and you have hindered those who were entering'** (11:52). The symbol of the scribes was a key. They claimed to be the ones who could interpret the law of God; they held the key to knowing God. Yet, said Jesus, not only had they not entered into the knowledge of God themselves, but they were proving a stumbling-block to all those who did want to enter in.

Jesus is the real key of knowledge. By knowing him, we can know God. How many so-called preachers of God today are, in fact, obscuring Jesus by claiming that many things in the Bible are the words and thoughts of man? They say, 'You have to take some of the Bible with a pinch of salt.' These people are in a very serious condition; not only do they not know the Lord Jesus Christ themselves, but they are leading others astray by promising them eternal life through taking the sacraments, by observing good works and putting themselves in subjection to men who have a religious 'handle' to their names.

No wonder that **'When Jesus left there, the Pharisees and the teachers of the law began to oppose him fiercely and to besiege him with questions, waiting to catch him out in something he might say'** (11:53-54). The forefathers of these religious leaders killed many of the prophets, whom they were pretending to revere even while they themselves were plotting to kill the Lord Jesus Christ — the greatest prophet of all time. In the parallel passage in Matthew 23:13 Jesus said, 'Woe to you, teachers of the law and Pharisees, you hypocrites! You shut the kingdom of heaven in men's faces. You yourselves do not enter, nor will you let those enter who are trying to.'

What about us?

It is all very well for us to condemn the behaviour of those religious people, but are we leading people astray? Are we meticulous in our religious observances and yet do we fail to give our time, money and talents to those in need? Do we make a show of keeping religious rules, and yet neglect justice and the love of God? Do we love to be noticed and made a fuss of, and yet fail to show a humble attitude in our lives? Do we look askance when someone hangs their washing out on a Sunday, and yet fail to lift a finger to help them do it on a Saturday? Do we revere what godly men of the past have said, and yet, by our spiteful words and actions kill those who come seeking to do God's work today? Do we claim to have the key to God's Word, and yet by the way we live our lives hinder seeking souls in their search for God?

Jesus pronounced six 'woes' upon the religious people of his day. Would it not be dreadful if he had to pronounce the same kind of 'woes' upon us in our day?

12.
Treasure in heaven

Please read Luke 12

What a wonderful world we live in! There are riches untold for all of us to obtain and enjoy. Not only are there the blessings of nature and the companionship of human fellowship, but there are many material things for us to delight in as well.

It.is at this very point that we are in great danger.

Beware of materialism (12:1-21)

Jesus tells us to beware of hypocrisy (12:1) and of greed (12:15). In speaking to his disciples about these dangers the Lord probably addressed not only the Twelve, but all of his followers who were with him at that time. Also listening were the crowds, who were so numerous that they were trampling upon one another in order to get near to Jesus.

It seems strange to our ears that the first thing that Jesus spoke about was 'yeast'. But in those days everyone would have known about the properties of this substance. They all baked their own bread and they knew that yeast was mixed with the dough to make it rise. When yeast is first added it does not seem to make any difference, but gradually it spreads throughout the whole of the dough. After a certain period of resting, the yeast causes the whole lump to rise up to several times its original size.

In Scripture yeast is almost always a symbol of evil (see 1 Cor. 5:6). This is why Jesus said that his disciples must be on their guard against the yeast of the Pharisees, which was hypocrisy. He meant that the hypocrisy of the Pharisees was undetectable, initially (in other words, everything about them seemed to be godly). However, their influence spread through all of those who truly wanted to serve God. Like yeast, the Pharisees swelled up with pride and tried to swamp all of those who would be followers of Jesus.[1]

What did Jesus mean by accusing the Pharisees of hypocrisy? Hypocrisy is acting out a part. A hypocrite is someone who wears a mask, someone who pretends to be something other than he really is. Actors in a play take on the traits of the characters they are portraying. Some actors even carry this on throughout their public life and everyone thinks that they are really like the persons they usually depict. This was the case with the crooner, Bing Crosby. In every one of his films he played a very kind, loving man. Yet some years after his death one of his sons announced that Crosby was actually mean and miserable, quite unlike the person that all of his 'fans' worshipped.

The point that Jesus was making was that the Pharisees were merely acting a part, and one day they would all be unmasked! That is why the Lord said, **'There is nothing ... hidden that will not be made known'** (12:2). Then he brought it nearer to his disciples by saying, **'What you have said in the dark** [when you thought no one could see or hear you] **will be heard in the daylight, and what you have whispered in the ear in the inner rooms** [the store rooms hidden away in the middle of the house, or basement] **will be proclaimed from the roofs'** (12:3). If they had had modern technology in those days Jesus would probably have said that their secrets would be 'flashed across the world by satellite television'.

So why did believers sometimes speak quietly? It was because they were frightened that they would be arrested for speaking about Jesus. But the Lord says, **'I tell you, my friends, do not be afraid of those who kill the body and after that can do no more. But I will show you whom you should fear: Fear him, who, after the killing of the body, has power to throw you into hell. Yes, I tell you fear him'** (12:4-5).

How foolish we are to fear what mere men can do to us! The believer has nothing to fear; he is safe with God in Christ (Col. 3:3). But what about those who do not know the Lord Jesus Christ as their Saviour? They need to take careful note of those words of Jesus, **'after that'** (12:4). What will happen after they have died? The

Scriptures say, 'It is appointed unto men once to die, but after this the judgement' (Heb. 9:27, AV). What does Jesus say about sinners who are unrepentant? He declares that God has the power to throw them into hell. The word he used was not the word for the sleep of death *(Hades)*. He spoke of *Gehenna* — the ever-burning fire. Everyone who lived in Jerusalem knew about the rubbish heap in the Valley of Hinnom. It constantly smouldered, and all decent people kept well away from it. Jesus said that God, not Satan, has the power to cast people into hell. Many people do not like hearing about hell but we should never treat lightly any of the Lord's sayings.

Then Jesus spoke words of encouragement to his disciples. He said, **'Are not five sparrows sold for two pennies? Yet not one of them is forgotten by God.'** Sparrows were cheap — two a penny (they were bought for food). But if anyone bought two pennyworth it seems that an extra bird was thrown in free. Even this free one is noticed by God.

The Lord followed up this saying with another example. **'Indeed, the very hairs of your head are all numbered'** (12:7). Campbell Morgan says that this sentence really means that all of the hairs of our heads are 'labelled';[2] this is a far more intricate task than numbering!

'So,' said the Lord, **'don't be afraid; you are worth more than many sparrows'** (12:7). God cares for all of his people. They might pass through many trials. They might often have a natural fear of man, and of death (or rather the act of dying) but what a comfort it is for us to know that God loves us and cares for even the most humble and insignificant of his people!

Jesus then tells his disciples about the importance of owning him as Lord and Saviour: **'I tell you, whoever acknowledges me before men, the Son of Man will also acknowledge him before the angels of God. But he who disowns me before men will be disowned before the angels of God. And everyone who speaks a word against the Son of Man will be forgiven, but anyone who blasphemes against the Holy Spirit will not be forgiven'** (12:8-9). To acknowledge Jesus means to affirm that he is the Messiah, the Son of God. How we should remember the folly of disowning Christ! This is the same word which was used of Peter when he denied that he knew Jesus when the Lord was being tried. But was Peter forbidden entrance to heaven because he denied the Lord? No. Nor will we be, because the blood of Christ (his atoning death) cancelled out all our sins when we trusted Jesus as our Saviour.

But what is the blasphemy against the Holy Spirit which will not be forgiven? (12:10). Every sin of a believer is forgiven even though he or she might on occasion speak against the Lord. But those who continually make up their minds to pay no attention to the prompting of the Spirit have placed themselves on the road that leads to perdition. Hendriksen says, 'The blasphemy against the Spirit is the result of a gradual progress in sin. Grieving the Spirit (Eph. 4:30), if unrepented of, leads to resisting the Spirit (Acts 7:51), which, if persisted in, develops into quenching the Spirit (1 Thess. 5:19). The true solution is found in Ps. 95:7-8, "Today if you would listen to his voice, harden not your hearts."'[3]

When we trust God, though faith in Christ and reliance upon the Holy Spirit, we will not need to fear anyone, or worry about saying the right thing. The Holy Spirit will teach us and lead us into saying and doing what is correct (12:12).

The dangers of greed

There was an interruption from someone in the crowd. He had a very important matter that he wanted to bring to Jesus' notice. It does not seem that this person had been paying much attention to what the Lord had been saying. He was concerned only about himself, and what he wanted. He said, **'Teacher, tell my brother to divide the inheritance with me'** (12:13). How rude he was! Probably their father had died and there was some dispute between these two brothers. We do not know who was in the wrong, or whether both of them were. But Jesus was not so much interested in that as in the man's attitude to money. However, he was not going to be drawn into this dispute. He said, **'Man, who appointed me a judge or an arbiter between you [both]?'** Rabbis judged in these kinds of cases and Jesus was not going to interfere in the work of the local religious teachers. Instead he gave a warning about greed: **'Watch out! Be on your guard against all kinds of greed; a man's life does not consist in the abundance of his possessions'** (12:15).

How up-to-date this is! People still squabble over possessions, but Jesus reminds them, 'Who will own these things after you die?' He goes on to tell a story about a rich farmer who had a bumper harvest. What did this man not do? He did not say, 'How much of this shall I give to the cause of God?' Nor did he say, 'How much of this shall I give to the poor?' What he did say was, **'I will tear down my barns and build bigger ones, and there I will store all my grain and my goods. And I'll say to myself, "You have plenty of good things laid up for many years. Take life easy; eat, drink and be merry"'** (12:18-19).

But then God had his say: **'You fool! This very night your life will be demanded from you. Then who will get what you have prepared for yourself?'** (12:20). There is a story about a Jew who asked his rabbi, 'When shall I repent of my sins?' The rabbi replied, 'A few minutes before you die.' 'But' said the man, 'I don't know when I will die; I might not receive any warning.' 'Well', replied the rabbi, 'You'd better do it now, then!'

None of us knows how much longer we have to live on this earth. We must be ready to meet with God. There is that 'after that' to be considered. The rich farmer thought only of himself. In the Greek there are twelve personal pronouns in the few sentences which this man uttered. He spoke about 'I' and 'my', and never about 'God' or 'others'. That is how life is for one who lives only for himself, who is full of greed. 'You can't take it with you,' is a very true saying. How important, then, it is for us all to be rich towards God! We can do that by giving everything to him: our time, our money and our talents. And we can seek to live our lives for God's glory alone.

Beware of looking inward (12:22-48)

Worry is destructive. The root of the word in verse 22 means 'to be torn apart'. It is a picture of a ship being tossed about in a dreadful storm. Corrie Ten Boom said, 'Worry does not empty tomorrow of its sorrow, it empties today of its strength.'[4]

Worry is a sin

Unbelievers have great cause to worry, because if they die without knowing Christ they will be cast into hell (cf. 12:5). But believers are safe from sin's condemnation; therefore they should not be over-anxious about anything.

However, for many people it is natural to worry. Yet Jesus commands his people, **'Do not worry.'** If we are doing so, then we are disobeying one of the Lord's clear commands. If we are worrying we are saying, in effect, 'Jesus does not understand me,' and we are turning our backs upon the Lord and his desires for us.

What do Christians worry about?

Christians worry about their life, about food and clothing. They are concerned when there is not enough money to buy the basic necessities of life. They worry about how they are going to manage to provide for their family and they worry about what people think of them. For those who are hard up, life can be one big worry. But even to these believers the Lord says, 'Don't worry.' However, when a Christian is faced with large bills and nothing to pay them with it is much easier to say, 'I will trust God to supply my need,' than to actually do it. On one occasion I was faced with an extremely large telephone bill (which was not of my making) and I was in despair. I had no idea how I would pay my debt and I even considered whether I should end my life. It was on that morning that I read from a book of daily readings, based on the works of Dr Martyn Lloyd-Jones, words to this effect: 'If the Lord has been with you, and provided for your needs right up until this present moment, do you think he will now turn his back upon you and fail to provide for your current needs?' The answer, of course, was 'No.' Nor has the Lord ever failed to meet even one of my, or my family's needs.

So what is the antidote to worry? Jesus says, 'Look around you. Consider the ravens' (12:24). They have no means of carrying out an agricultural programme, yet God sees that they get enough to eat; and every child of God is worth more than many birds.

Then the Lord turned to the wild flowers growing all around them and said, **'Consider how the lilies grow'** (12:27). They are so beautiful and so natural. Even Solomon, with all his gorgeous robes, was not as grandly dressed as the fields of wild flowers in springtime. But what happens to these lovely flowers? They bloom just for a few days and then they fade and die. After that men cut them down and use them as fuel in their ovens. 'Now,' said the Lord, 'if God causes the fields to be clothed so beautifully, don't you realize that he will provide suitable clothing for you? You are more precious to him than birds or wild flowers.'

So what is the point of worrying? We should remember that our almighty God is in control of all things. Can we add to the length of our lives (or our height) by worrying about it? (12:25) Of course not.

But what about unbelievers? They live their lives trying to obtain bigger, better and more possessions. 'Don't worry,' said the Lord, 'your Father knows about all of your needs' (12:30). For God to know about our needs is for him to provide for us. The thing that we should be concentrating upon is to **'seek his kingdom'** (12:31). If we try to glorify God in our lives then all the material things that we need will be given to us. Jesus is not saying that we should be lazy; he never encourages anyone to be a scrounger. He is merely saying, 'Don't be over-anxious; trust me to supply your every need' (see Phil. 4:19). Believers should keep their eyes fixed upon heaven. **'Do not be afraid, little flock, for your Father has been pleased to give you the kingdom. Sell your possessions and give to the poor. Provide purses for yourselves that will not wear out, a treasure in heaven that will not be exhausted, where no thief comes near and no moth destroys. For where your treasure is, there your heart will be also'** (12:32-34).

Service is a privilege

Jesus said that his disciples should always be ready to serve their Master. He paints a picture of an Eastern wedding ceremony, but he looks at it from the angle of the household servants who are left behind at home. Their master has gone to a wedding celebration which might last for many days but, even so, being good servants, they are always dressed ready for service. They have their long robes tucked up into their belts, so that their work will not be hampered. They also keep their lamps burning. They keep stocked up with oil. They maintain the flame. They are like the wise virgins in Matthew 25. They are constantly ready for their master's return so that when he does comes back, they can open the door immediately for him (12:36).

But what a surprising thing happens when they do this! The master himself puts on servant's clothing and he makes his servants recline at table and then he proceeds to wait on them.

What does this parable mean? Jesus was talking about his own return to this earth. He is speaking about the period between his ascension and his second coming. During this time each of his people (his servants) should be watching and waiting for his return. They should not be debating the manner and time of his coming. They should not be arguing whether there will be a secret rapture or not. Only one thing is required of them: they should be living 'holy and godly lives as [they] look forward to the day of God' (2 Peter 3:11). On earth he said, 'I am among you as one who serves' (22:27; cf. John 13:4-5,12-16), but he will return one day as King; he is the Servant King.

Then Jesus emphasizes the importance of all of his people being ready for his return. He says, 'It will be good for those servants whose master finds them ready, even if he comes in the second or third watch of the night' (12:42). In other words, Jesus said, 'I am talking to everyone who regards himself as one of my servants.'

The Lord tells us about what will happen to the false servants when he returns. He speaks about one who throws his weight around because he has been given great responsibility (cf. 1 Peter 5:3). But when the master returns and finds that the one he left in charge of his household (which would also include his business) has abused that privilege, he will punish him greatly and 'assign him a place with the unbelievers' (12:46). He speaks about a lesser punishment being given to the servant who knows what his master wants and yet does not get ready or do his master's will. Finally he talks about the few blows which will be given to the servant who does not even know what his master requires and, of course, in consequence, has not done it.

These are solemn words spoken to those who claim to be servants of Christ. A true servant seeks to obey his master in all things. He seeks to ascertain his master's will. He has no concern about his own wishes but is solely devoted to carrying out the wishes of his Lord and Master. For all those who fail to carry out the Lord's wishes there will be punishment. This may vary in intensity but all false servants will be punished and cast into hell.

Jesus said, **'From everyone who has been given much, much will be demanded; and from the one who has been entrusted with much, much more will be asked'** (12:48). Elders of churches are no more important than the humblest church member, but they do have more responsibility. If they sin their removal from office will be all the more public and their fall will be the greater.

Beware of imminent judgement (12:49-59)

When any of us go for a job interview we make sure that we are well prepared and have everything in order. Jesus wanted his hearers to be ready, not for a job interview, but for the Judgement Day.

Jesus' baptism

When the Lord spoke about his baptism he meant his death on Calvary. Baptism is being immersed. Just as Jesus was dipped under the water at his baptism in the River Jordan, so he was baptized into his death by his crucifixion. It would completely envelop him. His death was to be terrible, and he was distressed until it was done.

His baptism was also linked with fire. When John was baptizing in the Jordan, he declared that Jesus would 'baptize [his people] with the Holy Spirit and with fire' (3:16). This fire fell on each of the disciples in the upper room on the Day of Pentecost (Acts 2:3). Jesus came to this earth to bring about redemption, through his death upon the cross, and to endue his people with power, through the gift of the Holy Spirit.

When Jesus spoke these words to his disciples they must surely have remembered those Old Testament prophecies which speak of the ushering in of the new age of the Messiah. They were living in a world of conflict and turmoil. They were under the domination of the mighty Roman Empire. All around them were soldiers who had been placed in Palestine to ensure that the Roman peace was observed. But in the heart of each loyal Jew there was a great longing for the coming age of peace and prosperity which the prophets had often spoken about. Isaiah had written of the time when there would be an increase of God's government and endless peace. He also spoke of the Messiah reigning on David's throne and over his kingdom, 'establishing and upholding it with justice and righteousness from that time and for ever' (Isa. 9:7). Micah wrote about the time when the people would beat their swords into ploughshares and their spears into pruning-hooks. He said, 'Nation will not take up sword against nation, nor will they train for war any more' (Micah 4:3).

Those who were listening to Jesus knew that he was the promised Messiah. How amazed they must have been then when he said to them, **'Do you think that I have come to bring peace on the earth? No, I tell you, but division'** (12:51). He said his presence would cause division in households. That was what Roman families feared most of all. They hated divisions, especially in families. Their own religion made room for as many gods as were wanted. Any Roman would have been happy to place Jesus alongside all the rest of his gods, and he would have worshipped him with equal devotion.

'But the essence of Christianity is that loyalty to Christ has to take precedence over the dearest loyalties of this earth.'[5]

The Jesus said, **'From now on there will be five in one family divided against each other, three against two and two against three. They will be divided, father against son and son against father, mother against daughter and daughter against mother, mother-in-law against daughter-in-law and daughter-in-law against mother-in-law'** (12:52-53). Jesus was not teaching that we should neglect our families; he was saying that he must have first place in the allegiance of each of his people. All true believers discover that, sooner or later, their loyalty to Christ will bring division, even within their own families. Jesus put the same thing another way in Luke 16:13 where he said, 'No servant can serve two masters. Either he will hate the one and love the other, or he will be devoted to the one and despise the other. You cannot serve both God and money.'

Observing signs

How often is the weather forecast correct? We complain when it is not. For generations past people have had ways of predicting what the weather would be like. Some hung up seaweed and felt it to find out if it would rain or not. Some would look at the sky and say, 'Red sky at night, shepherd's delight. Red sky in the morning, shepherds take warning.' The very same kind of things happened in Palestine. Everyone knew that when there was a cloud rising in the west (over the Mediterranean Sea) the rains were on their way. Likewise when the south wind was blowing (from over the desert lands), then they knew they were in for a hot, dry spell of weather.

Knowing this is how the people behaved, Jesus turned on them and called them hypocrites. We have already seen that a hypocrite is one who is living a life of pretence, merely acting out a part (see 12:1). Jesus called them hypocrites because 'They could interpret nature's physical signs of approaching storm or scorching heat [but] they could not read the sign of the moral and spiritual storm that was blowing around them.'[6] They were hypocrites because they pretended not to understand what God was so clearly telling them. Judgement was coming, just as it had come upon their forefathers when they rejected the words of the prophets. Leon Morris puts it like this: 'They understood the winds of earth, but not the winds of

God; they could discern the skies but not the heavens. Their
religious externalism prevented them from seeing the significance
of the coming of Jesus.'[7]

Isaiah had said something similar to the people of his day,
hundreds of years beforehand:

'The ox knows his master,
    the donkey his owner's manger,
but Israel does not know,
    my people do not understand'

(Isa. 1:3).

The reason they did not understand was because they were
hypocrites. They were pretending that everything was all right with
them. They were surely thinking, 'We are God's chosen people; no
harm can come to us.' However, subsequent history tells us of their
seventy years of judgement while they were in exile, away from
their beloved land and temple. Now Jesus was saying to his audience
that a similar judgement was going to come upon the Jews of his day.
The Romans were going to overthrow Jerusalem and scatter God's
people far and wide. In fact, all this did happen in A.D. 70. The
destruction was so great that not one stone was left standing upon
another.

Because all of these things were going to come upon them, Jesus
made this impassioned plea for his hearers to get right with God.

A picture of a lawcourt

The Lord said to them, **'Why don't you judge for yourselves what
is right?'** (12:57). Then he told a story about someone who is on his
way to court to be tried. This person is obviously in the wrong and
he knows he is going to be found guilty. 'Now', implies Jesus to his
hearers, 'any man who has a bad case in the presence of God (the
Judge of all things), if he is wise, will make his peace with God while
there is still time.' If people do not get things settled out of court they
will be thrown into prison and will not be let out until they have paid
the last penny (here Jesus used the name for the smallest coin then
in use. This was not the same word as he used in verse 6). The Lord
meant that someone who is thrown into this prison will never be able

to get out. They will stay there for ever, suffering because they have no means of earning money to buy their way out of their confinement.

What Jesus said to his hearers so long ago is very relevant to all of us today. He is speaking about the need for everyone to get right with God, even though this may cause division in our families. If our friends no longer accept us because Christ takes first place in our lives, then they must leave us. We cannot, and we must not, leave Jesus. He loved us and gave himself for us. We must abide faithful to him.

Jesus is also speaking to us about the coming judgement. The sin of the world is going to bring in a day of judgement. There will be eternal division then and we must make sure that we are sheltering under the blood of Christ because when the great Judge of all the world comes he will not look at our good works. He will examine our clothing. Only those who are wearing the righteousness of Christ will be exempt from his judgement. That means that only those who have fled for mercy to the cross of Christ will be saved.

Jesus is also speaking about hell. So many people do not like to mention this awful subject. But Jesus speaks about it. In verse 5 Jesus said, 'Fear him who ... has the power to throw you into hell.' And here he says, of those who die unrepentant, **'You will not get out.'** The Bible nowhere speaks of an escape from hell. It is not medieval thinking to say that there are only two places to spend eternity — heaven or hell. It is the reality which Jesus Christ himself speaks of and which anyone ignores at his or her peril.

13.
Time is running out!

Please read Luke 13

The urgency of repentance (13:1-17)

Quite often when we talk to people about the Lord Jesus Christ they ask a question which is designed to steer the conversation away from their need of Christ. They will say things like, 'If only you didn't insist that God created the world in seven days, I would be able to believe what you say.' Or they say, 'I can't believe that the Bible is infallible; if you weren't so dogmatic about that then I would become a regular churchgoer.' However, as important as these things are, they serve to divert attention from the central question: 'Who is Jesus, and what is my response to him?'

An irrelevant question

Jesus was on his way to Jerusalem. He had an appointment to keep there — an appointment with death. The disciples had warned him about going to the capital city. They knew that the religious leaders were determined to have him put to death, but despite all of this the Lord steadfastly set his face to go to Jerusalem.

He knew that it would be unwise to get involved in political matters. Later on when someone tried to catch him out regarding the payment of taxes he avoided that issue (20:20-26). In this section we find that there were some people in the crowd who were trying to get the Lord to launch an attack upon an injustice which Pilate had earlier carried out upon some Galilean worshippers. The governor had caused the blood of these worshippers to be mixed with the blood of the sacrifices which they had brought to the temple.

Although this incident is not recorded elsewhere in the pages of history, we know of other cases where Pilate's orders had caused people to be killed in the temple. The blood of these particular worshippers had certainly run down on to the animals which they had brought to offer as sacrifices.

However, we can see that, in reminding Jesus of this incident, the people in the crowd were out to cause mischief. For a start, they chose a case where the victims were from the north of the country. (The people of Judea did not think very much of those who lived in Galilee.) The other way in which they were trying to trap Jesus was by attempting to make him pass judgement about the behaviour of Pilate. But the Lord refrained from being drawn into any political discussion. Instead he asked the people around him, **'Do you think that these Galileans were worse sinners than all the other Galileans because they suffered this way?'** (13:2).

In asking this, the Lord put the onus onto them. In a sense he was saying, 'Don't talk to me about those who have died. I'm not going to say whether these were worse sinners than those who were not murdered. What I am going to remind you of is that you are all sinners.' He meant, 'Stop worrying about those from the past and start thinking about your own relationship to God.' Then, with great solemnity he said, **'Unless you repent, you too will all perish'** (13:3).

To reinforce what he was saying, Jesus reminded them of a case where some Judeans were killed. Apparently the tower near the Pool of Siloam had fallen and killed eighteen people, and these were all from Jerusalem. 'So,' he seems to be saying, 'it was not only Galileans who died in accidents, was it?' Jesus was saying that death and sickness do not always come about as a judgement from God (see John 9:1-3). The thing to consider is whether these Galileans, or these citizens of Jerusalem, were greater sinners than those who were not killed. He meant that everyone is a sinner in God's sight, and all need to repent and turn to God.

A fruitless tree

This parable is about a fig-tree planted in a vineyard (cf. Isa. 5). Jesus was pointing out, through this parable, that God's people must not

only repent; they must also produce good fruit by living their lives
for God's glory. The fig-tree is a picture of the nation of Israel and,
perhaps, particularly of the religious leaders of the nation.[1]

The owner of the vineyard had this particular fig-tree planted in
his vineyard because the soil was fertile and he expected a good crop
of fruit from it. That was the only function of the fig-tree; it had to
justify its existence. If it was going to take up space and draw
nourishment from the ground and the air, then it would have to show
it was worth having. The harvest it produced must be good and
regular.

The tree would have been three years old before it could hope to
give a harvest. Then, according to Leviticus 19:23-25, the fourth
year's crop must be given to the Lord. Therefore it was not until the
fifth year that the owner could expect to enjoy the fruit of the tree for
himself. But, in the case of this tree the owner went to look for fruit
on it, but he found none (13:6). Jesus was saying that God has a right
to expect a return from the people of God, and especially from those
who are religious leaders.

Because of the lack of fruit on the tree the owner of the vineyard
said to the man who took care of it, **'For three years now I've been
coming to look for fruit on this fig-tree and haven't found any.
Cut it down! Why should it use up the soil?'** (13:7). The owner
had a right to say, 'Cut it down.' He had given it a good chance, but,
to his mind, the tree was obviously useless. In fact the sense of the
owner's words is, 'Dig it up so that there is no possibility of it
beginning to grow again.'[2]

God had the right to pass judgement on the unfaithful and
unfruitful rulers of Israel, and likewise he has the right to pass
judgement upon us as well. He has planted us (individually) in his
vineyard (the church) with the purpose that we can produce a harvest
for his glory. If he keeps coming to us and finds that we are
unfruitful, then he has the right and the power to say, 'Cut him down,
why should he use up space?'

Jesus then tells us of the gracious mercy of the Lord. The
vinedresser in the story (who is evidently a picture of the Lord Jesus
Christ) says, **'Sir, leave it alone for one more year, and I'll dig
round it and fertilize it. If it bears fruit next year, fine! If not,
then cut it down'** (13:8-9). How gracious is our God! He knows that
we are failures, but he gives us a little more time to prove ourselves.
God has the authority and the power to destroy us, yet he is so kind

and gracious. Peter tells us that '[God] is patient with [us], not wanting anyone to perish, but everyone to come to repentance' (2 Peter 3:9).

In verse 3 of our chapter the Lord said, 'Unless you repent, you too will all perish.' In verse 5 he says it again: 'Unless you repent, you too will all perish.' And then, in case anyone is saying, 'Oh, there's plenty of time to think about repentance later on!' he says, 'If it bears fruit next year, fine! If not, then cut it down' (13:9). What does he mean by 'next year'? He means 'any time, or soon'. The message is that we must all repent now, and go on repenting every day of our lives. We can never produce anything useful to God unless we are living holy lives and seeking to please him in everything we do, and say and think.

A crippled woman

In verse 10 we read of the last recorded incident of Jesus visiting a synagogue. In this building the elders would sit at the front and all of the important men would be in prominent positions. The women would sit at the back, or in some out-of-the-way place.

Somewhere in this synagogue was a crippled woman. She was bent over and could not straighten up at all. For eighteen years she had been like that. (This is the second time that Luke uses the number eighteen in this chapter — see 13:4.) Being bent over, she could not look anyone in the eyes and most people, through embarrassment, would have looked the other way when she was about. But, despite her infirmity she still went to the synagogue; worship was very important to her.

Once again Luke draws our attention to someone in need; again it is a woman. He was concerned to show us that Jesus cares for all kinds of people, even crippled women. Despite all of the crowds and the fact that she must have kept in the background Jesus saw her — as he sees everyone, especially those with deep needs. The Lord called her to come forward, even though she would rather have stayed in the background. He did not do this to embarrass her. He did it to show to everyone that she was going to be healed, and restored to full fellowship in the community again. That is why he said, **'Woman, you are set free from your infirmity'** (13:12).

Then Jesus put his hands on her. He was not ashamed to touch her. He did not despise her. He treated her with respect and love, and

'**Immediately she straightened up and praised God'** (13:13).

But this miracle caused the ruler of the synagogue to object. Perhaps he felt that his authority was being overruled. He addressed the people, but he was getting at Jesus. He said, '**There are six days for work. So come and be healed on those days, not on the Sabbath'** (13:14). He was ignoring the fact that Jesus had not been there on those other days and no one else had healed her on a weekday. However, Jesus turned angrily upon him and said, '**You hypocrites!'** Again he was talking about all religious leaders. He accused them of pretending to be what they were not. They were hypocrites because they cared more for their interpretation of the Bible than that a sick woman had been healed. He emphasized this by saying, '**Doesn't each of you on the Sabbath untie his ox or donkey from the stall and lead it out to give it water?'** (13:15). He meant, 'You regard your animals as more valuable than this poor woman. If God's Word says that it is all right to feed and water domestic animals on the Sabbath day, then it is in order to bring healing on the Sabbath day.'

Then Jesus told them the real cause of the woman's illness. It was not her sin, or the sin of her fathers, which had brought about this deformity: it was Satan (see 13:16). No wonder this statement and action caused humiliation to his opponents, and delight to the crowds (13:17).

Jesus set this woman free from that which had bound her, but Satan still has very many people in bondage today. Some are in bondage to fear. They are frightened of living and they are frightened of dying. Some are in bondage to a habit or a drug which controls their lives, or an obsession which uses up all their money, time and effort. But Jesus can still break the power of Satan's grip. He can still set people free.

The growth of the kingdom (13:18-35)

Jesus compared the kingdom to a mustard seed — the very smallest seed that farmers used in those days. This tiny seed, given favourable conditions, can grow into a large plant; so large that birds can even perch on its branches, or leaves. In speaking about this the Lord was saying to his disciples that his work would grow very large indeed. This is what did happen in the first century of its existence.

The second illustration which Jesus gave was of a woman making bread.

Often yeast is a symbol of evil which is making inroads into the world, but here it is a picture of inward growth. When a small amount of yeast is mixed into a large amount of flour, it grows and swells — from within. Jesus was teaching that, not only will the church make rapid outward numerical growth; it will also expand from the inside. Inward, spiritual growth is even more important than growth in numbers. We all like to see more and more people coming to church, but that, on its own, is not enough. All of God's people must be making progress in their love for Christ as well. Peter tells us to 'grow in the grace and knowledge of our Lord and Saviour Jesus Christ' (2 Peter 3:18). We need to ask ourselves questions like, 'Do I love the Lord, and the people of God, more now than I did at this time last year?'

Inside the kingdom

Jesus was journeying through the region of Perea, the land beyond the River Jordan. He had been teaching the people all of the while (13:22). His desire was to bring people to repentance and faith in God but someone asked him, **'Lord, are only a few people going to be saved?'** (13:23). They raised this because, up until that time, it had been assumed that every Israelite belonged to God. However, the teaching of Jesus had made them think; it had made them realize the awful truth that not every Jew would automatically be saved. And one of the first steps in anyone's salvation is when they realize that they are not real Christians after all.

The question that this person asked Jesus was, perhaps merely an intellectual one. But the Lord did not give him an intellectual reply. He did not just want to stimulate his knowledge of theology. He was concerned about this man's soul. So he turned the question back upon him and, in effect, said, 'Never mind about how many people will be saved, what about you? Will you be among that number?' He put it like this: **'Make every effort to enter through the narrow door, because many, I tell you, will try to enter and will not be able to'** (13:24).

Jesus used a Greek wrestling term when he said, 'Make every effort to enter.' The word translated 'to enter' means 'to agonize'. Jesus did not mean that we can be saved through our own efforts. He meant that we all need to seek the Lord and his salvation, and to do it rigorously and urgently. He also reminded his hearers that there is day coming when the door will be shut and finally bolted. The number of those who are saved will be complete. He means that after that time no one else will enter heaven. The angel of God says, 'Let him who does wrong continue to do wrong; let him who is vile continue to be vile; let him who does right continue to do right; and let him who is holy continue to be holy' (Rev. 22:11).

It will be a very sad time for those who are outside of the door on that day. They will be like the foolish virgins in Matthew 25:1-13. On the great Day of Judgement those people who are left outside will hammer on the door and plead, **'Sir, open the door for us.'** But the Lord will answer, **'I don't know you or where you come from'** (13:25). And all their pleadings and explainings will be in vain. They will try to gain admittance by saying, **'We ate and drank with you, and you taught in our streets.'**

What greater connection could anyone have had with Jesus than to have actually been one of those five thousand who ate of the five loaves and two fish? What closer links could they have had with the Lord than to have stood in their home town and heard, with their own ears, Jesus teaching them about the kingdom of God? Yet the Master said to these very people, 'I don't know you.'

We all know the Queen. At least we know who she is, and what she looks like, but how many of us can say, 'The Queen knows me'? On the Day of Judgement, it will not be good enough to say to God, 'I know who the Lord Jesus Christ is.' The real question is, 'Does he know me?' Have I been to him in repentance and faith, and has he looked directly into my soul and said, 'Your sins are all forgiven you'? How awful it will be for those of whom Jesus said, **'You will stand outside'!** (13:25).

On the Day of Judgement all those who assume that they are Christians, and are not, will be furious. There will be weeping (but not the weeping of repentance) and there will be gnashing of teeth. Yet, to make the pain even worse, although the door will be fast shut, those outside will be able to look in and they will see Abraham, Isaac, Jacob and all the prophets in the kingdom of God. But they, themselves, will be thrown out. They will not be annihilated (and so unaware of anything). They will see who is inside, and they will know that they are outside because they, who thought that they had a place guaranteed in the kingdom, will be **'thrown out'** (13:28).

They will be humiliated further still. They will see people coming from all the four corners of the earth and taking their places in the kingdom of God. They will also see Jews, who they thought would have the first place, having to give way to Gentiles, who they thought were inferior, and even 'beyond the pale' (that is the meaning of 'last'), but who are in fact taking the first places (13:30).

The Lord's sorrow for Jerusalem.

As Jesus was saying these things some Pharisees came and said, **'Leave this place and go somewhere else. Herod wants to kill you'** (13:31). How strange that Pharisees, who had become bitter enemies of the Lord, should now appear to be concerned about his welfare! But Jesus was not taken in by them. He said, **'Go tell that fox, "I will drive out demons and heal people today and tomorrow, and on the third day I will reach my goal"'** (13:32). He called Herod 'that fox' (literally 'that vixen'). Herod was the only person of whom Jesus ever spoke in such a disparaging manner. A fox is a sly, cunning, crafty creature. Jesus knew that Herod only wanted to be entertained. He knew that Herod had no concern about his own salvation. But Jesus also knew that no one, however powerful, could harm even one of the hairs of his head, until God ordained it.

It is the same with us. If we are living our lives with the aim of pleasing God, then he has us continually in his care. There may be dreadful things happening to us, but we always remain under the protection of our heavenly Father. An old hymn puts it like this:

Sovereign ruler of the skies,
Ever gracious, ever wise;
All my times are in thy hand,
All events at thy command.

Plagues and death around me fly;
Till he bids, I cannot die;
Not a single shaft can hit,
Till the God of love sees fit.[3]

Then Jesus spoke about Jerusalem, the holy city. He said, **'For surely no prophet can die outside Jerusalem!'** (13:33). Just as

others of God's messengers had been murdered in the holy city, so
would he be. Then he sang a lament for Jerusalem: **'O Jerusalem,
Jerusalem, you who kill the prophets and stone those sent to you,
how often I have longed to gather your children together, as a
hen gathers her chicks under her wings, but you were not
willing! Look, your house is left to you desolate. I tell you, you
will not see me again until you say, "Blessed is he who comes in
the name of the Lord"'** (13:34-35).

Jesus spoke so tenderly about Jerusalem. He longed for its
deliverance. He offered it his own protection. He was like a chicken
holding out its wings to gather in all of her chicks. How different is
a chicken from a fox! (See 13:32). Yet the sad fact was that Jesus said
of the city, 'But you were not willing' (13:35).

He further adds, 'Look, your house is left to you desolate' — just
as the temple was left desolate in the days of the exile (Hag. 1:4,9).
When Jesus was in the temple at the age of twelve he had said to his
parents, 'Didn't you know that I had to be in my Father's house?'
(2:49). But he no longer called the temple 'my Father's house'; here
he called it 'your house'. That is why, from that day onwards, it was
desolate. It was no longer God's house. The glory of the Lord had
departed from it. All this happened because the Jews had rejected the
Lord Jesus Christ. Unconverted Jews (together with unconverted
Gentiles) are to remain outside of the door of God's kingdom unless
they repent and turn to Christ in faith. Jesus will reveal himself no
more to them until the time of his second coming. On that day all will
be compelled to say, **'Blessed is he who comes in the name of the
Lord'** (13:35). Believers will say it willingly, but unbelievers will
say it reluctantly. Paul, writing to the Romans, quotes the Old
Testament Scriptures:

> '"As surely as I live," says the Lord,
> "Every knee will bow before me;
>   every tongue will confess to God"'
>
> (Rom. 14:11).

To the Philippians he also wrote,

> 'At the name of Jesus every knee should bow,
>   in heaven and on earth and under the earth

and every tongue confess that Jesus Christ is Lord,
to the glory of God the Father'

(Phil. 2:10-11).

The call to everyone is: 'Do not remain outside of the door of Christ. Do not be among those who are not willing to be gathered under the protection of the Lord.'

14.
The great invitation and our response

Please read Luke 14

God's gracious invitation (14:1-24)

No one is good enough to be entitled to enjoy the blessings of heaven. The Jews often thought of the coming of the Messiah as the culmination of all things. They spoke of the time when the Great Day of the Lord would come and they would receive their reward by sitting down to a great heavenly banquet in the presence of the Lord. They saw this as something reserved especially for the Jews — and their places of honour would be worked out in accordance with how much merit they had earned while they were here on earth. But Jesus smashed those ideas. He taught that the great feast which God will give on the day of his appearing will be only for those who have accepted his gracious, and free, invitation to join with him.

A Sabbath meal

Jesus was attending a meal given by a prominent Pharisee (14:1). This kind of invitation had been extended to him before (7:36); and it seems that this one was given with the same motive. The Pharisees wanted to catch Jesus out. They were hoping that he would break one of their Sabbath prohibitions.

Jesus would have known that he was being watched very carefully (14:1). Nevertheless he accepted the invitation and walked openly into the house. When he entered the house he found someone else there — a man suffering from dropsy. This was a dreadful

illness which affected the kidneys, heart and liver. Those who had
this incurable disease found that the tissues of their bodies filled up
with water and swelled up.

Obviously this poor man had been 'planted' by the Pharisees. He
was **'in front'** of Jesus (unlike the woman in 13:11). The Pharisees
knew 'that Jesus could not be in the presence of human suffering
very long without doing something about it.'[1] So Jesus turned to the
Pharisees and the experts in the law (apparently there were many of
them also invited to the meal) and asked, **'Is it lawful to heal on the
Sabbath or not?'** After this question they were all speechless
(14:4).

They must have known what had happened on the previous
occasions when Jesus had healed people on the Sabbath day. There
are seven recorded miracles of Jesus healing on the Sabbath; five of
them are in Luke (4:31,38; 6:6; 13:14; 14:1) and two are in John
(John 5:10; 9:14). Many times Jesus had shown that when he healed
people it was not God's laws which were being broken, but man's
traditions. Evil men, like the devil, never give up their work of trying
to stop God's people from doing good.

As there were no spoken objections, Jesus took hold of the man,
healed him and then sent him away (14:4). The man had obviously
not been invited to the meal and Jesus wanted him to be faced with
no further embarrassment. The Lord then turned to the religious
people and said, **'If one of you has a son or an ox that falls into a
well on the Sabbath day, will you not immediately pull him out?'**
(14:5). Again **'They had nothing to say'** (14:6). They had got the
point. It went home to them because it was personal. Jesus did not
ask, 'What do people do if their son, or their animal, falls into an
open well on the Sabbath day?' He said, 'What would *you* do if *your*
son or *your* animal was in danger of drowning?' Of course, the
answer was obvious. They would immediately run to rescue their
son, or their animal, before he drowned.

Why, then, were these religious people upset? All that Jesus did
was to rescue a man from drowning in the water which was in his
body — but he did it on the Sabbath day. It might have been too late
had Jesus waited until the Sabbath was over. And, in any case, was
it in keeping with the love of God to keep the man in pain one
moment longer than he needed to be? How sad it was that these religious leaders were much more concerned about man-made religious
conventions than about showing the love of God to the needy!

A lesson in humility

Jesus had noticed the undignified scramble which had taken place in order to get the best places at the feast. Everyone wanted to be thought of as important, and the seats were all graded: the highest one was next to the host, and the lowest one was furthest away from him. What a scandal it was that these people were so conscious of status!

So Jesus said, **'When someone invites you to a wedding feast, do not take the place of honour, for a person more distinguished than you may have been invited. If so, the host who invited both of you will come and say to you, "Give this man your seat." Then, humiliated, you will have to take the least important place. But when you are invited, take the lowest place, so that when your host comes, he will say to you, "Friend, move up to a better place"'** (14:8-10).

In saying this the Lord was only reiterating what the Jews' own Scripture taught. Proverbs 25:6-7 says,

> 'Do not exalt yourself in the king's presence,
>   and do not claim a place among great men;
> it is better for him to say to you, "Come up here,"
>   than for him to humiliate you before a nobleman.'

Then Jesus said an oft-repeated phrase, **'For everyone who exalts himself will be humbled, and he who humbles himself will be exalted'** (14:11).

Following this parable Jesus applied its teaching by enquiring into the motives which people had for giving invitations to parties. He said, 'Do you just invite people to your party who are in a position to invite you back?' And he concluded that such behaviour is only selfishness. 'It is so much better', said the Lord, 'to invite the poor, crippled, the lame and the blind.' These people are not in any position to return the favour to you. If you invite such people to your house, you will receive great blessing. They cannot repay you, but, if you are truly humble and have genuine love for the outcast, then God will repay you at the resurrection of the righteous (14:14). The resurrection of the righteous will be for all those who have been pronounced righteous by God on the basis of Christ's atonement, because they have demonstrated their faith by their actions (cf. Matt. 25:34-40).

The great banquet

One of the guests said, **'Blessed is the man who will eat at the feast in the kingdom of God'** (14:15). Jesus then took up this theme of the feast which will be held at the last time, the day of the end of all things, when the righteous will enter the kingdom of God. The Lord told a parable about a certain man (a picture of God, the Father) who invited many guests to the feast he was preparing. In those days the person giving the feast would send out prior invitations saying when and where the feast would be held. But the exact time of day would not be stated. Presumably the people invited to this feast had said that they would attend. That is how the host would know how much food to prepare. The people would wait until they heard the servant of the man who was giving the party going around the neighbour-hood saying, **'Come, for everything is now ready.'** The the people would respond — just as children do when mum calls out, 'Dinner's on the table and getting cold.'

But, on this occasion, the sad thing was that they all began to make excuses (they were not reasons). The first said, **'I have just bought a field, and I must go and see it. Please excuse me'** (14:18). What a thin excuse! He could have seen his field at any time and, in any case, can we imagine a Jew (of all people) spending money on a field without actually seeing it first?

The second said, **'I have just bought five yoke of oxen, and I'm on my way to try them out. Please excuse me'** (14:19). This was another feeble excuse! He could try them out at any time, and besides, surely he would have done so before he handed the money over?

The third said, **'I have just got married, so I can't come'** (14:20). But that was a lie. He could have gone and taken his wife with him! These men gave the same kind of paper-thin excuses that people still give today for not accepting God's gracious invitation to come to Christ for salvation.

Having had all of these refusals, the servant came back and reported them to his master, and not surprisingly, the owner of the house became angry. He had gone to so much trouble. He had even checked up first with everyone and they had all said that they would attend the feast. To give such weak excuses was nothing less than insulting.

So the host ordered his servants, **'Go out quickly into the streets and alleys of the town and bring in the poor, the crippled, the**

blind and the lame.' These were the same kinds of people that Jesus
had been speaking about in verse 13. These were imperfect Jews
whom society regarded as outcasts. The poor did not get invited to
banquets. The crippled did not get married. The blind did not go out
to examine fields; and the lame did not test oxen.[2]

Then the servant returned and said, 'Sir ... **what you have
ordered has been done, but there is still room. Then the master
told his servant, "Go out to the roads and country lanes and
make them come in, so that my house will be full"'** (14:22-23).
The servant was not to 'make them come in' by force (as was done
in the Spanish Inquisition). His task was to persuade, by every
means, those who were outside to come to the feast which was
waiting for them to enjoy. The master wanted his house to be full.

The meaning

God has sent out his prior invitation to the gospel feast through the
Old Testament prophets. When Jesus came to this earth for the first
time he said, 'Come, for everything is now ready.' He meant that
there is nothing more that needs to be done. The feast is waiting for
the guests to come, as a result of the invitation. But the pious,
religious Jews, in rejecting the Lord Jesus Christ, also rejected the
kingdom prepared for his people. It is the same today; the servants
of God are sent out urgently with the gospel message: 'Come to me,
all you who are weary and burdened, and I will give you rest' (Matt.
11:28). Jesus also said, 'If anyone is thirsty, let him come to me and
drink' (John 7:37). The only sensible response for anyone to make
is to say, 'I come, Lord Jesus.'

The gospel invitation goes out in all kinds of ways. It is sent out
to those in the town (14:21), that is, the Jews who are in all kinds of
situations; and it goes out to those in the countryside (14:23), that is
the Gentiles who never received the first invitation. This is a
wonderful feast, to which all kinds of people are invited, and the
only qualification is that people come just as they are and that they
do not delay in answering the invitation!

The cost of discipleship (14:25-35)

Jesus had now left the house of the Pharisee (14:1) and a large crowd
started travelling with him. But suddenly Jesus stopped and turned

to the people, almost certainly startling them as he said, **'If anyone comes to me and does not hate his father and mother, his wife and children, his brothers and sisters — yes, even his own life — he cannot be my disciple'** (14:26). He said these last words three times in this passage (14:26,27,33). He pulled the crowd up in their tracks because he did not just want hangers-on. He wanted people to follow him who would be fully committed to him and learn from him, as an apprentice learns from his master. He was not saying that his disciples should turn against all of their loved ones; that would be contrary to the fifth commandment and also his own teaching. He meant that all his followers should love him more than they loved their own families. Those who want to be his true disciples must give him first place in their lives.

Jesus then reinforced this statement by saying, **'And anyone who does not carry his cross and follow me cannot be my disciple'** (14:27); he had spoken similar words in Cæsarea Philippi (9:23). The Lord meant that if any of us are to be true disciples of his then we must die to selfishness, ambition and pride. He knows that such a thing will be painful for his followers — just as his own crucifixion was going to be agonizing for him. In the same way Paul was to say, 'I have been crucified with Christ and I no longer live, but Christ lives in me' (Gal. 2:20).

How would any of us feel if we were being led out to be crucified? What plans would we make for the future? We would make none — because our lives would shortly come to an end. In the same way, anyone who becomes a true follower of Jesus automatically forfeits control of his own life and hands it over to Christ.[3] The cost of being a disciple is total commitment to him. This means that when loyalty to our parents, our spouses or our employers conflicts with loyalty to Christ then we have to make sure that we put Christ first in our lives, even if it means upsetting those to whom we are also committed. This is hard — and many are failing do it. Numerous church leaders are saying today, 'My biggest problem is the lack of commitment of our church members.'

Two parables

Jesus was not trying to put anyone off from following him. He was merely being honest with them. He wanted to make it clear to them what discipleship would involve. He did not want anyone to be half-hearted in their loyalty to him, nor unaware of the cost of commitment. That is why he made this statement about the cost, and then went on to tell these stories recorded in verses 28-30.

In the first story the man needed to build a tower. No one builds a tower just because it seems a good idea. Perhaps this particular man had a vineyard and he needed a watch-tower so that intruders could be seen and warned off. Jesus never said that he was foolish to build the tower, but he did say that he would be unwise if he did not first of all sit down and work out the true cost of the project. He should actually sit down and work out the sums very carefully. He should only proceed if he had enough money to complete it.

In the same way each disciple of Christ must very carefully weigh up the cost of following Jesus. Following Christ is a serious business and it must not be undertaken lightly. There are so many people who start well and then backslide into the world. This causes both them and the church to be objects of ridicule. How awful for anyone to say of us, 'He started out well, but he wasn't able to keep up the pace; so he turned his back upon Christ and the church.' How many people there must be who have not first of all counted the cost of being a disciple of the Lord and have fallen away and now feel utter failures! It is all the harder for them to come back.

Jesus then told a similar parable, but this one had more disastrous consequences (14:31-32). In this story there is a king who wants to go out and fight against another one, but the second king has a much stronger army. The obvious thing to do is for the first king to sit down (as the man did in verse 28) and calculate the cost of the war. If he realizes that there is no hope of him winning, then the only sensible thing to do is to sue for peace.

Both of these parables speak about the importance of counting the cost. In the first story the man risks only ridicule from his community and possible loss of financial investment. But 'The man who fails to realize that he is outnumbered in battle risks losing his kingdom, his soldiers and his life.'[4]

Salt

In verses 34-35 Jesus speaks about salt. This was, and still is, a very useful commodity. It is a preservative, a purifying agent, an antiseptic and something which makes people feel very thirsty.

Disciples of Christ are to be all of these things. They must help to preserve the truth of God's Word and always seek to retard the growth of evil and decay. They must seek to bring purity into this world by acting in Christ-like and holy ways. They should act like antiseptic, seeking to cleanse wounds from infection. They ought to try to heal the broken spirits of those who are cast down, and they must seek to make people thirsty. Warren Wiersbe says, 'By our character and conduct, we ought to make others thirsty for the Lord Jesus Christ and the salvation that he alone can give.'[5]

If we do not measure up to these standards then we are not fulfilling our responsibilities as disciples of Christ. Indeed the Lord says that if we have lost our saltiness then we are useless. We are not even of any use on the compost heap. The only thing that can be done with us is to throw us out as rubbish.

The Lord was not saying that a failed disciple will be cast out of heaven. Those who are true disciples are safe for all eternity. But how sad if on the Judgement Day the Lord had to say of any believer, 'You did not live as a disciple of mine should live.'

Then the Lord concludes, **'He who has ears to hear, let him hear'**(14:35). God's people must ask themselves, 'Am I listening to what the Lord is saying to me today?' He is calling us all to a complete commitment to him. He must take first place in our lives. And we must obey his voice rather than the voice of our loved ones. We should obey our earthly masters, but we must not love our work, even our Christian work, more than we love our Lord.

We who live in the West cannot really understand this call as many of those who live in the East do. For them commitment to Christ means everything. In some communities when people become Christians they are thrown out of their families, their jobs and even their home villages. Sometimes believers are even hunted down and killed.

Following Christ means committing everything to him and placing the whole of our being into his loving care. Listening to his voice means obeying him and following him whatever the cost to ourselves might be.

15.
Lost and found

Please read Luke 15

God's seeking love (15:1-10)

'All religions lead to God,' is a popular saying. The Hindu pictures man's religious quest as a mountain climb. Everyone is working his way up the pathway which leads to the mountain-top. It is a long, hard and tortuous struggle; but at last, perhaps after many reincarnations, the summit is reached and the enjoyment of eternal bliss begins. 'But,' says the Hindu, 'when the seeker after truth reaches the top of the mountain, he looks down and sees that the path which he has taken is not the only one. From his high vantage-point he can see that there are many, many paths, all hidden from one another, but each one leading to the top of the same hill.

That is a very popular scenario. It is well liked because it teaches that it does not matter what anyone believes; those who sincerely seek the truth will find it. It is also admired because it emphasizes man's search after God. It shows that reward is given to those who work hard and gain merit for their soul's eternal welfare. It makes salvation something which all human beings can obtain, if only they work hard enough for it. However, this kind of teaching is quite contrary to that of Jesus.

A popular teacher

Jesus was well liked, and many people gathered around him (15:1). Included in the crowd were despised tax collectors and those whom the religious people called 'sinners'. Luke does not tell us that they wanted to be healed, or desired some material blessing for themselves. They gathered around the Lord for the express purpose of hearing him teach.

But by encouraging ordinary people to gather around him, Jesus caused annoyance to the Pharisees and the teachers of the law. These 'holy people' were very concerned to keep themselves pure. They pulled their cloaks around themselves very tightly to prevent any 'sinner' from brushing against them and thus causing them to be defiled. They knew the scripture: 'Be holy, because I am holy' (Lev. 11:44) and their main concern in life was to make sure that they were separate from all those who might defile them by coming into contact with them.

It is no wonder that they were astounded that Jesus not only welcomed sinners, but actually ate food with them. To their minds 'sinners' (i.e. tax collectors, prostitutes and sick people) were all to be avoided. But Jesus turned religious conventions on their head. By his actions, he was showing that God cares even for those who do not come to him by the pathway of formal religious observance. He showed that those who could not help themselves could still be made welcome by God.

It is the same today. Religious people tend to look down their noses at those who do not practise religion as they do. They welcome those who dress in smart clothes and who conform to the religious traditions of the day but they shun those who come into church wearing jeans, tee-shirts and trainers. However, Jesus looks beyond conventions and judges the condition of the heart.

Jesus would have known the kind of thinking that was going through the minds of the religious people; so, to shatter their false conceptions, he told them a parable (15:3).

He did not tell three parables. He told one parable which was in three parts. Each of these stories illustrates the wonderful grace of God. Each one speaks of something which has been lost and then found again, and each one ends with great rejoicing. This one parable is told from three different angles. The first two stories were revolutionary in their depiction of God. Jesus showed that God is not some great, far off, passive being who is waiting for each individual, by his own strenuous effort, to find him. Jesus tells us something which no other religion in the world does. He says that it is God who is seeking people. Jesus likens God to a shepherd, a woman and a father. Under each of these figures he tells how God is seeking those who are lost. In every other religion God is depicted as one who is passively waiting for man to find him.

If the fact that Jesus welcomed and ate with sinners upset the religious teachers, then surely this parable would have made them absolutely furious. Although shepherds were often spoken about in the Old Testament (e.g. Ps. 23; Isa. 40; Ezek. 34), by the time of Jesus they were a despised profession who were not even trusted to testify in court.[1] Women too, were not worth a second thought to the 'pious Jew'. And, as for receiving back a wasteful son who had brought disgrace upon his family and his religion, that would have been far too much for 'pure' religious people to have accepted.

The lost sheep

This first aspect of God's grace is shown in a man (the word 'shepherd' is not mentioned here) who had a hundred sheep, but one of the sheep had become lost. It was lost because of its own stupidity. It wandered astray from the pathway. Unlike cats or dogs, apparently sheep do not have the sense to try to find their way back home. Sheep are some of the most stupid of animals; try looking into the face of a sheep! In calling Christians the people of his pasture, God was not being very polite. The fact is that when any person is wandering far away from God, he is like a sheep; he does not have the sense or the ability to find his way back to safety. The Hindu can urge him all he can to climb the hill of destiny in his effort to reach the top. The Buddhist can encourage him to tread the eightfold path in his search for true happiness. The Muslim can bully him into following the five pillars of Islam in the hope that on the Day of Judgement he will escape the fires of hell. But only the God of the Bible actively goes out to seek and to save the one who is lost — and actually finds him, putting him joyfully on his shoulders and taking him home with rejoicing. Our God never says, 'I have ninety-nine sheep; that will be enough.' God, our loving heavenly Shepherd, cares about each and every one of his sheep. He sent his only begotten Son to go all the way to Calvary to die for each lost and wandering one. Jesus is the Good Shepherd who lays down his life for his sheep (John 10:11).

The return of one lost sheep brings joy to the heart of the Shepherd. **'When he finds it, he joyfully puts it on his shoulders** and goes home. Then he calls his friends and neighbours together and says, "Rejoice with me; I have found my lost sheep"' (15:5-6). Jesus contrasts the Father's attitude with that of the Pharisees. They were so concerned about keeping rules and regulations that they did not have any love in their hearts for those who come back to God. Repentance is a wonderful thing. Over and over again in the Gospels we have the call to repentance. This is what God desires for all people. He calls them today to stop short in their ways, turn their backs upon their old pathways and start moving towards himself. He tells them that he is waiting to receive all who truly repent of their sin.

Jesus said, '**There will be more rejoicing in heaven over one sinner who repents than over ninety-nine righteous persons who do not need to repent**' (15:7). Jesus did not mean that the Pharisees did not need to repent. He was using a kind of sarcasm. He meant that they did not think they needed to repent. The fact is that they were in a very dire and dangerous position, and it may have been that the stories which Jesus told may have caused some of them to stop and think, and then to return to the Lord.

The lost coin

Again, Jesus tells a story about one missing object. In the previous story one sheep was missing from a collection of 100. Here one coin is missing from a group of ten, and in the next story one son is missing from a set of two. These silver coins would have been worth ten drachmas each. In those days that would have been a considerable sum of money and so ten would have represented something of great value. This would have been especially so if the coins were joined together in a headband. In that case they would have been the equivalent of an engagement ring.

When it was discovered that one was missing, an immediate search was instigated. Looking for lost things is something which most of us know about. It is usually in the five minutes before our sons or our daughters should have left for school in the morning that the loss is discovered.

This woman lit a candle, swept the house and searched carefully until she found it. All the people listening to Jesus would have been able to picture the scene. The would have known about the small huts with tiny openings for windows. They would have been able to smell the dust as they imagined the woman carefully sweeping the rush mats on the mud floor. They would also have been able to catch the thrill of excitement as Jesus told how the woman found her coin. They would have understood why she gathered her neighbours together and called upon them to rejoice at the discovery of the lost coin. 'In the same way,' said the Lord, 'there is rejoicing in the presence of the angels of God over one sinner who repents.'

Do we get excited when someone is converted to Christ? There is rejoicing in heaven when such a great change takes place in a person's life. Someone has come home to God. It is because a man or woman, a boy or a girl has been saved — and saved for all eternity. It is not merely that he or she has decided to follow Christ. It is because God, their heavenly Father, has brought these people to himself and transformed them. They have been washed from their sins in the blood of Christ and been made God's children.

We do not know what the shepherd in the story had to go through to bring back the lost sheep into his fold, but we do know that the Lord Jesus Christ had to go all the way to Calvary to open up the way for each of his people to come back into God's fold.

God's welcoming arms (15:11-32)

Jesus is speaking to two groups of people in chapter 15 — religious, 'good' people, and irreligious, 'sinful' people. The bad people knew they were bad, and the Pharisees and the teachers of the law had told them they were. But the religious people, who thought they were good, had, in fact, wandered far off from God. We know this because they complained about Jesus when they said, 'This man welcomes sinners and eats with them' (15:1).

In the first part of this parable we have seen the seeking love of God at work, under the guise of a shepherd and a woman. In the second part Jesus told a story about a son who deliberately and wilfully left his loving father, solely to satisfy his own selfish desires. There are various reasons why people become lost. Some get lost because of their own foolishness, others because of the circumstances of life, and yet others through their own rebellion. But here Jesus is showing the first step in anyone's salvation is that he or she must return to God.

One wandering son

The story is about a man who had two sons, the younger of whom demanded his share of the family estate. Deuteronomy 21:17 tells us that when a father died his elder son must receive twice as much inheritance as any other son. This was because the elder son was obliged to carry on the family business when his father died; he had no choice in the matter. It was only fair, therefore, that he should have a double portion of his father's property; otherwise he might not have sufficient funds to maintain the business.

When Jesus said, **'So he divided his property between them'** (15:12) we can imagine that his listeners would have been amazed because the father had not yet died.[2] Apparently it did sometimes happen that a division of property was made before the death of the father, but in such a case the children were not allowed to use the capital while their father was still alive.

The elder, more responsible son, stayed at home. He was a good boy. He worked hard. He never put a foot out of place. He never pestered his father for hand-outs. He never even asked for a young goat so that he could have a feast with his friends (15:29). He seldom wandered very far away from his father's side.

We can imagine the Pharisees and teachers of the law identifying themselves with this nice young man. They too, lived lives which were upright and pure. In fact they felt very proud of their loyalty to God. If anyone had suggested that they had wandered away from God, they would have been horrified. They had always kept near to the temple and had obeyed the law of the Lord perfectly, 'right down to the last icicle of truth'.[3]

But the story that Jesus told centred initially upon the younger son. Not long after he received his share of the money, he **'set off for a distant country and there squandered his wealth in wild living'** (15:13). He found that, as any child in a school playground holding a bag of sweets discovers, all the while that he had something that others liked, he had friends in abundance. But when the prodigal son's money ran out, so did his friends! To make matters worse, a famine hit the land at the same time. This meant that the younger son began to be in need. All the while he had money, he had no wants. While everything was going well for him he was happy. But when his money ran out, so his circumstances got worse.

It is the same with us today. All the while we have our health and strength we take them for granted. It is only when they begin to deteriorate that we give them a second thought. It is only when we lose them that we show any appreciation of them.

However, the lad eventually obtained work — feeding pigs! We can imagine the disgust on the faces of these religious people as Jesus came to this part of the story. Pigs were 'unclean' animals (Lev. 11:7). Fancy stooping so low as to feed pigs!

Not only that, the boy was so hungry that he was even tempted to eat the pods that were meant as food for the pigs. Yet no one gave him anything (15:16). We can imagine how he must have felt, but the situation was one of his own making. If only he had stayed at home, been more sensible with his money and had saved something for a rainy day, things would have been better.

As they heard the story the self-righteous Pharisees would certainly have said to themselves, 'Serves him right. He deserved everything that he got.' And we have the same attitude today towards those who wander away from a good home. We look at the drunkard, the drug addict and the bored teenager with the same kind of self-righteous smugness as those religious people must have had. Everyone condemned this lad — except the one he had sinned against the most. No one had any time for him — except his own father, who, all the while he was away, was waiting for him to come home.

The story turns at verse 17. There we read, **'When [the younger son] came to his senses...'** He had been in a kind of mad abandonment before but now he came to his senses. He said, **'How many of my father's hired men have food to spare, and here I am starving to death! I will set out and go back to my father and say to him: "Father, I have sinned against heaven and against you. I am no longer worthy to be called your son; make me like one of your hired men"'** (15:17-19).

It was at this point that the boy began to think. He shut out all other noises, and thought about his father and his home. D. L. Moody comments, 'There is always hope for a man when he begins to think.'[4]

How sad it is that today people do not want to think! They do not dare to think. They are too frightened to think. So they shut out thought by listening to very loud music and looking at puerile video tape films. It seems that few people want to stop and give serious thought to their own lives and where they are heading for.

This young man **'got up and went to his father'** (15:20). He said, 'I will ... go back to my father.' This is a picture of repentance; it means, 'to think again'. Before people can be saved they have to be brought up short in their tracks, consider where their lives are leading them, and then turn away from their hopelessness and despair and turn towards God in faith. Helmut Thielicke said, 'The repentance of the lost son is ... homesickness; not just turning away from something, but turning back home.'[5]

The waiting father

'While he was still a long way off, his father saw him and was filled with compassion for him' (15:20). The father had been waiting and watching every day. That is why he saw him when he was still a long way off. He knew, in his heart, that he would come home one day.

In the first two stories Jesus told about God taking the initiative and actually going out and bringing back his sinful children. Here Jesus tells how the sinful child has to come to the point of repentance and God, his heavenly Father, is waiting for his return. And, even though it is right that the sinner should be eager to demonstrate that he or she is repentant, God never makes the returning process difficult. He welcomes with open arms sinners who come home, without even waiting to hear their recital of wrongdoing.

The religious people of those days would have been astounded at the welcome the father gave his son. If they had been in the position of the father who had been wronged so much, they would have made the lad beg for forgiveness. They would have been amazed that the father ran to meet his son. That was a most undignified thing for any Eastern patriarch to do. But Jesus wanted his audience to see that God is far, far more welcoming than their cold, unloving hearts could ever imagine.

So the father gave his son a wonderful homecoming. Whatever he had done, the prodigal was still his son. He called for the best robe to be put upon him, to show that he was welcomed as an honoured member of the family. He put a ring on his finger, to show that he had authority (see Gen. 41:42). He put sandals on his feet, to show that he was a son, not a slave. (Slaves went barefoot. The negro spiritual goes, 'All God's chillen got shoes' — shoes were a sign of freedom.) And the fattened calf was killed, to show that there was joy at the return of the lad. Everyone began to celebrate. And because the father was happy, then so was everyone else — or nearly everyone!

The scene moves to a field

We read, **'Meanwhile, the older son was in the field. When he came near the house, he heard music and dancing. So he called one of the servants and asked him what was going on. "Your brother has come," he replied, "and your father has killed the fattened calf because he has him back safe and sound"'** (15:25-27). Then the older brother became angry, and refused to go into the house. So, just as the father had run out to greet his lost son, he now went out and pleaded with his older son (15:28).

This was very strange behaviour for a father in that particular culture. It seems incredible that such an honourable old man should be seen running, going out and pleading with a son who had brought shame on the family. Such things were unheard of in those authoritarian days. But Jesus wanted to show how loving, gracious, forgiving and welcoming our heavenly Father is to those who have gone far away from him, and have begun to return home. However, this welcome extends not only to those who have strayed publicly. It also applies to those who, while they appear respectable on the outside, have wandered away from God, just as much as those who have committed dreadful, outward misdeeds.

However, the elder brother complained bitterly to his father. We can see his pride and selfishness as he said, **'Look! All these years I've been slaving for you and never disobeyed your orders. Yet you never gave me even a young goat so I could celebrate with my friends. But when this son of yours who has squandered your property with prostitutes comes home, you kill the fattened calf for him!'** (15:28-29). He was so full of all that he had done as he made accusations against his brother. He was certainly correct in stating that his brother had squandered his father's property, but was he right in asserting that his brother had wasted money on prostitutes?

By his outburst the elder brother was showing his dirty mind. He assumed that his brother had been with immoral women. Perhaps he was envious of him. Let none of God's people entertain such thoughts. Jesus said, 'Anyone who looks at a woman lustfully has already committed adultery with her in his heart' (Matt. 5:28).

However, the father still had love for his older son, despite his rudeness and insulting behaviour. **'"My son," the father said, "you are always with me, and everything I have is yours. But we had to celebrate and be glad, because this brother of yours was dead and is alive again; he was lost and is found"'** (15:31-32).

We are not told what the elder son did then. Jesus left his hearers, both 'the sinners' and the self-righteous people, to work out their own response to this parable. But we have to consider the implications for ourselves. Whether we have wandered away from God and sinned openly, or have constantly lived a 'good life', we may be far off from God. The gospel message is not just for 'nice' people; it is for all kinds of men, women and children. Stuart Briscoe tells of plans that his church had to move to another area of their city. An objector at a public meeting said, 'We don't want this kind of church in our vicinity because they will bring undesirables into the neighbourhood.'[6] The coffee bar which our own church runs for youngsters who hang around the street corners has likewise been seen by some as causing 'undesirables' to gather. However, we read in 1 Timothy 1:15 that 'Christ Jesus came into the world to save sinners — of whom I [said Paul] am the worst.'

16.
Living in the light of eternity

Please read Luke 16

Preparing for the future (16:1-13)

We often read or hear about underhand financial dealing by people who abuse the trust their employers give to them. These people have 'lined their own pockets' while carrying out their daily work. Throughout the Bible we read of similar misappropriation of funds. Here in Luke 16 Jesus taught about the dangers of the wrong use of money. These principles apply equally to us today.

Teaching the crowds

Jesus had been speaking to tax collectors and 'sinners' in the hearing of the religious people and his own disciples (15:1). Now he turned specifically to his disciples and told them a story about money. This is a difficult story to interpret, but Luke, under the guidance of the Holy Spirit, has put it in his Gospel so that we may learn from it.

The story is about a landlord who had many tenant farmers, who each rented land from him so that they could work it and earn a living. The villain of the piece is the landlord's own steward (or manager). It was this man's job to run the estate for his master and see that it made a good profit. One day the rich man called his manager to him and told him of a rumour he had heard. This indicated that the manager had been wasting his master's possessions. So he demanded that he give him an account of his management, because he was to be dismissed (16:2). The manager was like the prodigal son in the previous chapter; he had wasted money.

When he realized that he had been 'found out', the manager did some quick thinking. He knew that he could do nothing to rectify the wrongs of the past, so he started to think about his future. He said to himself, **'I'm not strong enough to dig'**; perhaps he meant that he was not prepared to do hard, manual work. **'And I'm ashamed to beg.'** Then, a flash of inspiration hit him and he said, **'I know what I'll do so that, when I lose my job here, people will welcome me into their houses'** (16:4).

Having made his plan, he acted secretly and started to carry it out. He took the account books (it seems that he was given time to put the ledgers in order before he departed), and he called for all of his master's debtors to visit him. They were each to come on their own, and no one else was to know about it. The manager asked every one of them to reduce the amount they owed on their bill. They were to do this quickly before the master found out what was happening. It seems that the custom was that every tenant had to write out his own bill detailing what he owed, and then the manager counter-signed it on behalf of his master. That is why Luke tells us that they sat down and altered the bill.

We have two examples of tenants who had their bills reduced, but there were probably many more who were similarly treated. (A possible reason why the oil was reduced by 50% and the wheat by only 20% was because oil can be watered down and wheat cannot.)

Eventually, probably just before the manager was finally dismissed, the master found out what had been happening during the period since he served notice on his steward. But the strange thing about the story is that the master actually commended the dishonest manager for what he had done. Jesus does not say he was pleased with the man; we can be sure that he was not! But he praised the manager for acting shrewdly, or wisely.

This story does not teach us that it is in order for people to do wrong, provided they do it cleverly. (We can admire the skill with which a certain gang of thieves might carry out a cunning robbery, but that does not mean that we applaud them for what they have done.)

The master praised his manager when he understood why he

acted in this way. He could see that by reducing everyone's bill the manager, who would soon be out of a job, would have put each of these tenant farmers into his debt; they would owe him a big favour. And if he had nowhere to live when he was out of work, then they would be obliged to take him into their own houses (16:4).

The master could also see the cunning of the man in making the tenant farmers grateful to the rich owner. They were now beholden to him as well as to the manager. So the master could not even hint at suggesting that the earlier bills should be reinstated. He was now a much more respected and honoured man because it appeared that he had been very generous to them!

The teaching drawn out

Then Jesus made some comments about the people of this world and the people of the light. By **'the people of this world'** he meant the people who are fully occupied with the things of this life. Their sole concern is with the here and now. For them 'the future' means their old age or their retirement from work. They have no thought about any afterlife because they believe that the only thing worth thinking about, and planning for, is this life. How different are 'the people of the light'! By this phrase Jesus meant those who have been illuminated by the light of God. These people can sing with great meaning, 'The Lord is my light and my salvation — whom shall I fear?' (Ps. 27:1). Their minds, their hearts and their desires are not just centred upon this life. Their whole lives are filled with the light of the glory of God. He is the one who occupies their thoughts and their affections.

Jesus was saying that the people of this world actually plan and work for the future, even though they can see no further than the end of their time on this earth. They still take great care to plan for their old age when they can no longer earn their living. Jesus took this thought and taught that God's people, too, should take great care to plan for their future, but he does not just mean their future on earth. He means their future life in heaven. This is why he said, 'Do not store up for yourselves treasure on earth, where moth and rust destroy, and where thieves break in and steal. But store up for yourselves treasures in heaven, where moth and rust do not destroy, and where thieves do not break in and steal. For where your treasure is, there your heart will be also' (Matt. 6:19-21).

The meaning of the story

Jesus gave some practical instructions about how we should use our money. He said, **'I tell you, use worldly wealth to gain friends for yourselves, so that when it is gone, you will be welcomed into eternal dwellings'** (16:9). He was not saying that people can buy themselves a place in heaven; if that was the case then the poor would stand no chance of getting to glory at all. He is saying, 'Use your money wisely.'

We do not know much about heaven, but we do know that it is a place where Jesus is. And we also know that it is a place where God's people are. I wonder if, when we get to heaven, someone from a heathen tribe will come up to us and say, 'I am here today because years ago you sent missionaries to my land; you gave money so that literature could be sent to us which would tell us about Jesus and his death on the cross to take away our sins.'

Just as the dishonest manager saved people money in the hope that they would welcome him into their homes when he had none, so many of God's people who have been honest and generous with their money will find that they will, when they leave this life, 'be welcomed into eternal dwellings' (16:9).

Jesus then took the story of the dishonest manager and said that his disciples should act in the opposite way. Believers should copy this manager in the sense that he planned for the future, but they should not copy his dishonesty. **'If [we] have not been trustworthy in handling worldly wealth, who will trust [us] with true riches?'** (16:11).

What does Jesus mean by saying, 'If you have not been trustworthy with someone else's property, who will give you property of your own?' (16:12). He means that the money we have really belongs to God. Indeed everything that we have on this earth is only lent to us. Therefore we should use it wisely.

How do we use our money? Do we just use it for ourselves, and our selfish ends? Or do we use it to bring pleasure to others? If we could only grasp that everything that we have is given to us by God, then we would want to use it all for his glory.

Then Jesus spoke about two gods: the true and living God, and the god of money. Warren Wiersbe comments, 'If God is our master, then money will be our servant, and we will use our resources in the will of God. But if God is not our master, then we will become the servants of money, and money is a terrible master! We will start wasting our lives instead of investing them, and we will one day find ourselves "friendless" as we enter the gates of glory.'[1]

Money is not the root of all evil. It is 'the love of money which is the root of all evil' (1 Tim. 6:10, AV). We have been given money to use, not to worship. An old lady, whom I knew many years ago, used to work for various aristocratic families. She said to me once, 'The trouble with these newly rich people is that they do not realize that money has been given to them so that they can provide employment and use their money to help those who are poor.' When I lived in Kenya in the early 1950s I expressed surprise when I learned that a Christian friend of mine employed both a cook and a gardener. But he explained to me that, even though he could manage without either of them, it was his duty to employ them, otherwise they would have no income. Money has been given to all of us so that we should use it wisely. A neighbour of mine said to me one day, 'When I was young I was left enough money for my husband and myself to buy a house of our own. I would have loved to have done that but my husband said, "No. Let's use it to help with our children's education instead."' That is what they did and each of those children benefited greatly because of their parents' wise use of the money. They all now have well-educated children of their own.

Godly Bishop Ryle said this about people who try to serve God and at the same time keep their affections chained down to earthly things: 'They have too much religion to be happy in the world, and they have too much of the world in their hearts to be happy in their religion.'[2] So let us use our money, our talents and our business sense for the benefit of others and for the glory of God. Jesus was talking to his disciples about the dangers of loving money. He was concerned that all of his people should be faithful stewards of the gifts which had been given to them. Paul said, 'It is required that those who have been given a trust must prove faithful' (1 Cor. 4:2).

Facing the future (16:14-31)

The Pharisees were trying to do what Jesus said was impossible. They were professing to love God, and yet they adored money at the same time (16:13). They thought that they were observing the law of Moses; and one of the ways they assumed they were doing this was by keeping well away from the common people. But they also loved money; it was a powerful thing to be rich. They could afford to live in the better part of town — away from the riff-raff. They had the money to dress flamboyantly so that it could be seen that they were better off than the people who only wore rough clothing. And they had the means to give expensive parties and invite the most important people into their houses.

So when Jesus said that no man can serve two masters, the Pharisees refused to accept that the love of God and money were incompatible. This is why they began sneering at him (16:14).

Jesus not only sensed what these religious people were thinking; he spoke severely to them. He told them, **'You are the ones who justify yourselves in the eyes of men, but God knows your hearts. What is highly valued among men is detestable in God's sight'** (16:15). The things that the Pharisees held to be precious were detestable to God. Jesus illustrated what he meant by telling the story of the rich man and Lazarus.

But first he explained that since John the Baptist appeared the good news of the kingdom of God had been preached, and, as a consequence, many were seeking to enter it. By saying, **'Everyone is forcing his way into [the kingdom],'** Jesus meant that vast crowds were attending to him and obeying his injunction to 'make every effort to enter through the narrow door' (13:24). However, because the kingdom of God was being preached, this did not mean that the law had been done away with. Jesus said, **'It is easier for heaven and earth to disappear than for the least stroke of a pen to drop out of the law'** (16:17). The small marks on Hebrew letters look very insignificant, but if they are omitted the whole sense of a word or phrase can be completely changed. The coming of Jesus did not mean that some of the things in the law would be changed, but through Christ the law would be fulfilled. His life and atoning death on the cross would bring the law to its full fruition.

Then Jesus gave an example. Divorce was very slack in those days. But Jesus was saying that despite men's twisting of the law, 'Adultery was still adultery, still unlawful and still sinful.'[3] The only reason that Jesus allowed for divorce was when marital unfaithfulness occurred (Matt. 19:9).[4] Following this Jesus returned to the theme of the love of money, together with the need to obey the Law of Moses and the Prophets (i.e, the Scriptures, see 16:29).

The rich man and Lazarus

The story has main two characters. One was a very rich man who dressed in purple and fine linen. Purple was an expensive dye. (This is how we know that Lydia, in Acts 16:14, was a rich woman.) Only royalty, the nobility and very rich people could afford to wear material of this colour. By saying that he wore fine linen, Jesus meant that this rich man wore undergarments which were soft and cool, and consequently very expensive to buy.

But this man not only dressed very ostentatiously; he lived in luxury as well. He had everything that his heart could desire. Furthermore his expensive lifestyle was something which he enjoyed every single day of his life. Other people might have fine clothes to wear on special days, and delicious food to eat on particular occasions, but this man wallowed in extravagance every day of his life.

The other man in the story was exactly the opposite to the rich man. He was in a very sad state. Not only did he have none of this world's goods, but it seems that he was crippled, because we are told that he had to be laid at the gate of the rich man. This is the only parable that Jesus told (if it was a parable) where we are given the name of the main character. He was called Lazarus. This was not the same Lazarus who was the brother of Mary and Martha. The name means, 'God is my helper.'

This poor man was laid outside the very beautiful ornamental gate of the rich man's house. And every day he lay there longing to get hold of some of the food which fell from the rich man's table. People did not eat with knives and forks in those days. They used their fingers and then wiped them on pieces of bread, which they afterwards threw on the floor. It was some of these scraps which Lazarus was hoping to get hold of.

Furthermore Luke (the medical doctor) tells us that the poor man was **'covered in sores'** and even the dogs came and licked them (16:21). When they heard this the Pharisees would have been even more repulsed by the character of Lazarus. Dogs were useless animals; it was a name used to describe unclean Gentiles.

The next scene in the story describes the end of their earthly lives. Everyone has to die (unless Jesus returns to this earth first). Thomas Adams said, 'Death takes away the difference between king and beggar, and tumbles both the knight and the pawn into one bag.'⁵We know that this beggar went to heaven when he died; we are told, **'The angels carried him to Abraham's side.'** This means that Lazarus went to the place of blessedness, the abode of all those who 'die in the Lord'.

We can imagine the funerals that each of these men had. Jesus tells us that after the rich man died he **'was buried'** (16:22). He certainly would have had a most expensive and lavish funeral. Many women would have been paid to weep long and loud for him. But I wonder how many people shed genuine tears of sorrow at his death? Those who live only for themselves are seldom missed when they die. But what about the funeral of Lazarus? Not many people would have missed him, except perhaps those who had carried him to the rich man's gate. His body may even have been thrown on the ever-burning rubbish heap in the Valley of Hinnom outside Jerusalem.

But the thing that really matters is not the kind of funeral that a person has, but whether he or she enters heaven or hell. The rich man went to hell (or *Hades*). Because Jesus believed that those who reject him go to hell, then so must we accept this teaching. Jesus often refers in the Gospels to this awful place.

There are five things about hell which are mentioned in this passage.

1. Hell is far off from the abode of the righteous; Lazarus was seen far away (16:23).

2. It is a place of torment; four times the word **'agony'** or **'torment'** is used (see 16:23,24,25, 28).

3. There is a great gulf fixed between heaven and hell (16:26).

4. The sufferings of hell are great (16:24). The fire of hell is unquenchable; it devours for ever. Yet hell is elsewhere called the place where darkness dwells (see Matt. 8:12; 22:13; 25:30; Jude 6).

5. But perhaps the most awful thing about hell is that there will be no escape from it (16:26). No one can cross over from it. Albert Barnes says of hell, 'It is a dark, obscure, and miserable place, far from heaven, where the wicked shall be punished for ever.'⁶

We can observe several things about the rich man in hell. He called out to Abraham. Although he could not reach him, he could see him — just as those outside the door in Luke 13:28 could see Abraham, Isaac, Jacob and all the prophets inside the kingdom of God. For many years Lazarus had been outside the rich man's door.

There he had been totally ignored. How different is the situation now! From his place in hell the rich man could see Lazarus sitting at the side of Abraham — the man whom all Jews regarded as their father. How awful it is for anyone to be outside of the kingdom — and to know it!

The rich man asked Abraham to send Lazarus to him so that he could dip the tip of his finger into water to cool the rich man's tongue. Despite his dire situation he had not learnt his lesson. He still regarded Lazarus as a servant and he ignored the fact that Abraham had said that no one could go from heaven to hell, or the other way round.

Finally, the rich man said, **'Then I beg you, father, send Lazarus to my father's house, for I have five brothers. Let him warn them, so that they will not also come to this place of torment'** (16:27-28). For the first time in this story we hear of the rich man showing concern about someone other than himself. Or was he? Why did he not want his brothers to join him in hell? Surely he realized that their presence would have increased his suffering further; they would have blamed him for leading a life on earth which did nothing to warn them of the need to repent and seek the Lord.

Abraham said, **'They have Moses and the Prophets** [the Scriptures]; **let them listen to them'** (16:29). But the man said, **'No, father Abraham ... but if someone from the dead goes to them, they will repent'** (16:30). Abraham replied, **'If they do not listen to Moses and the Prophets, they will not be convinced even if someone rises from the dead'** (16:31).

But of course, someone did come back form the dead — perhaps not very long after Jesus told this story. The other Lazarus, the brother of Mary and Martha, came back to life (John 11:44). But he only had an extension of life; he eventually died again. Later on Jesus himself rose from the dead, and now he is alive for evermore. He has lived on this earth, and he has warned us about the terrors of hell. How foolish people are not to pay attention to what he said!

17.
Watch yourselves!

Please read Luke 17

Watch your attitude (17:1-19)

In chapter 16 Jesus had taught about money. In the first part he spoke to his disciples about this, and in the last part he spoke to the Pharisees about their attitude towards it. But here in chapter 17, Jesus returns to addressing his disciples. He spoke about their attitudes, to others and to God.

The importance of right living

Temptations cannot be avoided. The closer a person lives to God, the greater are the temptations he faces. However, God's people must not be cast down because evil thoughts sometimes pass through their minds. The devil will use all kinds of methods to tempt believers to think about the pleasures of wickedness. Advertising, in all its forms, often has the aim of stimulating wrong desires within us; for what other purpose is the bikini-clad girl on the new fast motor car? And the filthy talk of our fellow men and women frequently makes us consider, with sensual excitement, things which we know are wrong. These temptations frequently pass through our minds, but let us make sure that they keep going and pass right on through them. Never let us spend time drooling over things which can cause us to sin. We should say to the tempter, 'Get thee behind me, Satan.' The message is that all believers need to watch themselves. Complacency is a great danger; those who think they are strong in the faith need to be careful that they do not fall (1 Cor. 10:12).

But in this passage Jesus taught about the person who causes God's people to be tempted. Young believers (i.e. the 'little children' of verse 2) are especially susceptible to things which cause people to sin. But the people who are going to be judged are those who cause others to sin. In fact, Jesus says of the person who leads others astray that, rather than be tried for the evil he has done, **'It would be better for him to be thrown into the sea with a millstone tied round his neck than for him to cause one of these little ones to sin'** (17:2).

How can we cause others to fall? First, we can be loose in our *behaviour*. We might think, 'One little drink will not harm me,' but a weak believer might be watching us, and that one small drink could encourage him to start drinking, and he might not know when to stop! Second, we might be loose in our *speech*. Even though we might think that one dirty joke is rather funny, it could still lead a less mature Christian back into his old pre-conversion ways. Third, we can be loose in our *attitudes*. We might think that it is all right for us to walk the other way when we see our awkward neighbour coming down the street, but our action might lead a younger Christian to think it is all right to treat others with contempt. Let us never forget these words of Jesus: **'Watch yourselves.'** We should watch our thinking, our actions and our attitudes.

Jesus then told his disciples to be prepared to forgive those who truly repent. First of all, he said we must rebuke those believers who commit sin. When we see a fellow-Christian doing something wrong (particularly if it is someone we do not particularly like), it is all too easy to ignore what he is doing. We can say to ourselves, 'I know I ought to say something, but let him find out the hard way.' Jesus said that it is our duty to rebuke those who fall into sin (17:3). We must do this for the good of the person concerned, and also because of the good name of Christ. However, we should never reprimand anyone with a judgemental attitude — as though we were more holy than the person who is doing wrong. Paul said, 'Brothers, if someone is caught in a sin, you who are spiritual should restore him gently' (Gal. 6:1). We should always speak the truth, but we must do it in love (Eph. 4:15).

Then if, after our words, the person repents, we should forgive him. That was the main reason for rebuking him in the first place.

We should never have that self-righteous attitude which says, 'Well, now I've done my duty, that's all there is to it.' We should be thrilled when someone returns to God. Our attitude should be like that of the father in the parable of the lost son, who welcomed his son home with tears of joy; it should never be like that of the elder brother, who was upset with the way his father received back his sinful brother. Even if the wayward man afterwards sins again and again, and keeps on repenting, we should still forgive him. If he sins and repents as much as seven times a day (i.e. an infinite number of times) we should continually forgive him (Matt. 18:22). After all, if God keeps forgiving us, then it is only right that we should always forgive those who do wrong to us.

Next the disciples said to the Lord, **'Increase our faith'** (17:5). They did not say, 'Increase our love'; it was more faith that they asked for. So in reply, Jesus said, **'If you have faith as small as a mustard seed, you can say to this mulberry tree, "Be uprooted and planted in the sea," and it will obey you'** (17:6). Here the Lord was talking about the quality of faith, not its quantity. This is one of those Eastern pictures which we find rather difficult to understand. Our minds do not think like that. What the Lord means is, 'It is not so much great faith in God that is required, as faith in a great God.'[1]

The way we serve God

Jesus told his disciples a parable: **'Suppose one of you had a servant ploughing or looking after the sheep. Would he say to the servant when he comes in from the field, "Come along now and sit down to eat"? Would he not rather say, "Prepare my supper, get yourself ready and wait on me while I eat and drink; after that you may eat and drink"? Would he thank the servant because he did what he was told to do? So you also, when you have done everything you were told to do, should say, "We are unworthy servants; we have only done our duty"'**(17:7-10).

Although none of these disciples was particularly rich, they would have known people who had enough money to employ at least one servant. After a hard day's work in the field it was the servant's duty to get his master's meal, before he had his own. The servant (he may have been a slave) would not have expected to be thanked for doing what, after all, was his duty. So, said Jesus, why should you expect to be thanked for serving God?

The Lord was teaching that it is an honour for us to be servants of God. We should gladly serve him in his church and in the world; and we should not do this merely to receive his thanks. Nor should we do it because we are going to be rewarded for our efforts. We should do it gladly because we love serving our heavenly Master. Warren Wiersbe says, 'If a common servant is faithful to obey the orders of his Master who does not reward (thank) him, how much more ought Christ's disciples obey their loving Master, who has promised to reward them graciously!'²

Luke next tells us about a miracle. Jesus was on his way to Jerusalem. The author of this Gospel is constantly reminding us that the cross was getting nearer. The Lord, at that time, was travelling along the border between Samaria and Galilee. Samaria was a place much despised by the Jews, and Galilee was a district where Jews were, more or less, accepted as the authentic people of God. But Jesus carefully kept both Jews and Samaritans at a distance. He was like the ten lepers whom he met as he was going into a village. They **'stood at a distance'** (17:12) because they were required to do this by the law (Lev. 13). These men had a highly contagious disease and it was only sensible that they should not approach people and spread their illness. They must have recognized Jesus, and they certainly seem to have heard about his healing powers. The amazing thing was that they did not call out to him for healing. Instead they said, **'Jesus, Master, have pity on us'** (17:13)

But **'When [Jesus] saw them, he said, "Go, show yourselves to the priests"'** (17:14). Why did he say this? It was because a wonderful thing had happened to them; the Lord had healed them. Only the priests had the authority to examine them, pronounce that they were healed, and then allow them to mix freely in society once again (Lev.14). Jesus was concerned that these lepers should obey God's law. But unlike the leper in Luke 5:12-14, Jesus did not touch them; nor did he say the words, 'Be clean.' He just told them to show themselves to the priests. The remarkable thing was that **'As they went, they were cleansed.'** They were healed as they made their way to the priests — as they obeyed the law. It was when they did as Jesus said that they were cleansed.

Then **'One of them, when he saw he was healed, came back, praising God in a loud voice. He threw himself at Jesus' feet and thanked him'** (17:15-16). He showed gratitude for his healing. Then, at this point, Luke drops the bombshell: he says of this particular man, **'And he was a Samaritan.'** But the Jews had no dealings with Samaritans, and the feeling was mutual. However, Jesus overcame all barriers, and he still does. Those same arms of love still reach out to all peoples as they did then. The other nine former lepers were presumably Jews, but only this foreigner returned to give praise to God.

Then the Lord said to the Samaritan, **'Rise and go; your faith has made you well'** (17:19). It would seem that he then went to show himself to the priests. But he had first praised God and thanked Jesus.

He can teach us all about the need to show gratitude to God for the gracious and bounteous salvation we have been given in Christ. How feeble it is to murmur, 'Thank you, Jesus'! How much better it is to praise God for who he is, and then thank him for what he has done by sending his Son to Calvary to wash away our sin!

The coming of the kingdom (17:20-37)

An enquiring mind is a good thing. Children who ask sensible questions are likely to learn and make progress throughout their lives. Likewise, all believers should be asking the Lord what he wants to teach them through his Word and the events of their lives. The Pharisees constantly asked the Lord questions. However, unlike the questions of young children, theirs were asked with the wrong motives. They were hoping that Jesus would say something contrary to the Scriptures. The Pharisees were not humble people. They had evil minds. They never enquired of the Lord, 'What must we do to be saved?' They never said, 'Show us how we can honour God more in the way we live our lives.' They were proud, arrogant and boastful people, and they despised all whom they regarded as inferior.

On this occasion they asked Jesus when the kingdom of God would come. They did not say, 'How can we be ready for the kingdom?' They were too self-righteous to think that there was anything in their lives which needed to be altered. What they wanted to know was, 'When will the kingdom of God come?' Jesus answered by saying, **'The kingdom of God does not come with your careful observation'** (17:20). He meant that God was not saying, 'Oh, those wonderful Pharisees are looking for me to come!

I'd better not keep them waiting any longer.' Jesus added, **'Nor will people say, "Here it is," or "There it is"'** (17:21). He intended them to realize that the kingdom of God was not 'a thing' which could be observed or ignored as people wished. On the contrary Jesus said, **'The kingdom of God is within** [or among] **you.'**

Jesus was saying, 'It's here now.' The kingdom can be known by the presence of the king, and Jesus was that King and he was there in their midst. They expected the kingdom of God to come in with great pomp and splendour, and they assumed that, when it did arrive, they would be sitting in the best seats as honoured guests. Not only that, they surmised that many signs would be given before the coming of the King. But Jesus was saying to them in effect, 'You are blind.' He was the King, and he was right there with them. He had performed many, many signs by healing the sick and showing his power over nature, but they did not recognize him for who he was. This meant that they, who thought themselves to be so holy, were excluded from the kingdom of the God whom they professed to serve. Instead, the poor, the sick and these disciples, whom they regarded as ignorant followers of Jesus, were already members of that kingdom.

Teaching for the disciples

Then Jesus turned his attention to his followers and he gave them more details of the kingdom. He pointed out that there is another aspect to the kingdom: 'then', as well as 'now'. There is the present ('The kingdom of God is among you'); that is the part which he told to the Pharisees. But there is also the future, when the kingdom of God will be ushered in with great pomp and glory. Then Jesus implied that there are things which are going to happen to these same disciples which will be so terrible that they will long to see one of the days (or the first day) of the Son of Man (17:22).

He means that his own disciples will, some time in the future, suffer great persecution. And in their torment they will yearn for the time of the Messiah — that day when he will return to this earth and cause their pain and agony to come to an end. This second coming of the Lord will be the final triumph over everything that is evil and sinful.

However, the Lord gave his disciples a warning. He said, **'Men will tell you, "There he is!" or "Here he is!"'** Down through the ages there have been impostors who have claimed to be the Messiah. They have come with a religious message and have gained many followers. But Jesus said, **'Do not go running after them'** (17:23). **'You will not see it'** (17:24). It is to come later.

So how will anyone know when the Great Day of the Lord has come? Jesus made it unmistakably clear. He says, **'The Son of Man in his day will be like the lightning, which flashes and lights up the sky from one end to the other.'** There will be no doubt in anyone's mind when Jesus returns to this earth. It will be like a tremendous flash of lightning which comes suddenly and very quickly. One minute everything will be calm and peaceful. Everyone will be behaving in a normal way, and then, in an instant, everything will be changed. Christ will have returned to this earth. Lightning comes unexpectedly, without any warning. People will be sleeping, or working in the fields, and then without any prior notice, Christ will be manifested on this earth in all his majesty and power.

Lightning is also very public; everyone is aware of it. The coming of Christ will be like that. John tells us,

'Look, he is coming with the clouds,
    and every eye will see him,
even those who pierced him;
    and all the peoples of the earth will mourn because of him.
                    So shall it be! Amen '
                                    (Rev. 1:7).

But before any of these things could happen Jesus reiterated that first of all, **'He must suffer many things and be rejected by this generation'** (17:25). He had already told them about his coming death many times (5:35; 9:22,43-45; 12:50; 13:32-33). It is only through his death that the sins of his people can be washed away.

Two men

To emphasize the importance of people being ready for the second coming of Christ, the Lord gave two examples from the Old Testament Scriptures. He said that in the days of Noah, **'People were eating, drinking, marrying and being given in marriage'** (17:26). We can imagine the disciples thinking, 'And what is wrong with that?' The answer is, 'Absolutely nothing.' These are perfectly wholesome things for anyone to be engaged in. But if that is all a person's life consists of, then he had better beware. There is more to life than enjoyment. There is the judgement awaiting. One day while the people of Noah's time were doing these legitimate things, **'The flood came and destroyed them all'** (17:27).

Then Jesus went on to remind his disciples about the days of Lot. The **'people were eating and drinking, buying and selling, planting and building'** (17:28). Again, there is nothing wrong with any of these things — unless that is all there is to the lives of the people concerned. The person who only thinks about material things is in a very sad condition. Jesus reminds them, **'The day Lot left Sodom, fire and sulphur rained down from heaven and destroyed them all'** (17:29).

In both of these cases Jesus mentions 'the end'. In these examples everyone who only cared for this life and what it holds was completely destroyed. The Lord then went on to ram home his message. He told them that when the Son of Man is revealed there will be a great judgement upon everyone. He gave several illustrations to show that no one will escape the judgement of God **'on that day'**, which is surely and relentlessly coming. In 2 Peter 3:10 the apostle says, 'The day of the Lord will come like a thief. The heavens will disappear with a roar; the elements will be destroyed by fire, and the earth and everything in it will be laid bare.'

What a picture of destruction that is! Then what will a man do who is having his siesta on the top of his flat roof on that day? In the face of sudden destruction will he run down to the house to select which of his possessions he wants to take with him? Of course not! There will not be time. It will be the same for all those who are alive when the great day of God's judgement comes.

This shows us what value we all place upon 'things'. How we ought to devote more time, energy and attention to the Lord and the things of God!

In the same way, anyone working in the fields on that day should not go back for anything. Jesus adds, **'Remember Lot's wife!'** (17:32). She lingered because she loved the pleasures of Sodom. She was loath to leave them behind, and because she looked back with longing, she was turned into a pillar of salt. What a dreadful sign this is to all those who want to hang on to the possessions of this life when the end comes!

Then Jesus repeated the saying Luke quotes in chapter 9:24: **'Whoever tries to keep his life will lose it, and whoever loses his life will preserve it'** (17:33).

Finally, the Lord gave his disciples two more illustrations, but this time he emphasized the fact of separation on that day. First, he talked about two people in one bed at night. They may have been two men, but it is more likely that he is referring to a husband and wife asleep together. Whatever the case, they are obviously two people who are closely related. However, even their family tie does not preserve them from being separated from one another on that day. This is because one of them knows and loves the Lord and the other has rejected God's salvation.

In the same way Jesus told about two women grinding grain together. They may well have been very good friends, but he says, **'One will be taken and the other left'** (17:35). Jesus does not tell us whether the one 'taken' is to be destroyed (because she is an unbeliever) or to go with the Lord (because she belongs to him). 'What is clear is that no matter how close two people may be in life, they have no guarantee of the same eternal destiny. One may go to judgement and condemnation, the other to salvation, reward and blessing.'[3]

To close this section Luke tells us that Jesus quoted one of the sayings of those days. After they had listened to the Lord's teaching the disciples asked, 'Where, Lord?' And Jesus replied, **'Where there is a dead body, there the vultures will gather'** (17:37). He seems to mean that the Second Coming will be as obvious, when it happens, as the gathering of vultures around a carcass.

Where there are dead bodies, there has been death (vultures only eat dead meat). The second coming of Christ will happen when people least expect it. It will cause a separation between those who know, love and honour God, and those who are only concerned about this life and what it has to offer. The point for all of us to take note of is that we should 'be ready for the day of his appearing'. We should make sure that we are true believers in the Lord Jesus Christ and we should be living our lives in a way which pleases God. Peter said, 'Since everything will be destroyed ... what kind of people ought you to be? You ought to live holy and godly lives as you look forward to the day of God and speed its coming' (2 Peter 3:11-12).

18.
How to come before God

Please read Luke 18

The mercy of God (18:1-17)

How can people like us approach God? When we take an honest look at ourselves we realize that there is nothing in us to commend us to the Lord. But it is people like us whom God calls into his kingdom. Not many of us are wise by human standards, or influential, or of noble birth. However, Paul tells us, 'God chose the foolish things of the world to shame the wise; God chose the weak things of the world to shame the strong. He chose the lowly things of this world and the despised things ... so that no one may boast before him' (1 Cor. 1:26-28).

The importance of persistence

'**Jesus told his disciples a parable to show them that they should always pray and not give up**' (18:1). Sometimes the pressures of life make us wish we could give up our Christian faith. There are demands put upon us by other people and these tempt us to want to turn from following the Lord, and then there is the sheer unfairness of everything around us.

The widow in this parable was under tremendous pressure. Everything was against her. She was a woman. She had no husband. She was poor, and she had been unjustly treated. The judge in the story would not have been a Jew because the Jews had elders to deal with their local problems. So he must have been a Roman or some other Gentile. What we do know about him is that he neither feared God nor cared about men (18:2).

What a person to have in such an important position! However, he was there and he had all the authority of mighty Rome behind him. So why did he take no interest in this widow? It was because she was poor, and therefore she did not have sufficient money to pay for a court hearing. Once again we see Luke selecting a story concerning the underprivileged — a poor widow. And, in doing so, he was saying, 'God cares about such people.'

Eventually, because of the woman's persistence, the judge gave in and told her that he would see that she received justice. He did not promise that he would find in her favour. He merely said that she would get justice. In other words he would allow the case to be heard fairly. Why did he change his mind and do this? It was because the woman was persistent in urging him to help her. Despite all of the difficulties in reaching him, she never gave up. She was not put off because she had no money to bribe him (as was the usual practice). Neither was she deterred because the judge's servants made it difficult for her to see him. The fact that she was a 'nobody' and he was a very powerful member of society did not hinder her and her request. She persisted because she knew that justice was on her side, and her continual demands paid off.

After Jesus told this parable he said, **'Listen to what the unjust judge says. And will not God bring about justice for his chosen ones, who cry out to him day and night?'** (18:6-7). This is rather like the parable of the friend at midnight recorded in Luke 11:5-8. It is a parable of contrasts. It is not telling us that God will only answer our prayers if we keep on badgering him. This story is teaching the very opposite; as Jesus says, **'Will [God] keep putting them off?'** (as the unjust judge did) **'I tell you, he will see that they get justice, and quickly'** (18:7-8). 'God will not delay his support of the chosen ones when they are right.'[1] Righteousness will be established. Wrongs will be put right. God does hear and answer prayer.

After the parable Jesus uttered a plaintive cry: **'However, when the Son of Man comes, will he find faith on the earth?'** He does not mean, 'Will he find Christians on the earth?' He means, 'Will he find in those believers faith that perseveres in prayer and loyalty?' In Matthew 24:9-13 Jesus told his disciples, 'You will be handed over to be persecuted and put to death, and you will be hated by all nations because of me. At that time many will turn away from the faith and will betray and hate each other, and many false prophets will appear and deceive many people. Because of the increase of wickedness, the love of most will grow cold, but he who stands firm to the end will be saved.'

The importance of penitence

Jesus next addressed the people around him, who probably included some religious leaders. Luke tells us what Jesus was thinking: **'To some who were confident of their own righteousness and looked down on everybody else, Jesus told this parable: "Two men went up to the temple to pray, one a Pharisee and the other a tax collector"'** (18:9-10).

There was a great contrast between these two men. One was naturally religious, and the other was naturally ungodly. One was familiar with the temple and its ritual, and the other was only able to stand at a distance from the altar (18:13) — like the lepers who were standing at a distance from Jesus (in 17:12). One stood up and prayed about himself (18:11). How proud he was! But the other **'would not even look up to heaven, but beat his breast'** (18:13). One told God how good he was; he prayed about himself: **'God, I thank you that I am not like other men — robbers, evildoers, adulterers — or even like this tax collector'** (18:11). He also told God about his own good deeds. He said, **'I fast twice a week** [while the law only demanded a fast once a year; on the Day of Atonement], **and I give a tenth of all I get'** (18:12). (The Pharisees prided themselves that they even gave away a tenth of their garden herbs!) But all the other man could cry out to God was: **'God have mercy on me, a sinner!'** (18:13).

Jesus must have greatly surprised his audience when he said, **'I tell you that this man** [the tax collector], **rather than the other, went home justified before God. For everyone who exalts himself will be humbled, and he who humbles himself will be exalted'** (18:14). Jesus actually said that this sinful tax collector went home justified before God!

The Pharisee was so full of himself, but the tax collector was full of God. He had no good works to plead before the Almighty. He knew that he was a sinner, but the thing that enabled him to go home with peace in his heart was the fact that he cried out to God for mercy

— and he found it. This sinner found mercy in God, not because he was humble, but because he was aware of his sin and he cast himself upon the mercy (i.e. the loving pity) of God.

The importance of dependence

At this point (18:15) Luke again starts using incidents which we also find in the other Gospel accounts. Here we read of people (fathers as well as mothers) bringing babies to Jesus to get him to touch them. Obviously those parents desired the very best for their children. That is why they brought them to Jesus. They wanted the Lord to touch their children so that they would receive Jesus' blessing.

But **'When the disciples saw this they rebuked them'** (18:15). They did this because they were conscious that the Lord was in need of rest. They probably also thought that little children were not important enough for Jesus to bother about. But the Lord had other views on the subject. He did not tell the disciples off (in the way that his followers had rebuked the parents). He said, very graciously, **'Let the little children come to me, and do not hinder them, for the kingdom of God belongs to such as these'** (18:16).

Then he used the children to teach his disciples and others who were listening. In Luke 9:46-48 he had taken a little child and used him as a teaching object. There he placed the child next to him and said, 'Whoever welcomes this little child in my name welcomes me.' Here he said, **'I tell you the truth, anyone who will not receive the kingdom of God like a little child will never enter it'** (18:17). He was teaching everyone the value of the qualities which innocent children possess. A little child is completely dependent upon his parents or others; that is how we should be towards God. Our attitude should not be, 'Look at all I've done for you, Lord.' It ought to be, 'God, have mercy on me, a sinner.'

A little child is also full of trust. He has not yet learned to be suspicious of what is offered to him; that is how we should be towards God. We should trust him fully and accept all that he gives us, knowing that it is for our good.

Next, a little child is completely sincere; he has no false motives for anything that he does. We too should be sincere with everyone. We should have no hidden ambitions. We should be straightforward and frank in all that we do.

Finally, we should remind ourselves of how a child receives a gift: he receives it as it is. He does not ask, 'How much do I owe you for this?' or 'What do I have to do to earn this?' A little child receives it willingly, freely and openly. For each of God's people, 'The kingdom of God must be received as a gift; it cannot be achieved by human effort. It can be entered only by those who know they are helpless, without claim or merit.'[2]

God's mercy is a gift

We need to persevere in prayer and be determined to press on in the things of God, whatever difficulties may come to us. We need to come to God with humility and penitence. We must acknowledge that we are sinners in God's sight, that even our best efforts are useless so far as gaining acceptance by God is concerned. We need to remember that we must depend upon God as a little child relies upon his parents for everything.

Blind eyes opened (18:18-43)

In this section of Luke's Gospel we have three incidents of blindness. The rich young ruler had nothing wrong with his natural eyesight, but he could not see what was keeping him from receiving eternal life. The disciples did not understand that Jesus had to suffer and die; their eyes were not opened to the reason for that until after his resurrection. And, finally, the blind man at the approach to Jericho was made to see physically.

The rich young ruler

The story of this man is mentioned in all three Synoptic Gospels but Luke is the only one to tell us that he was a ruler — an official of some kind. He must have been very clever, or especially favoured, to have been given such responsibilities while still young.

This man, like so many others, asked Jesus a question. In this case, he was perfectly open and honest; he did not seem to be wanting to trap the Lord into saying something which could incriminate him. He obviously had a high regard for the Master, because he ran up to him and fell on his knees before him (Mark 10:17) and said, **'Good teacher, what must I do to inherit eternal life?'** (18:18).

He called Jesus, 'Good teacher'. This was very unusual because no rabbi would have been called 'good'. Rabbis knew that only God could be described like this. That is why Jesus reminded the young man of this fact. However, the Lord was not denying that he was God. He was merely getting the man to think of the implications of what he was saying. He was testing him to see if he fully understood that Jesus was, indeed, God in human form.

As this ruler was interested in knowing what he should 'do' to obtain eternal life, Jesus asked him what he had done. The Lord then listed five of the six commandments which are about man's duty to his fellow men. The ruler quickly replied that he had kept them all. He had never committed adultery, or killed anyone, or stolen anything. He had never told lies before a court of law, and he had always respected his parents. This is why he said, **'All these I have kept since I was a boy'** (18:21).

What a clean-living young man he was! When we think of all the pressures there must have been upon him to break some of those commandments, we realize what a good life he had lived. Could we, with utter truthfulness, say, 'I, too, have kept all of these laws, all of my life'?

But Jesus then said to the man, **'You still lack one thing.'** The ruler must have realized that; otherwise he would not have asked, 'What must I do to inherit eternal life?' He desperately wanted to be certain of his eternal salvation. So when Jesus said, 'You lack one thing,' we can imagine him wanting to say, 'Tell me what it is, Lord. I'll do anything or go anywhere if only I could gain the assurance that I will inherit eternal life.' He was full of heroics. He almost wanted to show off so that he could be assured of his place in heaven.

It is interesting to notice that Jesus never asked him about his attitude to the tenth commandment. This says, 'You shall not covet' (Exod. 20:17). Coveting is having 'an eager desire to possess'. But this man already possessed great riches, and he wanted to hang on to them. The Lord knew that the young ruler would do anything that he was asked, except give up his possessions!

That is why the Lord told him, **'Sell everything you have and give to the poor, and you will have treasure in heaven. Then come, follow me'** (18:22). But we read, **'When he heard this, he became very sad, because he was a man of great wealth'** (18:23). And, whatever else happened, he was not prepared to give up his riches. He would certainly make a contribution to the temple funds;

he would even give generously to the poor, but he could not bring himself to make the great sacrifice of giving away all of his money.

That is why Jesus looked at him (cf. 22:61), and said, **'How hard it is for the rich to enter the kingdom of God! Indeed, it is easier for a camel to go through the eye of a needle than for a rich man to enter the kingdom of God'** (18:24). The Lord was not saying that it is impossible for rich people to be saved. Abraham, Solomon and many other Old Testament characters were very wealthy people, but they all belonged to God. There have also been some very rich men in recent centuries who have become true Christians. What Jesus meant was that those who persist in letting their riches come between themselves and their allegiance to God can never be saved.

Whoever heard of a large camel being able to go through the eye of a needle? The commentators give us some very clever expla-nations of what Jesus meant about camels and needles, but I believe Jesus was using this illustration to show how impossible it is for people who trust in their riches to become real Christians. This does not mean that those of us who are not rich can learn nothing from this saying. The same principles apply to us all. If there is anything in our lives to which we cling more than we do to our love for the Lord, then that thing is a barrier to our salvation. If we are not prepared to part with it, it will keep us out of heaven. Our prayer should be like that of William Cowper:

> The dearest idol I have known,
> Whate'er that idol be,
> Help me to tear it from thy throne
> And worship only thee.[3]

At this point some of the Lord's followers asked him, **'Who then can be saved?'** If a clean-living young man like this rich young ruler could not be saved, then, they wondered, what hope was there for anyone else? But Jesus replied, **'What is impossible with men is possible with God!'** (18:27). God is the God of the impossible. He can do miracles and change men's hearts. He can open their eyes to spiritual truth.

Then Peter added, **'We have left all we had to follow you!'** He probably meant, 'Does that mean that we cannot be saved because we are poor and, therefore, cannot give away so much money as this ruler?' But Jesus replied, **'No one who has left home or wife or brothers or parents or children for the sake of the kingdom of God will fail to receive many times as much in this age and, in the age to come, eternal life'** (18:29-30).

The sacrifice at Jerusalem

Luke tells us that Jesus then took the Twelve aside and told them what would happen at Jerusalem (18:31). He had previously spoken to them about these things (9:22,43-45). Everyone was travelling to Jerusalem for the Passover feast. They were all going to offer sacrifices for their sins and many of them would have been taking their choicest lambs to offer on the altar in the temple. 'Jesus too [was] now "going up to Jerusalem," to bring himself as an offering for "the sin of the world". See Isa. 53:10 and John 1:29.'[4]

Again the Lord explained to his disciples that **'Everything that is written by the prophets about the Son of Man would be fulfilled'** (18:31). But this time he adds a new element. He speaks of being handed over to the Gentiles. This was a degrading thing for a Jew, but the point was that only the ruling Gentile powers had the authority to put anyone to death. In fact, everything that Jesus told his disciples did happen, but he never mentioned his death without speaking of the certainty of his resurrection. We too, should never talk or preach about the cross of Calvary without also telling our hearers about the power and certainty of the resurrection.

But the minds of the disciples were blinded to what he was telling them. We are told this in three different ways: **'The disciples did not understand any of this. Its meaning was hidden from them, and they did not know what he was talking about'** (18:34).

The blind beggar

By this time there must have been quite a large crowd going up to the Passover festival at Jerusalem. But Luke focuses our attention, not on the crowds, but on a **'blind man ... sitting by the roadside begging'** (18:35). He was poor. He could not work and he depended on the gifts of others for his sustenance. Yet this useless man is the only one who seems to have had eyes to see who Jesus really was. He asked the people around him what all the commotion was about, and they said, **'Jesus of Nazareth is passing by'** (18:37). He obviously had heard of Jesus; someone had told him about the Lord. But he addressed the Saviour as **'Jesus, Son of David'**. 'Son of David' was a title for the Messiah, and this blind man saw that Jesus was the long-awaited Saviour who had been promised for many centuries past.

However, when he called out, those who were at the head of the procession told him to be quiet. They rebuked him (cf. 18:15) because, to them, he was of no account. What use was a blind man to anyone? But it was this blind man who saw who Jesus really was, and he would not keep quiet about it. This is why the Lord ordered the man to be brought to him. He had been calling for mercy. He was like the one in the temple who cried, 'God, have mercy on me, a sinner' (18:13). He called for mercy because he knew that he could do nothing to earn his salvation.

Jesus then asked him plainly, so that there could be no mistake, **'What do you want me to do for you?'** (18:41). The man did not have to stop and think about his answer. He said, **'Lord, I want to see.'** So **'Jesus said to him, "Receive your sight; your faith has healed you." Immediately he received his sight and followed Jesus, praising God. When all the people saw it, they also praised God'** (18:43).

Everyone praised God because a physical healing had taken place, but what about this man's spiritual healing? He had had the eyes of his heart opened so that he could see Jesus for who he truly was, the chosen one of God (see Eph. 1:18).

In this second half of Luke 18 we have seen three incidents of blindness. The rich young ruler, having encountered Jesus, was not prepared to open his eyes to the glorious future of following Christ. 'He went away sad, because he had great wealth' (Matt. 19:22). The disciples had spent three years with Jesus witnessing his healing and teaching ministry, yet they did not understand until after he had risen from the dead and the Holy Spirit was poured out upon them at Pentecost. And finally, blind Bartimæus (cf. Mark 10:46) saw the real Jesus even before his physical eyes had been opened. The question is, 'What about us?' Are we still blind to who Jesus really is, or do we understand, but refuse to get rid of those things which are in our lives, preventing us from following him as we should?

19.
The King comes to his own

Please read Luke 19

The responsibilities of servants (19:1-27)

In this opening part of Luke 19 we see how a very rich rogue behaved after he had met with Jesus: he gave half of his possessions to the poor, and paid back four times the amount he had cheated people out of (19:8). The other story concerns ten servants who were trusted with a fairly small amount of money while their master went away. During that time most of the servants worked hard, using the money to gain more and so increase the wealth and importance of their master.

The story of Zacchæus

Jesus met Zacchæus in his home town of Jericho. This was a city near to Jerusalem. During the time of Joshua a curse had been placed upon it (Josh. 6:26) but someone had rebuilt it—or at least had built a new city right next to it. It was through this city that Jesus passed (19:1). The only reason why Jesus went to Jericho, or so it seems, was to meet and heal a poor blind man (18:43) and to confront and transform a rich chief tax collector, who had climbed a tree so that he could see the Lord (19:4). From these stories we can learn that Jesus calls both the rich and the poor to be his people. It may be very hard for rich people to become Christians (18:24), yet, by God's grace, this sometimes does happen (18:27).

Zacchæus was a determined man. We do not know what he had

heard about Jesus, but he knew something about him, otherwise he would not have run ahead of the crowd and thrown aside his dignity by climbing a leafy, shade-producing sycamore tree.

There is nothing in the story to suggest that this tax collector wanted to hide from Jesus, but we can be sure that he was not liked by the majority of the people. We can tell that by the way in which they all began to mutter when Jesus went to be a guest with a man who, in their estimation, was a **'sinner'** (19:7). Tax collectors were notoriously corrupt. They would tend to let the rich off some of their taxes, and demand extra money from the poor, who had little money to use to bribe the officials. However, Zacchæus was not just an ordinary tax collector (like Matthew/Levi); he was the chief one in that large area. But it seems that he had gained his riches (19:2) by underhand methods because a chief tax collector would be well off, but not wealthy.[1]

Jesus stopped under the very tree which Zacchæus had climbed and called out, **'Zacchæus'** (19:5). The Lord knew his name, and everything else about him, and told him to **'come down immediately'**. There was an element of command in his voice as he added, **'I must stay at your house today.'** The Lord did not ask if it was convenient; nor did he say, 'I'd like to come.' He gave one of those divine 'musts' which are emphasized throughout the whole of this Gospel.

When Jesus spoke, Zacchæus hesitated no longer. He was very quick to respond to the call of Jesus. He did not plead his unworthiness, but when he approached Jesus he welcomed him into his house without saying, 'Give me time to get it ready, Lord.'

We are not given any details of the interview, but we do know that as a result of meeting Jesus, Zacchæus became a changed man. His whole life was transformed. It is this element of change which speaks most clearly about anyone's conversion to Christ. If someone claims to have become a Christian, and yet there is nothing different about the way he or she thinks, speaks and acts, then I believe there may be some cause to doubt that the person has been truly converted.

Zacchæus declared that, for him, things would now be different. That is why Luke says, **'Zacchæus stood up'** (19:8). He was making his stand for Jesus and a new way of life as he said, in the hearing of all of the people, **'Look, Lord! Here and now I give half of my possessions to the poor.'** Since his conversion he had a deep compassion for those who were less well off than himself. He did not want to be seen to be living a lavish, ostentatious way of life, while others were starving.

Zacchæus also added, **'And if I have cheated anybody out of anything, I will pay back four times the amount'** (19:8). The law only required that a person repay the original sum stolen, plus one fifth (Lev. 6:5; Num. 5:7), but Zacchæus cheerfully agreed to give back much more than was necessary. He was doing what was laid down for theft with killing or selling an animal (Exod. 22:1; 2 Sam. 12:6). He had become much more generous because Jesus had entered his life. Whenever people come to know the Lord Jesus Christ as their Saviour then everything takes on new meaning and they face up to new responsibilities and exhibit new values.

Not only did Zacchæus himself speak, Jesus also made a declaration concerning him. He said, **'Today salvation has come to this house, because this man, too, is a son of Abraham.'** Zacchæus was a Jew, by birth, but Jesus now declared that he had become a son of Abraham because he now walked in the footsteps of Abraham's faith (Rom. 4:12).[2] He now believed God, as Abraham had believed when things seemed totally impossible (see Rom. 4:3).

Zacchæus was one of the lost souls whom Jesus, the Son of Man, had come to seek and to save (19:10). Many have missed their way. They do not know where to go, or what to do, but God still sends his Son to seek them out and save them. The Lord God Almighty stoops down and takes the initiative; and the same God who made such a difference in Zacchæus' life is still in the business of changing people today.

The ten minas

This parable is unique. It is the only one which Jesus told which is known to have some basis in historical fact. Some years earlier, King Herod the Great had died. In his will he left the kingdom of Judea and Samaria to his son, Archelaus. But, because of the foreign occupation, Archelaus had to travel to Rome to seek permission from Cæsar Augustus to have himself appointed as king. However, shortly after his departure a delegation of fifty Jews also set out for Rome. They went on behalf of the Jewish people to tell Cæsar that they did not want Archelaus to reign over them because he was just as cruel as his father had been (see Matt. 2:16). The outcome was that

Archelaus returned to Judea with authority to rule the province, but without the title, 'King'. But that did not stop him being known as 'the King of the Jews'. Everyone would have known that story. There were also other similar instances in Jewish history.

The parable which Jesus told had a similar outline — only the whole situation was different. Luke tells us that, while the crowds were listening to the declaration of Zacchæus and the statement by Jesus, the Lord went on to tell everyone this parable. He told it because he and his disciples were nearing Jerusalem and their long journey was reaching its climax. Also **'The people thought that the kingdom of God was going to appear at once'** (19:11). Because of these things Jesus told the people this story. In it a man of noble birth **'went to a distant country'** (19:12), and, naturally, he was away for a very long time.

The nobleman in Jesus' parable was certainly not like Archelaus; this nobleman was a picture of Jesus himself. After his resurrection the Lord left this earth to receive a crown; he had his coronation at his ascension. Unlike Archelaus, he did receive from his Father his kingdom, his crown and his title; and even now he is in heaven waiting to return to this earth.

In the story that Jesus told, the nobleman gave ten of his servants one mina each. A mina was one hundred drachmas, a drachma being the weekly wage of a working man. Therefore, one hundred drachmas would have been the equivalent of about three months' wages. This was not an enormous amount of money, unlike that in the parable of the talents (in Matt. 25:14-30). There each servant received a different sum of money and there were huge amounts involved. Here Jesus is speaking about a comparatively small sum of money, and each of the servants was given the same amount.

After the nobleman had gone to a distant country to have himself appointed king, a group of his subjects who hated him sent a delegation after him to say, **'We don't want this man to be our king'** (19:14). However, their plea was ineffective. The nobleman was made king, and he returned to his home country.

It was when he arrived home that the ten servants were called before the king to tell him how much they had gained from the money they had been given. This should not have surprised them because, before he went away, their master had said, 'Put this **money to work ... until I come back'** (19:13).

The first man came and showed that his mina had been set to

work in such a way that it had gained ten more. The nobleman was pleased, and because the servant had been faithful in this small thing, he was rewarded. But he was not told to go and have a rest. Because he had discharged his duties well in a fairly small matter, his reward was to be given even more responsibility: he was put in charge of ten cities.

Then the second servant showed that his mina had gained five more. He, likewise, was given more responsibility: he became ruler of five cities. **'Then another servant came and said, "Sir, here is your mina; I have kept it laid away in a piece of cloth. I was afraid of you, because you are a hard man. You take out what you did not put in and reap what you did not sow." His master replied, "I will judge you by your own words"'** (19:21-22). He did not say that he agreed with the statement of the unfaithful servant. He merely took the man's words and used them to judge him. He said, **'You wicked servant! You knew, did you, that I am a hard man, taking out what I did not put in, and reaping what I did not sow? Why then didn't you put my money on deposit, so that when I came back, I would have collected it with interest?'** (19:23). And, because this man had not served him well (he had not put the money to work) the king took his one mina away from him and gave it to the one who had ten minas.

But those standing by said, **'Sir... he already has ten!'** The master replied, **'I tell you that to everyone who has, more will be given, but as for the one who has nothing, even what he has will be taken away'** (19:26). This sounds so strange to our ears, but we need to remember that Jesus was not talking about rewards; he was referring to responsibilities. Those who fail to use 'the mina' which the Lord has given to them will have it taken away. So what is 'the mina' which each of God's people have been given? It is not a natural talent or a spiritual gift; not everyone receives these in the same quantity (see Matt. 25:14-30 which speaks about abilities). What is it that every Christian receives in exactly the same measure? It is the gospel message. We have all been given this glorious message of salvation so that we can declare it to the lost. Faithful servants of God use it to lead many people into the blessings of Christ. They do this by witnessing to them of God's love in sending the Lord Jesus Christ down to this earth to bring salvation. That is how one mina can be increased to five or ten.

We have looked at the faithful servants of God, and we have also considered what happens to the gift of the unfaithful servants. But there is a third group of people in this parable. These are the enemies of the king. They did not want this man to be king over them. Because of this Jesus says that they will be utterly destroyed; and this will happen in front of the king. He will be their judge and he will see that his righteous judgements will be carried out.

Each of these three groups of people challenges us about our attitude to the Lord Jesus Christ. We must ask ourselves, 'To which group do I belong?' Are we faithful servants of Christ? Are we unfaithful believers, who are saved — but only by the skin of our teeth? Or are we among those who will, one day, be utterly destroyed because they spit out those dreadful words: 'We don't want this man to be our king?' (19:14).

The King rejected (19:28-48)

Jesus has been nearing Jerusalem for some while, and in verse 28 Luke tells us that Jesus **'went on ahead, going up to Jerusalem'**. On the Friday evening, before sunset, he would have arrived at Bethany, just a mile or two outside of Jerusalem. Here was the home of Mary, Martha and Lazarus (John 11:18). On the day after the Sabbath the Lord sent two of his disciples to a neighbouring village to collect a colt (John calls it a young donkey — John 12:14). There had evidently been some arrangements made because they were to give a kind of password to anyone who asked them what they were doing. They were to say, **'The Lord needs it.'** This is stated twice (19:31,35).

The triumphal entry

How was Jesus going to go into Jerusalem? Most of his disciples wanted him to arrive in the city unobtrusively. They all knew that the religious leaders wanted to catch him out (19:47) and they had tried to dissuade him from going near the city during Passover time. But the Lord had steadfastly set his face to go to Jerusalem (Luke 9:51, AV). He was determined to reveal himself to the people on this particular occasion. Often in the past he had instructed the people whom he had healed to go away and tell no one who he was, because 'his time had not yet come'. But now his time had come. He could now let everyone know that he, the real King of the Jews, had arrived in the holy city. So, on that first Palm Sunday morning he prepared himself to ride into Jerusalem in triumph.

The disciples threw their cloaks on the colt and put Jesus on it. No one had ever ridden this animal before and the clothes would have made it more comfortable for Jesus to sit upon.

Just as no one had ridden this animal before, so Jesus had been born into a womb in which no one else had been carried; and before long his dead body would be laid in a tomb in which no other body had been buried. There was nothing haphazard about the triumphal entry. Everything had been carefully planned and was in order — just as it should be.[3]

Jesus did not climb on to the colt; his disciples put him on to it. They may not have understood the significance of this action but they willingly assisted in it. They knew that he was their Master and they obeyed him, even when they were uncertain about the wisdom of his action.

The journey that Jesus undertook that day was very significant too. The people spread their cloaks on the road. They did this before the procession came in sight of Jerusalem. The followers of the Lord were not just trying to impress the citizens of the capital. They wanted to make the journey comfortable for Jesus; the road was very rough and uneven, and their clothes would have made it less likely that the colt would stumble. Matthew tells us that they also spread palm branches on the road (Matt. 21:8) just as today we put down the red carpet for any distinguished visitor.

When they all reached the place where the road began to go down the Mount of Olives, **'The whole crowd of disciples began joyfully to praise God in loud voices'** (19:37). This was the point at which they came over the brow of the hill and caught their first glimpse of the holy city shining in the sunlight. Something about its splendour sparked off inside them a great song of praise to God.

They also praised the Lord because of all the miracles they had seen (19:37). Blind Bartimæus had been made to see again only a few days before and, even more recently, Lazarus had been brought back from the dead (John 11:45). This is what the crowds sang: **'Blessed is the king who comes in the name of the Lord!'** which is from Psalm 118:26. This psalm refers to the coming of the Messiah. Did they sing this because they recognized Jesus as the long-promised deliverer who was to set them free?

They continued, **'Peace in heaven and glory in the highest!'** At the announcement of the birth of Jesus the angels sang, 'On earth peace' (Luke 2:14). Now the cry of peace and glory is to be heard in heaven also. This was a prophetic cry of the people that the long-awaited work of redemption would soon be accomplished.

Some objections

At this point some of the Pharisees started to complain. They said, **'Teacher, rebuke your disciples!'** (19:39). These religious leaders objected to the people applying Messianic words to Jesus. The crowd recognized that Jesus was the longed-for King — even though they had the wrong idea of what Jesus had come to do. But the religious people objected, just as all through the ministry of Jesus the Pharisees had complained about him.

Jesus replied to his enemies by saying, **'I tell you ... if they** [the disciples] **keep quiet, the stones will cry out'** (19:40). He did not mean that stones would miraculously come alive and begin to shout. Rather, the city itself would be a witness of his glory. Habakkuk had said the same words about Jerusalem in his prophecy (Hab. 2:11).

As Jesus approached Jerusalem and saw the city, **'He wept over it'** (19:41). This was because its inhabitants had rejected him. They did not really want him to reign over them. The people were excited because they thought that he had come as the Messiah for the purpose of raising up a great army and driving out the Romans. Jesus wept because of the materialism of the people. He knew that many in this same joyful crowd who were shouting, 'Blessed is the King who comes in the name of the Lord!' would a few days later on be shouting, 'Crucify him! Crucify him!'

This is why he said that the people of Jerusalem were blind: **'If you, even you, had only known on this day what would bring you peace — but now it is hidden from your eyes'** (19:42). Then he went on to prophesy, in exact detail, what the Romans would do some thirty or forty years later: **'The days will come upon you when your enemies will build an embankment against you and encircle you and hem you in on every side. They will dash you to the ground, you and the children within your walls. They will not leave one stone on another, because you did not recognize the time of God's coming to you.'** This is why the city was going to be destroyed, because the people were blind and did not recognize the time of God's coming.

Jesus at the temple

Jesus went straight to the temple area — the centre and symbol of
all Jewish religion. Luke had begun his story in the temple.[4]
Zechariah was chosen by lot to go into the temple to burn incense.
There he was told of the birth of John. It was to the temple, on two
separate occasions, that Jesus was taken as a child (2:22, 41). And
now, towards the end of his Gospel, Luke tells us that Jesus began
driving out those who were selling things in the place of which it was
written, **'My house will be a house of prayer.'** The traders had
made the temple **'a den of robbers'**.

Jesus would have made himself very popular with the ordinary
people by this action. They knew that the outer courts of the temple
were being used to make a great deal of profit out of ordinary
worshippers. When people came to the temple at Passover time they
would bring a lamb to offer as a sacrifice to make an atonement for
their sins. But this lamb had to be pronounced suitable by the priests;
no animal was allowed to be sacrificed if it had a blemish or
imperfection in it. However, if anyone did bring an unsuitable
animal all was not lost; authorized animals were on sale in the Court
of the Gentiles (the outer court, the part where anyone could go). The
catch was that these animals were sold at very exorbitant prices.
And, for each one sold, Annas (the former high priest) and the other
leading religious people got a sizeable 'rake-off'.

How sad it was that the priests seemed to be more concerned to
get money for themselves than to carry out the work God had given
them to do! 'Instead of praying for the people, the priests were
preying on the people!'[5] David Gooding puts it like this: 'Instead of
being priestly intermediaries to help men find worship and be
blessed by God, they had become middlemen, turning their priesthood into a commercial monopoly in order to make financial profit
out of men's quest for God.'[6]

It is no wonder that Jerusalem was rejected by the Lord. The
priests were acting falsely. They were plotting to kill the genuine
Messiah, while many of the people, who had welcomed the true
King on that day, had said in their hearts, 'We will not have this man
to reign over us.'

They were looking for material answers to the problems they
faced. They only wanted a Messiah to drive out the Roman invaders
and set up a Jewish kingdom once again. They did not realize that
the kingdom of God would only be established when men's hearts

were made right and people were reconciled to God. They did not recognize that their real problem lay within themselves. They would not admit that they were sinners who needed to repent and turn to God in faith.

And, because the city of Jerusalem had rejected Christ, he rejected it. However, he did not do this lightly. Jesus, just like Jeremiah long centuries before, wept over Jerusalem (see Jeremiah 9:1 and the whole of the book of Lamentations).

Up until that point Jerusalem had been the holy city, where God's presence had dwelt in a very special way, but its inhabitants had finally turned their backs upon the Messiah. Now Jesus renounced it. He showed that he had cast it off by refusing even to sleep within its walls any more (21:37).

But still the people **'hung on his words'** (19:48). However, they did not do this for very much longer. Jesus knew all men's hearts. He was not deceived by flattery. How many of those same people who lapped up his teaching in those early days of 'Holy Week' would, a few days later, cry out for his blood?

They must have wondered why he entered Jerusalem on a colt, instead of a war horse. Kings about to go into battle always rode powerful steeds. But Jesus rode into the city on that day, 'gentle and riding on a donkey' (Matt. 21:5). These Jews surely knew the prophecy of Zechariah 9:9. They would have known, too, that 'Only in war did kings ride upon a horse; when they came in peace they came upon an ass.'[7] Why, then, did they only think of the Messiah in political, military terms?

It must have been because, even though they hung on his every word, they were not spiritually-minded people. They were only seeking physical gain. They did not realize that Jesus had come, as Messiah, to bring peace. He said, '"My kingdom is not of this world"' (John 18:36). He came as King to rule in the hearts and lives of all those whom he delivers from the bondage of their sin. He came to dwell in people's hearts. He came to bring peace.'[8]

20.
Questions and answers

Please read Luke 20

Who has authority? (20:1-19)

In verses 1-8 we see that representatives of all the religious parties in the Jewish council ganged up against Jesus. It was probably the Tuesday after his triumphal entry into the city, and Jesus was teaching the people in the temple courts, and preaching the gospel. This obviously irritated the religious people. So a group of them came up to him and said, **'Tell us by what authority you are doing these things?'** and **'Who gave you this authority?'** (20:2).

The reason they asked this was because Jesus was not an officially recognized rabbi. He had no authority from the synagogue to engage in teaching within the temple courts; and in any case, 'these things' to which they were objecting included riding into Jerusalem as though he was the promised Messiah. How was he going to answer their questions? He could have said, 'God has sent me,' but he knew that they would not accept such a statement. Or he could have kept silent and refused to answer at all. But that was the cowardly way out. Their own disciples were to take that line later on (20:26). Instead Jesus asked them a question.

He said, **'Tell me, John's baptism — was it from heaven, or from men?'** (20:4). He knew that many of the people believed that John was a great prophet and had been sent from God. He knew also that these religious leaders would have known that John had declared that Jesus was the Lamb of God, who had come to take away the sin of the world (John 1:29).

By asking them about the authority of John, Jesus was putting them on the spot. If they said that John's baptism was from heaven (they meant 'from God') then Jesus would ask them, **'Why didn't you believe him?'** (20:5). But if they said that John's baptism came from men, then all the people would have been angry and stoned them. They knew that the vast majority of the people were persuaded that John was a prophet. So they dodged the issue and said, **'We don't know where it was from.'** John Blanchard sums it up like this: 'They pretended that they were incapable of coming to a decision on the matter. Jesus refused to trade words with such hypocritical liars (v.8). He was under no obligation to answer dishonest questions.'[1]

The parable of the tenants

Now that the Lord had all these religious leaders around him he issued them with a challenge. He told a story about an absentee landlord. There were many people like this in Palestine during those days. They were rich farmers who owned land and sowed crops in it. But, instead of waiting for the harvest, they went far away and left the tending of the plants to tenant farmers. The understanding was that the tenants would work hard on the land; the better the crop, the more they would be able to keep for themselves, as their proportion of it. They knew too that at harvest-time the owner would return for his portion of the produce. The system worked well. The farmer owned the land, purchased the seed and planted the vineyard; it belonged to him, so he had his return on his money. The tenant too got his reward for his hard work.

These Jewish leaders would not only have known that this arrangement often took place, but more importantly they would have been aware that a vineyard was frequently used by the prophets of old as a picture of the nation of Israel, God's favoured people. They would have been familiar with scriptures like Isaiah 5:1-7, 'My loved one had a vineyard on a fertile hillside... [He] planted it with the choicest vines' (see also Ps. 80:8-16). So they would know that Jesus was going to speak about God's people by means of the parable he was about to tell them.

They, as the custodians of the religious welfare of the people, were represented in the parable as 'the tenants'. Consider how the tenants behaved in Jesus' parable. When it drew near to harvest time, the owner sent a servant **'so they would give him some of the fruit of the vineyard'** (20:10). But the tenants **'beat him and sent him away empty-handed'** (20:10). Because of this the owner sent two more servants; and each one was treated worse than the previous one. Why did this happen? It can only have been because of the greed of the tenants; they wanted to keep all of the produce for themselves.

Finally, the owner sent his beloved son. **'Perhaps they will respect him,'** he said to himself. But when the tenants recognized the son coming they said, **'Let's kill him, and the inheritance will be ours!'** (20:14). They must have assumed that the owner had died, and his son had come as the new owner to claim his inheritance. They knew, too, that if they killed the heir then, following Jewish tradition they, as occupiers for more than three years, 'could presume to own it in the absence of an alternative claim'.[2] So they threw the son out of the vineyard and killed him. Why did they throw him outside before they killed him? J. Duncan Derrett says that 'It was important that they did not kill him in the vineyard, for this would have defiled the ground with the corpse and made it more difficult for them to sell their produce.'[3]

At this point Jesus issued the challenge to his hearers. He asked them, **'What then will the owner of the vineyard do to them?'** The religious people would have recognzed that Jesus was talking about Israel when he spoke about the vineyard. They would have known that the owner was God and they would have worked out that the tenants were themselves, the religious leaders into whose care the nation of Israel had been entrusted (20:19). They would have understood that the three servants whom the owner sent were the Old Testament prophets, and it must have begun to dawn on them that the owner's son, who was killed outside of the vineyard, was Jesus, the person who was telling them the story. Therefore, when the Lord asked the religious leaders what the owner of the vineyard ought to do, they would, in all honesty, have had to say, 'Kill the tenants,' because of the way they had rejected the owner, misused the servants, treated the son and planned to obtain the vineyard for themselves. But, if they said that, they would be seen to have condemned themselves.

However, Jesus went on to tell them what the owner would do. He said, **'He will come and kill those tenants and give the vineyard to others'** (20:16). The owner would come in judgement, and the vineyard would be taken away from those tenants who were then in occupation, and given to others who were outside the circle of the former tenants.

As he delivered this shattering news to them, the Lord looked directly at them and asked, **'Then what is the meaning of that which is written: "The stone the builders rejected has become the capstone"? Everyone who falls on that stone will be broken to pieces, but he on whom it falls will be crushed'** (20:17-18). We can understand why, when they heard this, **'The teachers of the law and the chief priests looked for a way to arrest him immediately.'** It was **'because they knew he had spoken this parable against them'** (20:19).

The Lord had told a parable which had highlighted their failure to honour God, and then he backed up his accusation with Scripture. He quoted from the same 118th Psalm which the pilgrims had sung when Jesus entered the holy city a few days before. These religious people were supposed to be the builders of God's house (Israel), yet they had rejected Jesus, who was the very stone that God had chosen to be the foundation, and also the chief centre-stone which would tie together the whole of the main archway of the building of God (see 1 Cor. 3:11; Eph. 2:20-22; 1 Peter 2:6-8).

We can also understand why they were horrified when Jesus said that the vineyard would be taken away from the tenants and given to others. This is why they said, **'May this never be!'** (20:16). But it was going to be. The Jewish nation, with their leaders, had rejected God's chosen one, the Lord Jesus Christ. Everyone who stumbles at the knowledge that Jesus is the Messiah will be broken to pieces. One day the Lord will fall in judgement on all who reject him as the Son of God and they will be crushed (20:18).

Why, then, did the priests not arrest him immediately? It was because they were frightened of the people. They knew that Jesus still had a wide following. All the while that Jesus spoke against the deceit of the religious people, the crowds would accept him as their champion. Here at last was someone who was speaking up for the poor downtrodden ordinary Jewish people.

But they knew also that the Roman authorities were looking down into the temple courtyards from their vantage-point, high up in the Tower of Antonia at the corner of the temple. At the slightest sign of any disturbance Pilate, the governor, would cancel the whole eight-day feast of the Passover, and everyone would have to go home without having their Passover meal or being given the opportunity of offering their sacrificial lambs in the temple. This is why the religious people wanted to arrest him when he was in a quiet place and kill him outside Jerusalem.

Did they realize that they were going to do just what the tenants did in the parable? **'They threw him out**[side] **of the vineyard and killed him'** (outside). The writer to the Hebrews, later on, would refer to the Old Testament sacrifices and say, 'The high priest carries the blood of animals into the Most Holy Place as a sin offering, but the bodies are burned outside the camp. And so Jesus also suffered outside the city gate to make the people holy through his own blood' (Heb. 13:11-12). Mrs Alexander makes the same point in her hymn, 'There is a green hill far away, outside a city wall.'

Jesus had often predicted that he would have to suffer and be killed, and now the time was drawing near. But one further question remains for us to consider, 'Who are the others who are going to be given the vineyard when the occupying tenants are killed?' The owner in the parable could have been so angry at the rejection of himself and his son by the tenants that he completely destroyed the vineyard. It would have been understandable for him to have said, 'Well, because of the way you have treated me, no one shall have it.' But he did not. He gave it to others.

This is, therefore, yet another indication that the Jews had turned their back upon the blessings of God — they rejected his only Son. But God does not withdraw his blessings completely. They are 'simply removed from the Jews as a nation and given to the church universal',[4] and this church consists both of Jews and of Gentiles (non-Jews).

Some lessons that we can learn

We can learn that Jesus is Lord; John the Baptist testified of that fact. Therefore, we should always accept Christ's authority over every area of our lives. All Christians have a responsibility to care for their fellow believers. When we are converted God puts us to work in his vineyard. He expects us to work hard and produce fruit for his glory. We can do that by working hard for him through witnessing to his goodness.

But we must always remember that the owner is coming back again one day to claim what is his by right. He will come in judgement. Jesus warned the Jews that 'They will shortly have to do with God, the Almighty Owner and Lord of All — to their fatal undoing. The Jewish leaders (and along with them the unbelieving part of the people) will be visited by the judgements of God.'[5]

Should taxes be paid? (20:20-47)

No one likes paying taxes, but in the time of Jesus the amount that everyone had to pay was a very small annual sum. The money was for the upkeep of the Roman army, and every Jew wanted to see these invaders gone from their land. This tax, therefore, was a constant irritation. The teachers of the law and the chief priests wanted to trap Jesus, so they asked him, in front of the crowds, whether it was right to pay it or not. They knew that, in answering this question, he would be forced to say the wrong thing. If he said, 'You must pay this tax,' then he would lose credibility with the people. They would say, 'We thought he was God's chosen one who would violently oppose these dreadful Roman oppressors.' But, on the other hand, they knew that if he was to say, 'No. It is quite wrong to pay this tax,' then someone would be sure to slink away and tell the Roman authorities that he was stirring up the people to rebel against the power of Cæsar.

It is interesting to note that the religious people did not go to Jesus themselves; they sent spies (probably some of their own disciples) and these spies came with very smooth talk. They said, **'Teacher, we know that you speak and teach what is right, and that you do not show partiality but teach the way of God in accordance with the truth'** (20:21). However, Jesus knew that they were not speaking sincerely; they were using demeaning flattery.

Naturally, the Lord did not fall into their trap. Luke tells us that **'He saw through their duplicity'** (20:23). He said to them, **'Show me a denarius.'** This was a small coin, such as a man might earn for one day's labour. On one side of it there was an image of the ruling emperor, Tiberius, and also these words: 'Tiberius Cæsar Augustus son of the divine Augustus.' On the reverse was written, 'High Priest (or 'Supreme Ruler').[6]

This was one of the many coins then in circulation which could not be taken into the inner part of the temple, and put into the temple treasury. The reason for this was that it had a picture of a man

(Cæsar) on it. That was a breach of the commandment: 'Thou shalt not make unto thee any graven image, or any likeness of anything' (Exod. 20:4, AV). It also had the dreadful inscription which said that Cæsar was divine and the supreme ruler in spiritual as well as religious realms.

It is very significant that Jesus did not produce a coin from his own purse and say, 'Look at this.' Of course, this was partly because he carried no money; he was very poor in this world's goods. But neither did he say to any of his disciples (to Judas, for example), 'Pass me a coin.' Instead he said to the lawyers, 'Show me a denarius.' It is amazing that they were not embarrassed to be carrying on their persons such a 'blasphemous' object. Nor did they try to disguise the fact that they used such money in their daily business transactions. They meekly produced a denarius. It was at that point that the Lord trapped them. **'Whose portrait and inscription are on it?'** said Jesus. **'Cæsar's,'** they replied. **'Then give to Cæsar what is Cæsar's',** said the Lord.

He meant, 'If you are going to use the goods and service of this world, then you had better pay for them with this world's currency.' The Lord was saying what Peter and Paul were both to say, later on, in regard to obeying the powers that are over us. Earthly, political administrations exercise their power with the permission of God; all the while God's laws are not being contravened, his people should obey those who are rulers over them.[7]

But Jesus also said, **'Give ... to God what is God's'** (20:25). This means that we should pay our taxes because we owe the civil authorities for the services they provide. However, we should be just as ready to give to God because of all the blessings he bestows upon us. How can we pay God for what he gives to us? We cannot ever discharge our obligations to him, but we should give to the Lord the praise and honour which are due to him.

After the object lesson which Jesus gave, we are not surprised to learn that the spies were silenced by his answer (20:26). But that was not the end of the questions. There were others waiting to try to trap the Lord.

The resurrection and marriage

Some Sadducees had a question. Sadducees were very influential people. They were wealthy priests who held a majority on the ruling

Jewish council. For them, retaining favour with the Romans was even more important than upholding biblical truth. Most commentators say that they only accepted the first five books of the Bible (the books of Moses) as divinely inspired.

They began by saying, **'Teacher ... Moses wrote for us that if a man's brother dies and leaves a wife but no children, the man must marry the widow and have children for his brother'** (20:28). They were quoting what is written in Deuteronomy 25:5. They knew that every Jew accepted this law; although there are only a few recorded instances of its actually being carried out. Also there is no evidence that the practice was still in operation at this time.

The Sadducees went on to build upon this instruction from Deuteronomy. It seems that they invented a case. They said, **'Now there were seven brothers. The first one married a woman and died childless. The second and then the third married her, and in the same way the seven died, leaving no children. Finally, the woman died too'** (20:29-32). Their question was, **'At the resurrection whose wife will she be, since the seven were married to her?'** (20:33).

Why were the Sadducees asking this question? They believed neither in the resurrection, nor in angels or demons, nor in any afterlife. So they could only have asked this to test Jesus, in an effort to try to catch him out.

The Lord replied by talking about **'this age'** and **'that age'**. From studying the New Testament we can see that there is a vast difference between the two. He had said the same kind of thing in chapter 18:29-30. There he spoke about the blessing his followers will receive in 'this age'. He then went on to say that they will receive eternal life in 'the age to come'.

We see from this that the Lord knew all about these Sadducees but he did not refute their wrong teaching; he merely stated the truth. He knew that their problem was that they were worldly in their thinking. They only thought of things in the terms of this life, whereas Jesus taught that the age to come is totally different from this age. The religious people of that day merely imagined heaven was a continuation of this life (but without its sorrows), but Jesus was teaching that the afterlife will be a completely new realm.

As an example we can take sex. In this life we can see the attractions of sex continually being bombarded at us from advertisements on hoardings, in newspapers and on our television screens.

But, as wonderful as God's gift of sex is for this age, it will not exist in 'the age to come'. Roy Irving says, 'It is difficult for people to become interested in heaven if sex is their chief pleasure and they are told that heaven is "sex-less"'. He adds, 'Actually the joys of heaven will be far more satisfying than even the best marriage relationship.'[8]

Then Jesus spoke about those who are **'considered worthy of taking part in that age and in the resurrection from the dead'** (20:35). He does not mean that people go to heaven because they think they are worthy of that place, rather that God himself is the one who declares that those who are in heaven are worthy. The reason the saints are worthy is because they have repented of their sins and trusted in Christ for salvation.

Next Jesus said that there will be no marriage in heaven. This is because there will be no need for marriage in heaven. God's people in glory will receive their love, comfort and strength from the Lord himself, whom they will see as he is (1 John 3:2). Paul tells us that we shall see him face to face (1 Cor. 13:12). There will also be no marriage in heaven because there will be no children born there. This is because there will be no death in heaven. John tells us a great deal about this in Revelation 21 and 22. In heaven we shall not be angels, but we shall be like the angels in this respect that we shall neither marry nor die.

Then Jesus gave these Sadducees another quotation from the books of Moses. He reminded them of **'the account of the bush'**. (He had to put it like that because they had no chapter and verse divisions in their Bible.) In that story, Moses shows that the dead rise because he calls the Lord the God of Abraham and the God of Isaac and the God of Jacob (see Exod. 3:6). At that point Jesus devastated the arguments of the Sadducees by asserting that **'[God] is not the God of the dead, but of the living, for to him all are alive'** (20:36). When Jesus said this, even some of the Pharisees had to say, **'Well said, teacher!'** Unlike the Sadducees, they agreed with this particular teaching of Jesus, but the Sadducees were silenced. **'And no one dared to ask him any more questions'** (20:40).

Whose son is the Christ?

Jesus then reinforced his teaching that he is, indeed, the Christ (the Messiah). He asked, **'How is it that they say the Christ is the Son**

of David?' (20:41) and proceeded to quote from a psalm of David:

'The Lord said to my Lord:
    Sit at my right hand
Until I make your enemies
    a footstool for your feet'

(Ps.110:1).

To the religious people he said, **'David calls him "Lord". How then can he be his son?'** He received no answer. The reason, no doubt, was because they did not want to accept that Jesus was, and is, the Messiah. The first mention of the Lord in this psalm is printed in capitals in most translations of the Bible. The Lord spoken of here is Jehovah. When the psalmist says, 'My Lord' (the one whom the Jews regarded as the Messiah) he speaks of him being invited to 'sit at God's right hand'.

The Pharisees had no problem with the Messiah sitting at the right hand of God in his triumph over all his enemies. They had no difficulty in accepting that the Messiah was the Son of David — because David's line was the royal line. So what did they make of the fact that David called his own son, 'my Lord'? The brothers of Joseph bowed down to their younger brother (then prime minister of Egypt) and called him 'lord', but Jacob, his father, never called his son 'my lord'. The only answer to the question was that Jesus (the one whom Bartimæus had called 'Son of David' in 16:39 and the crowds on Palm Sunday had also declared to be 'the Son of David' in Matthew 21:9), was indeed the long-expected deliverer — the Christ. However, we are not told that the religious leaders made any response.

Jesus went on to point out a few things about the teachers of the law. He told his disciples to **'beware'** of them. **'They like to walk around in flowing robes and love to be greeted in the market-places'** (with great adulation) and they like **'to have the most important seats in the synagogues and places of honour at banquets'.**[9]

How different should be the demeanour of God's people! Each one of us should be filled with humility. Our behaviour should be that which does not draw attention to ourselves. No priestly robes are necessary for the servants of God. They should not be eager to be seen in the forefront of society; rather they should be taking the more humble places at religious gatherings (see James 2:1-7). Money, power and authority should never be the marks of any Christian — especially one who is in leadership in the church. None of us should ever be guilty of an open show of religiosity. Let us not be like those who love to hear people say of them, 'What a holy person he (or she) is!' Let our prayers be simple, clear, humble and to the point. Jesus said, 'Blessed are the poor in spirit, for theirs is the kingdom of heaven' (Matt. 5:3).

21.
Signs of the times

Please read Luke 21

'I am with you' (21:1-19)

The Jews have experienced much persecution throughout their history. Their land has been occupied by many nations, as it was in the time of Jesus. But through all these times of trial and grievous testing, all faithful Jews had turned their thoughts and their eyes towards the holy temple which stood on Mount Zion in Jerusalem. We can learn this from Jonah when he called out from inside the great fish,

> 'In my distress I called to the Lord...
> From the depths of the grave I called for help...
> I have been banished
> from your sight;
> yet I will look again
> towards your holy temple'

(Jonah 2:1-4).

Since the time of Solomon a temple had stood in Jerusalem as a symbol of the presence and the power of the Lord in the midst of his people. It had been destroyed by the pagan armies of King Nebuchadnezzar, but it was rebuilt again on the very spot where it had once shone out in all its glory. Later King Herod the Great, in an endeavour to please the Jews and, no doubt, to gain glory for himself, had beautified it and put much beaten gold into its decoration.

It was in this same temple that Jesus taught up until the Thursday of that last week of his earthly life. Luke tells us, 'All the people came early in the morning to hear him at the temple' (21:38).

The widow's offering

At the beginning of this chapter we are told that Jesus was sitting down in the court of the women. This was the part of the temple where non-Jews were forbidden access. They could go as far as the court of the Gentiles, which was the outer court of the temple, but they could proceed no further. The Jewish women could go as far as the court of the women, but no further. Closer in was the court of Israel, where only Israelite men could go; only the priests could go beyond that point.

It seems that Jesus had been sitting down and was resting his head in his hands (no doubt he was feeling very tired because of all the teaching he had been giving, and the questioning he had endured). But then he looked up (21:1) and saw the rich people putting their gifts into the temple treasury.

In the court of the women were thirteen large collecting boxes. These were shaped like trumpets which were upside down. They had the narrow end open to receive the monetary gifts of the people. Each of them was for a different collection.

As Jesus was observing these rich people, who were probably making a great show of the large gifts they were putting into the boxes, he saw someone else. Few other people would have taken any notice of her. She was a poor widow. As we have regularly seen, Luke often draws our attention to the ordinary poor people; and especially to those who were among the downtrodden of society. Many of the women he wrote about were widows. He had just been recording that flamboyant religious men often 'devoured widows' houses' (20:47); no wonder so many of these bereaved women were poor! But this widow did not show any bitterness towards God. She came with a very small offering, and she gave it to the Lord.

We can imagine the rich people looking down their noses at this lady. They would have despised the small amount which she gave, thinking that such a small sum would do no good — that is, if they noticed her at all. All that she put into the collecting box were two small, thin, copper coins which were worth practically nothing.

Jesus then called his disciples to him (Mark 12:43) and said, **'This poor widow has put in more than all the others'** (21:3). They would have been puzzled by this because they knew that the higher valued coins, which the wealthy people had donated, could buy a great deal more than the small coins which the widow had given. So how could this woman have given more than the rich people? By God's reckoning she had. The Lord measures not what we give, but what we keep for ourselves. These rich people had plenty of money left in their possession, but this widow had nothing over — not even enough to buy her next meal. She must have been tempted to keep one of the coins for herself, but she gave them both.

In his great passage on Christian giving Paul says, 'If the willingness is there, the gift is acceptable according to what one has, not according to what he does not have' (2 Cor. 8:12). This woman gave everything that she had to God. Had she known the hymn she could have sung (and meant it):

Take my silver and my gold,
Not a mite would I withhold;
Take my intellect and use
Every power as thou shalt choose.[1]

The persecution of God's people

Some of the disciples started to speak about the glories of the temple. Indeed it was a splendid building, but Jesus said, **'As for what you see here, the time will come when not one stone will be left on another; every one of them will be thrown down'** (21:6). This did, in fact, happen some forty years later. The Lord had cleansed the temple on the previous Monday, but by continuing to reject him, the Jews had caused the temple to remain defiled. So, because of their refusal to accept the King of glory, God decreed that the temple would be destroyed.

It seems that at this point Jesus and his disciples left the temple and went outside the city to the Mount of Olives. There he gave the address which occupies almost all of this chapter (up until verse 36). Matthew (in chapter 24) and Mark (in chapter 13) also record the same sermon but Luke gives a shortened version. He also leaves out some details which his non-Jewish readers may not have understood.

The disciples asked Jesus, **'When will these things** [the destruction of the temple] **happen? And what will be the sign that they are about to take place?'** (21:7). Before he answered them he gave a warning that they should not be deceived: **'Many will come in my name, claiming, "I am he," and "The time is near."'** There have been many who have claimed that they have been sent by God to save the world, but Jesus warned his disciples not to follow these false messiahs (21:8).

Then he went on to tell them about many signs which will occur. He speaks of wars, revolutions and nations rising up against nations, and kingdom against kingdom. But, he says, **'Do not be frightened.'** This is a call which echoes down through the ages: God's people must not fear. They must not be worried about the dreadful things which are happening around them. They must always remember that God is on the side of his people.

Isaiah had recorded the words of the Lord:

'Do not fear, for I am with you;
do not be dismayed, for I am your God.
I will strengthen you and help you;
I will uphold you with my righteous right hand'
(Isa. 41:10).

The psalmist had said, 'The angel of the Lord encamps around those who fear him, and he delivers them' (Ps. 34:7). None of God's people needs to be frightened, because he has promised to be with them whatever happens to them. And he has never yet failed to keep his promise.

Jesus said, **'These things must happen first, but the end will not come right away'** (21:9). He spoke of great earthquakes, famines and pestilences coming to various places. And certainly all of these kinds of things happened between the day Jesus spoke and the fall of Jerusalem in A.D. 70. Here is an example of some of them. In A.D. 61 there was a severe earthquake in Phrygia. In A.D. 63 Mount Vesuvius emptied itself and laid half of Pompeii in ruins (I, and many millions more, have seen it). There had been severe famines during the reigns of Claudius and Nero; and the war which led to the capture and destruction of Jerusalem had begun in A.D. 66.[2] Such things have been going on down through the centuries right up until the present day.

Jesus then spoke about the persecution which would come upon his disciples. They were all going to suffer on account of him. He said, **'Before all this, they will lay hands on you and persecute you. They will deliver you to synagogues and prisons, and you will be brought before kings and governors, and all on account of my name'** (21:13). All of this suffering would result in their being able to give testimony to Jesus and the salvation that he had come to bring. The word 'martyr' actually means 'witness'. Almost all of these twelve were going to be martyred, but each of their deaths would be a tremendous testimony to the Lord. Peter testified before the Sanhedrin (Acts 4:7-12). Stephen made a speech to the high priest (Acts 7:2-53) and Paul spoke of Jesus before Felix (Acts 24:10-25).

Jesus further said that, in circumstances like these, he will give his people the right words to say. Many since can testify that when they have been in very difficult situations the Holy Spirit has put into their mouths the exact words they needed.

All followers of Jesus must be prepared to be betrayed, even by close relatives (21:16). There may be circumstances when they find that all men hate them because of their allegiance to Christ, but they must remember that no hair of their heads can perish without God's divine permission (see Matt. 10:29-31).

'I am coming' (21:20-38)

The destruction of Jerusalem

Jesus said, **'When you see Jerusalem being surrounded by armies, you will know that its desolation is near'**(21:20). The things which are detailed in verses 20-25 actually happened some forty years after Jesus spoke those words. Some people say that the writer of Luke penned this section after the fall of Jerusalem, but if he had invented these words of Jesus later on then the details of the fall of Jerusalem would have been even more specific!

Jesus warned the Jews that they were to get out of the city at the first sign of danger. In times of trouble those who lived in the countryside usually fled into the big city for protection. But, said Jesus, 'When these things start to happen you must flee to the mountains.'

The great destruction which would come upon them was to be a fulfilment of prophecy. Many of the Old Testament prophets had predicted the fall of Jerusalem because down through the centuries its citizens had sinned grievously against God. Isaiah had spoken of the day of vengeance upon the city (Isa. 63:4). Jeremiah had told the people,

> 'This is what the Lord Almighty says,
> "Cut down the trees
>   and build siege ramps against Jerusalem.
> This must be punished;
>   it is filled with oppression"'
>
> (Jer. 6:6).

Similarly, Hosea had predicted,

> 'The days of punishment are coming,
>   the days of reckoning are at hand'
>
> (Hosea 9:7).

Despite all of this the inhabitants of Jerusalem had been complacent for many centuries, thinking that because they were God's people they did not have to worry about the purity of their lives. But God notices everything; no one will escape punishment simply because they belong to the people of God.

However, it was not only in Old Testament times that the people had sinned; in the days of Jesus Jerusalem had piled up yet more iniquity; and the most terrible sin they had committed was to reject the Lord Jesus Christ. He had ridden into Jerusalem on Palm Sunday, but we have seen that many were plotting in their hearts how they might get rid of him. So, in Luke 21, Jesus tells his disciples that punishment will come.

But even though these things will happen to the once holy city, the Lord takes no pleasure in its destruction. He says, **'How dreadful it will be in those days for pregnant women and nursing mothers!'** God always has compassion upon those who have to care for others; he was to pick up this theme again when he spoke to the Daughters of Jerusalem who wept when Jesus was on his way to be crucified (23:28-30).

He told them how terrible the destruction of Jerusalem was going to be: **'There will be great distress in the land and wrath against this people'** (21:23). It is very telling that the Lord spoke about 'this people', not 'my people' (cf. Hag. 1:2).[3] Jesus continued, **'They will**

fall by the sword and will be taken as prisoners to all the nations.' This actually happened in A.D. 70, and according to the Jewish historian Josephus, some 97,000 were taken prisoner and deported to other countries; in addition about 1,100,000 were killed during the campaign.

Jesus then told them about an even greater indignity: Jerusalem would be trampled on by the Gentiles. For the Jews to hear this about their holy city would have been a tremendous shock. They would have been even more distraught had they known that for many years (after A.D. 70) all Jews would be completely banished from the city. From A.D. 637 the actual site of the temple has been in Muslim hands, and today there are still two large Muslim mosques where the temple once stood. One of them, the Dome of the Rock, is the third most holy spot in the whole of Islam.

These things have all happened in fulfilment of this prophecy of the Lord Jesus Christ. He said that Jerusalem will be trampled upon **'until the times of the Gentiles are fulfilled'** (21:24). It is difficult to know exactly what these words mean, but certainly since the days of the Acts of the Apostles, millions of Gentiles have heard the gospel preached and many of them have responded and come to faith in Christ as their Lord. Although there are some Jewish (Messianic) Christians, it has mainly been non-Jews who have become believers in the Lord Jesus Christ. Some scholars believe that 'These times will end when God's purpose for the Gentiles has been fulfilled.'[4]

The Second Coming

Then Jesus gave his disciples further signs. These would happen much, much later than the destruction of Jerusalem. He had said, 'The end will not come right away' (21:9). Before that there will be many trying times. Paul lists some of the things which will happen before the coming of the Lord: 'People will be lovers of themselves, lovers of money, boastful, proud, abusive, disobedient to their parents, ungrateful, unholy, without love, unforgiving, slanderous, without self-control, brutal, not lovers of the good, treacherous, rash, conceited, lovers of pleasure rather than lovers of God — having a form of godliness but denying its power' (2 Tim. 3:2-5).

At the end of these days there will be terrible calamities in nature. **'There will be signs in the sun, moon and stars. On the earth, nations will be in anguish and perplexity at the roaring and** tossing of the sea. **Men will faint from terror, apprehensive of what is coming on the world, for the heavenly bodies will be shaken'** (21:25-26). Peter also tells us that 'The heavens will disappear with a roar; the elements will be destroyed by fire, and the earth and everything in it will be laid bare' (2 Peter 3:10).

It is when these things happen that the end will come. **'At that time,'** said Jesus, **'[the people on the earth] will see the Son of Man coming in a cloud with power and great glory'** (21:27); also we find this same scene described many years prior to this by the prophet Daniel (Dan. 7:13). When Jesus comes again in the clouds, all his people will stand and lift up their heads. This is because their redemption is drawing near (21:28). For then everyone who knows the Lord Jesus Christ as their Saviour will discover that the time of blessedness has begun. They will then be able to enter into the joy of their Lord. At that time the pains and sorrows of this life of toil will pass away, because the Lord Jesus Christ himself will have returned to this earth to claim his people for himself. That will certainly be a great and glorious day for all those who belong to him.

Instructions for life

To illustrate how believers should live in view of these coming events, Jesus told his followers a parable. He said, **'Look at the fig-tree and all the trees. When they sprout leaves, you can see for yourselves and know that summer is near'** (21:29-30). This is a very clear picture.

Jesus used this illustration because the fig-tree was one of the symbols of Israel. Therefore, the disciples would have known that Jesus was telling them that the blessed time for the Jewish people (the summer) was approaching. But why did Jesus speak of 'all the trees', as well as the fig-tree? It was because the blessings of redemption would not only be given to people from the Jewish nation; they would also be granted to people from all nations. From other scriptures we know that when the Son of Man (Jesus) comes back in power and great glory, then he is coming for his own people, to whatever nation, tribe and tongue they belong (see Rev. 5:9).

Then Jesus added, **'I tell you the truth, this generation will certainly not pass away until all these things have happened. Heaven and earth will pass away, but my words will never pass away'** (21:32-33). What did he mean by 'this generation'? A generation is usually thought of as a lifetime. 'From one generation to another' means something like thirty-five years, i.e. when a group of children have grown up into full adulthood, so that they, themselves, have given birth to a new generation of children.

Jesus could have meant that the destruction of Jerusalem will happen before the people of the disciples' age-group had all died; this certainly did happen. But it is more likely that Jesus was referring to this gospel age: 'the times of the Gentiles' will not come to an end before the Lord returns in glory at his second coming.

Next he said, **'Heaven and earth will pass away, but my words will never pass away'** (21:33). The abiding character of the Word of God is a great comfort and strength to God's people. Even though all material things will be destroyed, nothing will ever eradicate the Bible. Here every believer can find the stability upon which to build his faith and life. 'The word of the Lord stands for ever' (1 Peter 1:25).

Jesus then gave them a solemn warning. He says, 'Be careful.' Every believer needs to take care of what he says, what he does and what he thinks. Just because there is the certainty of salvation for all believers, this does not mean that we can live careless lives. We must not be tempted to live in unrestrained pleasure (dissipation) or drunkenness, nor must we be weighed down with the anxieties of life.

If we take our eyes off Jesus and only look at ourselves, then we shall not be ready for the return of the Lord. It will come upon us unexpectedly (even though we shall have many signs of Christ's coming given to us). It will spring on us like a trap, and try to catch us out. It certainly will trap and entangle all those who live on the face of the earth who are not looking for the return of Christ. Each of those who are not ready for his coming, because they do not believe in him, will have to face the Judgement Day on their own.

God's people are enjoined to **'Be always on the watch, and pray that you may be able to escape all that is about to happen'** (21:36). How can we escape all the calamity which is coming? We can hide in Jesus. If we know him as our Lord and Saviour then we will be safe in that day. When the Judgement Day comes God's people will be able to stand (to hold their heads up high) because they will not be pleading their own righteousness, but the righteousness of Christ. He has washed them from their sins in his precious blood and they have been made clean from every stain of unrighteousness.

22.
Betrayal and arrest

Please read Luke 22

The last Passover (22:1-23)

Do we sometimes wonder what we would like to be remembered for after our death? How did the Lord Jesus Christ wish to be remembered by his people?

His disciples had seen him perform many truly wonderful miracles. Is that what he wanted them to remember about him? They had observed his sinless life, which was full of concern and love for other people. Is that what Jesus wanted his disciples to remember about him? What about the wonderful teaching which he gave? Surely if everyone put that into practice then the whole world would be transformed. Is that what Jesus wanted to be remembered by? What about his glorious resurrection? He rose from the dead, the firstfruits of those who die. Is that what he wanted to be remembered for? No. 'He wants to be remembered, not for his miracles, nor by his life, nor by his teaching, nor by his mighty resurrection and ascension; but by his death!'[1]

The Lord said to his disciples in the upper room what he says to all of his people in every age, **'This is my body given for you... This cup is the new covenant in my blood... Do this in remembrance of me'** (22:19-20)

It is the glorious atoning sacrifice of the Lord Jesus Christ upon the cross which brings life and immortality to each of his people. That is what Jesus wants to be remembered for more than for anything else.

The mysterious actions of Judas

All over Jerusalem, and throughout the whole of Palestine, many people were preparing for a feast. The season was the eight-day Passover festival which was designed to remind the Jews of the deliverance of their nation from the slavery of Egypt. At this time every Jewish family gathered together for a special meal consisting of unleavened bread (which had no yeast in it), bitter herbs, salt water, an egg, haroset (a mixture of apples, nuts, cinnamon and wine), sprigs of parsley and some roast lamb. Each of these things was designed to remind the people of some aspect of the hardships which their forefathers had endured in Egypt, and also of the great deliverance which God had given them in rescuing them from that slavery.

Jews still gather together like this every Passover time. They do not realize that Jesus celebrated the last Passover of all in Jerusalem on the night before he was crucified. They do not know that he, by his death on the cross, fulfilled that which the Passover feast foreshadowed. Paul tells us that 'Christ, our Passover lamb, has been sacrificed' (1 Cor. 5:7). Because they will not accept that Jesus is the Messiah unconverted Jews are still looking for his coming.

But let us go back to Jerusalem at the time of Jesus. The religious authorities desperately wanted to kill the Lord. They had been plotting to arrest him for many days. This same group of people had often tried to trip him up (see 20:1-2) and they also attempted to discredit him in the eyes of his followers.

However, they had a problem: they were afraid of the people (22:2). Jesus was still far too popular for their liking. They knew that if they arrested him in public then there would be an outcry against them, and this might well cause the Romans to step in and cancel the Passover celebrations. The people would then have to go back to their home towns before they had the opportunity to celebrate the feast.

But, as these scheming religious leaders were looking for some way to get rid of Jesus, the thing that they least expected happened. One of Jesus' own disciples came to them and discussed with them **'how he might betray Jesus'** (22:4). Naturally they were overjoyed at this surprising turn of events. Little did they know the true meaning of the words in Psalm 41:9:

'Even my close friend, whom I trusted,
   he who shared my bread,
   has lifted up his heel against me.'

There have been many theories about why Judas turned against his Lord. He may have become disillusioned about the mission of Jesus. He may have felt that the Lord should have raised up a revolution to overthrow the Romans. Or he may have had an overwhelming desire to get more and more money for himself. (He is usually mentioned in the same breath as money.) We really do not know why Judas betrayed Jesus.

But this we do know: **'Satan entered Judas'** (22:3). Satan had tempted Jesus in the wilderness but the Lord had ordered him away. We, too, are exhorted to 'resist the devil' (1 Peter 5:8), and we are told that when we do that he will then flee from us (James 4:7). Judas obviously did not repel the Evil One. Instead he consented to receive money from the religious leaders (22:5; cf. Matt. 26:15; Zech. 11:12) and he **'watched for an opportunity to hand Jesus over to them when no crowd was present'** (22:6).

The Passover preparations continued

Every Jewish household planned a Passover meal, but Jesus did not tell his disciples where their meal was going to be held. If he had done so Judas would have had the opportunity to inform the religious leaders, and they could have arrested him in the privacy of that upper room. There would have been no one but the other eleven disciples to have raised any opposition to his capture.

Earlier in the day Jesus had sent Peter and John to make the preparations for the meal which Jesus (as head of the family) would be sharing with his disciples (22:8). This had to be done secretly so that the authorities would not know where they were going to meet. These two disciples had instructions to follow a man carrying a jar of water (22:10). (It would have been easy to spot him because normally only women did this kind of work.) They had to catch up with the man and then give him this password: **'The Teacher asks: Where is the guest room, where I may eat the Passover with my disciples?'** (22:11). When they did this he showed them the place. In this room Peter and John prepared the meal and arranged for the lamb to be slaughtered that afternoon.

The meal itself

Finally the hour came for them all to gather. This was probably the
first time that Judas and the rest of the disciples learned where the
place was. At the meal everyone would recline on one arm at the low
table. We know from John's Gospel that Jesus had washed each of
the disciples' feet (John 13:5). We know also that Jesus gave some
wonderful teaching in that upper room (recorded in John chapters
13-16). But Luke omits all of this and just concentrates on the last
Passover meal, and the first Lord's Supper.

Jesus said, **'I have eagerly desired to eat this Passover with
you before I suffer. For I tell you, I will not eat it again until it
finds fulfilment in the kingdom of God'** (22:15-16). The Lord
knew that he would soon have to endure the agonies of the cross. If
we had been in a similar position we should have dreaded anything
which would bring such a terrible death nearer, but Jesus was
eagerly looking forward to sharing this meal with his disciples
because it would be his last Passover until the coming of the future
kingdom. His death on Calvary would be the fulfilment of the
Passover meal. This meal itself looked back to the deliverance of
God's ancient people from the slavery of Egypt, and it looked
forward to the salvation of his new Israel (i.e. all those who are born
again through his sacrifice on the cross). The next time he would eat
it would be at the great wedding supper (Rev. 19:9), at which all of
God's blood-bought people, through all the ages, will enjoy the
blessings of his presence for ever.

At a Passover feast four cups of wine are symbolically drunk, as
the cup is passed round the table. After one of these cups had been
drunk (it may have been the last of the four) Jesus gave thanks and
said, **'Take this and divide it among you. For I tell you I will not
drink again of the fruit of the vine until the kingdom of God
comes'** (22:17-18).

The institution of the Lord's Supper

Then Jesus **'took bread, gave thanks and broke it, and gave it to
them, saying, "This is my body given for you; do this in
remembrance of me"'** (22:19). Luke wrote his Gospel after Paul
had penned his first letter to the Corinthians and so he would
probably have known the much fuller account of this feast in 1

Corinthians 11:23-29. Luke, alone of the Gospel writers, tells us that Jesus said, **'Do this in remembrance of me.'** This is the reason we hold communion services; it is because Jesus has commanded us to do it. And we do it because Jesus wanted us to keep on remembering his death.

When he said, 'This is my body,' he meant, 'This represents my body.' This must be so because, at that point, he was still alive. The bread was broken from a whole loaf (or a whole piece of unleavened bread) — just as his own body would soon be broken in death on the cross.

'In the same way, after the supper he took the cup, saying, "This cup is the new covenant in my blood, which is poured out for you"' (22:20). The Jews had been given a covenant by God in the early days of their history. The word covenant means 'an agreement'. God had said to Israel of old, 'If you obey me fully and keep my covenant, then out of all nations you will be my treasured possession' (Exod. 19:5). But their history was, sadly, one of disobedience to God's clear commands.

However, at the institution of the Lord's Supper, Jesus said that he was inaugurating a new covenant. Jeremiah had spoken of this many years before when he said,

> '"The time is coming," declares the Lord,
>   "when I will make a new covenant
> with the house of Israel
>   and with the house of Judah.
> It will not be like the covenant
>   I made with their forefathers
> when I took them by the hand
>   to lead them out of Egypt,
> because they broke my covenant,
>   though I was a husband to them,"
>   declares the Lord.
> "This is the covenant that I will make with the house of Israel
>   after that time," declares the Lord.
> "I will put my law in their minds
>   and write it on their hearts.
> I will be their God,
>   and they will be my people.
> No longer will a man teach his neighbour,

or a man his brother, saying, 'Know the Lord,'
because they will all know me,
   from the least of them to the greatest,"

                                                           declares the Lord.
"For I will forgive their wickedness
   and will remember their sins no more"'

                                                              (Jer. 31:31-34).

When Jesus said, **'This cup is the new covenant in my blood, which is poured out for you,'** he meant that through the shedding of his precious blood on Calvary all who believe in him will be washed from their sins. The cup of wine was to be a symbol of his blood, which was another way of saying his death.

He said to his disciples, **'My blood ... is poured out for you.'** That is why we continually celebrate the Lord's Supper. It is to remind us that it is only through the sacrifice of Christ's sinless body and the shedding of his cleansing blood that anyone can be saved. There is no other way to become a real Christian. It is not by 'taking communion' that people are made children of God. Communion is only of any value if we already know Jesus as our Saviour, Lord and Friend. But those who are in a right and living relationship with Christ are given the wonderful privilege of taking the bread and the wine at this feast. In any case, how can people remember the Lord, if they have never known him in the first place? 'Just as the Passover was a constant reminder and proclamation of God's redemption of Israel from bondage in Egypt, so the keeping of Christ's command would be a remembering and proclaiming of the deliverance of believers from the bondage of sin through Christ's atoning work on the cross.'[2]

Back to Judas

Throughout the whole of this time, there was a traitor among them. Jesus said, **'The hand of him who is going to betray me is with mine on the table'** (22:21). Matthew puts it like this: 'The one who has dipped his hand into the bowl with me will betray me' (Matt. 26:23). Both of these statements mean the same thing. Jesus went on to say, **'The Son of Man will go as it has been decreed.'** Jesus had to die. This was all in God's plan of redemption for his people. **'But woe to that man who betrays him,'** the Lord added (20:22).

The disciples began to question among themselves which of them it might be who would betray the Lord (22:23). None of the disciples knew of the treachery of Judas Iscariot. But Jesus was aware of it. 'He was in full control of the situation. He was not taken by surprise.'[3]

Although the death of Christ had been foreordained, that did not excuse the guilty betrayer. Because Judas did not truly repent, he had to die and his death was not an eventual annihilation; it was a condemnation to everlasting damnation (see Matt. 25:46).

We need to make sure that we never betray the Lord. Peter denied Jesus, but he did not betray him, and he truly repented. We, too, need to repent if we have been ashamed of owning that we belong to the Lord. One of the most clear ways we can declare that we truly belong to the Lord Jesus Christ is to do as he says and eat the bread and drink the wine in memory of him, and to carry on doing this until our death, or until he comes again (1 Cor. 11:26).

Subtle temptations (22:24-46)

Why is it that Christians sometimes argue and fall out with one another? It is because they are still people who have their old sinful natures dragging them back. None of us will be perfect until we reach glory, but that does not mean that we should not endeavour to honour the Lord in all we do, say and think.

In this passage there are a number of instances where the disciples succumbed to the temptations of the Evil One. The amazing thing is that this happened while the Lord Jesus Christ was still present with them — in the flesh!

Pride

The first temptation they fell under was pride. At the Lord's Supper God's people should experience peace. Jesus said, 'Do this in remembrance of me.' If we remember Christ in the bread and wine, we remind ourselves that he came to bring peace. Particularly we remember that believers should be at peace with one another, as they are at peace with their Lord.

If any of us have disagreed violently with another Christian then we should sort out our differences before we come to the communion service. The very word 'communion' means being in fellowship with Christ and with one another. 'How good and pleasant it is when brothers live together in unity!' (Ps. 133:1). But how disgraceful it is when two Christians cannot forgive one another, and when they persist in being at enmity with one another while they are in the same church fellowship!

However, at the very first Lord's Supper a dispute arose among the disciples (22:24). It was about who was the greatest among them. They had argued about this before in Luke 9:46. On that occasion Jesus took a little child and made him stand beside him and taught that whoever is 'least among you all — he is the greatest' (9:48). Obviously they had not learned that lesson. This dispute possibly arose over the seating arrangements at the supper. Everyone wanted to sit near to the Lord, who was the host at the meal.

The world of those days had its social order (see 14:7). The most important guest sat at the right-hand side of the host. The next in order of importance sat on his left-hand side. The third most important was placed at his right-hand side, next but one, and so on. But what a terrible thing it was that, of all people, it was the disciples who were squabbling over such worldly things!

Because of this, Jesus talked to them about the way the so-called 'important people' of the world behaved. He spoke about the kings of the Gentiles. These were all heathen kings. Most of them were despots who had complete control over their people. They could order anyone's execution without giving a good reason. Everyone knew that these Gentile kings lorded it over their people, and none of their subjects had the right to question their actions, or demand a just trial. Yet many of these heathen kings called themselves 'benefactors'. This was because they liked to be thought of as those who conveyed benefits upon their people. They enjoyed the praise and adulation of their citizens, but the honours they were given were hollow; they had not earned them.

Then Jesus said to his disciples, **'But you are not to be like that'** (22:26). He meant, 'Why are you trying to make out that you are so important?' In that society, as in many Third World countries still today, the elderly are the ones who are the most respected. These so-called backward countries do not shut their elderly relatives away in institutions. They are cared for by the whole family and are given a position of honour and great respect. In their society it is the young who are pushed into the more insignificant positions.

We, in the West, have reversed the situation. Here it is the young who often get far too much of everything (to the extent that many of them become spoilt, and unable to appreciate the true value of money), while the elderly are neglected.

It was because the youngsters in the days of Jesus were given the inferior positions, that Jesus said to his disciples, **'The greatest among you should be like the youngest.'** He was trying to teach these proud disciples the importance of humility. Pride always goes before a fall, so God's people should be those who 'do nothing out of selfish ambition or vain conceit, but in humility consider others better than [themselves]' (Phil. 2:3).

Then the Lord used another illustration. He asked, **'Who is greater, the one who is at the table** [waiting for his meal to be given to him] **or the one who serves?'** (22:27). The obvious answer was the person who was reclining at the table and being waited on by another. There was nothing difficult for them about that question — until they noticed who the waiter was! It was the Lord Jesus Christ himself who was serving them, just as he had washed their feet when they had arrived for the meal. Jesus said, **'I am among you as one who serves.'** He is the Servant King, and he set them an example to show how they should behave towards their fellow men and women.

Encouragement

Jesus said, **'You ... have stood by me in my trials.'** Jesus had been through temptation by the devil (4:13). He had suffered many hardships (9:58) and he had been rejected by the people (John 1:11). But throughout all of these things the disciples had stood with him. For all their imperfections, they had been by his side when difficulties arose. So the Lord told them, **'I confer on you a kingdom, just as my Father conferred one on me'** (22:29). The kingdom in some senses was already with them (because he, the King, was in their midst), but in its richest sense it is still yet to come. Then,

'At the name of Jesus every knee should bow,
    in heaven and on earth and under the earth,
and every tongue confess that Jesus Christ is Lord
    to the glory of God the Father'

(Phil. 2:10-11).

Each of these disciples will, on that great day, eat and drink at the table of the Lord and **'sit on thrones, judging the twelve tribes of Israel'**. What he means is that those who had stood with him through many difficulties will share in his kingly rule. They will judge in the same sense that the judges in the early days of Israel's history judged: they ruled the people justly and led them in right ways.

Then Jesus spoke particularly to Peter and gave him a warning: **'Simon, Simon, Satan has asked to sift you as wheat.'** Although he addressed Peter, he included all of the disciples, because the word 'you' is plural. He meant, 'Satan is going to sift all of you as wheat.' They would have known what happened to wheat. It was put into a large sieve and violently knocked from side to side. The idea was that the wheat itself would remain in the sieve and the chaff (which surrounds the wheatgerm) would be blown away (because it was not useful for food).

Jesus, by these words, was preparing his disciples for the many trials which they were going to face. Throughout the Acts of the Apostles we read about the severe persecutions that came to them. Many of them lost their lives for the sake of Christ. In those circumstances it must have seemed to them that they were in a large sieve and being battered from side to side to knock their faith out of them. However, no true Christian can completely lose his faith. Once we know the Lord as our Saviour we can never be lost. We can feel lost, and we can wander away from the truth, but eventually the Lord will bring us back into his fold. An old Puritan commentator, Trapp, put it like this: 'Jesus uses a fan, and sifts to get rid of the chaff; but the devil uses a fan and sifts to get rid of the wheat.'[4]

Jesus also gave Peter some personal encouragement. He said, **'I have prayed for you, Simon, that your faith may not fail.'** This must have been a great solace to Peter. Here the word 'you' is in the singular; it means 'you, Simon'. What a comfort it is to know that the Lord prays for us individually — particularly when we are about to pass through some great time of testing! How gracious our Lord is! We should praise his name and give him our love and adoration.

Then Jesus added some mysterious words. He said to Peter, **'And when you have turned back, strengthen your brothers.'** Peter would not have known at that time what those words meant. However, we know that he did actually become so frightened that, a few hours later, he denied that he knew his Master. Jesus said, 'When you have turned back'. In other words he is saying to him,

'You will recover from your denial of me, and then you will be able to tell others about your stumbling and my forgiveness of your failure.' But Peter, being Peter, said impulsively, **'Lord, I am ready to go with you to prison and to death.'** Jesus answered him, **'I tell you, Peter,'** (this was the only time the Lord actually addressed him as Peter) **'before the cock crows today, you will deny three times that you know me'** (22:34).

A change of tactics

The Lord then reminded the disciples about their work so far. They had gone out into the land **'without purse, bag or sandals'**. We saw that in Luke 9:3 and 10:4. As they travelled throughout Palestine, everything that they needed was provided for them by the people. **'But now'**, Jesus said, **'if you have a purse, take it, and also a bag; and if you don't have a sword, sell your cloak and buy one.'** Life was going to be tough from now on. They were not going to be treated so generously by the people. They were going to have to fend for themselves. They were even going to have to fight. This was because Jesus was going to suffer an ignominious death. He applied Isaiah 53 to himself. He said, **'It is written: "And he was numbered with the transgressors."'** These puzzling things were now beginning to come to pass.

So the disciples said, **'See, Lord, here are two swords.'** But Jesus said, **'That is enough.'** He meant, 'I don't want to hear any more talk about that kind of fighting.' From now on they were going to have to fight against evil powers, but they were not going to be using literal swords. Paul said, 'The weapons we fight with are not the weapons of the world' (2 Cor. 10:4). God's people are called upon to fight spiritual battles against the powers of darkness (see Eph. 6:12). After he said this, Jesus went out.

Jesus communes with his Father

By this time the Lord and the remaining eleven disciples had reached the Mount of Olives. Somewhere on the lower slopes of this hill was the Garden of Gethsemane (see Matt. 26:36). This was where Jesus slept on every night of that last week (21:37). Each of the disciples knew about this place, including Judas (who had now left them — see John 18:2). In this place Jesus gave them this

warning (which he afterwards reminded them about in verse 46):
'Pray that you will not fall into temptation' (22:40). He obviously
meant that they should pray that they would not be diverted from
their faith because of the great times of trial which were going to
come upon them. He exhorted them to keep on praying and looking
to God for strength to persevere during the coming struggles. But,
despite his urging, they eventually all fell asleep from exhaustion
and sorrow (22:45).

However, before they went to sleep they observed the Lord
praying. We come now to a most precious section of Luke's Gospel.
The disciples noticed that he went somewhere on his own, a little
way away from them (22:41). Then he knelt down and prayed. They
heard his words: **'Father if you are willing, take this cup from me;
yet not my will, but yours be done'** (22:42).

The cup he spoke about was his death. But how different was his
death from that of most men! He suffered unjustly. He did nothing
to deserve execution. And what a painful death he was going to
endure! The reason he asked God to take the cup of his death from
him was because he was going to have to undergo pain and
punishment for the sin of each one of his people. At that moment he
was going to have to experience, for the only time in his life,
separation from his Father.

It is no wonder that he cried out, 'If you are willing, take this cup
from me.' But he added, 'Yet not my will, but yours be done.' He
knew that it was God's will that mattered above all things. He knew
that there would be no hope for anyone unless he bore our sins in his
body on that cruel tree, and he gladly submitted to his Father's will.

What an example of obedience this is to us! Are we prepared to
do what God calls us to do, whatever we have to suffer in the
process?

But in the midst of his prayer, **'An angel from heaven appeared
to him and strengthened him'** (22:43). What a comfort that must
have been! We, too, find great strength in the presence of one of our
friends when we are in deep distress; it is a great blessing to have
someone with us in our pain and sorrow.

**'And being in anguish, he prayed more earnestly, and his
sweat was like drops of blood falling to the ground'** (22:44). But,
despite all of that, he still prayed. He maintained close communion
with his Father. Never once did he complain and say, 'I will not do
this.' He willingly and obediently carried out his Father's will. He
knew that it had to be.

How sad, then, it must have been for him to have returned and found his disciples fast asleep! **'Why are you sleeping?'** he asked. In other words, 'How can you sleep when such momentous things are about to take place?' And he woke them up and said, **'Get up and pray so that you will not fall into temptation.'**

We need to do all that we can to avoid the kind of sins those first disciples fell into. We should stop finding fault with our fellow-believers. We should always show them love, and be active in spreading peace. We should not use worldly methods for fighting evil and, above all, we should not keep falling asleep when our Lord commands us to be watching and praying lest we fall into temptation. We need to put into practice the words of Charles Swindoll: 'The sword of the Spirit is not meant to be used to fight against other Christians. It is to be used to fight against all wrong, and the enemy of souls, Satan.'

The trial of Peter (22:47-71)

There are two people on trial in this section: Jesus and Peter. Jesus had aroused the anger of the Jewish authorities, and now they had the opportunity to arrest him and put him to death. But the amazing thing is that, although Jesus is the one who was arrested and tried, it is to Peter that Luke draws our attention in a large section of this passage.

Jesus in Gethsemane

The Lord had been praying and had found his disciples asleep, and as he was rebuking them for their slothfulness **'a crowd'** came up the hill. This group included the servant of the high priest, some chief priests, the officers of the temple guard and elders of the Jews (22:52).

Also with the company was Judas (22:47). He is called **'one of the Twelve'** to show that he was supposed to be a friend of Jesus. Judas was leading the large group of people because he knew the place where Jesus was most likely to be found. Because the religious authorities did not want the embarrassment of arresting the wrong person, they took Judas with them to identify the Lord in the blackness of the night. The betrayer soon spotted Jesus and approached him with the intention of kissing him. The other Gospel writers tell us that he actually did kiss the Lord. Kissing was the normal way of greeting a rabbi; it showed affection and respect. Such behaviour sounds strange to British ears, but when I said 'Goodbye' to the pastor of the Free Evangelical Church in Corinth, after preaching there in early 1992, he kissed me on both of my cheeks. However, Judas did not kiss Jesus because he wanted to give him a warm, loving greeting; he did it to indicate which one of these men was Jesus.

In return Jesus asked Judas this poignant question: **'Judas, are you betraying the Son of Man with a kiss?'** (22:48). How dreadful it was for him to use a sign of love in an act of betrayal! Satan had certainly got control of this man, otherwise he could not have done such a terrible act. Albert Barnes comments, 'Perhaps few reproofs of crime more resemble the awful searchings of the souls of the wicked in the day of judgement!'[5]

'When Jesus' followers saw what was going to happen [it was so obvious] **they said, "Lord, should we strike with our swords?"'** We know that they had at least two swords in their possession (22:38). But, before the Lord could reply, **'One of them struck the servant of the high priest, cutting off his right ear'** (22:51). Presumably the man saw the sword coming and dodged to one side — not quite avoiding the blow. This is why his ear was cut off.

It does not surprise us that it was impetuous Peter who wielded the sword (John tells us this in John 18:10). After all, it was Simon Peter who had declared, a few hours earlier, 'Lord, I am ready to go with you to prison and to death' (22:33). **'But Jesus answered, "No more of this!"'** (22:51). He had already told them that he wanted to hear no more talk about swords (22:38).

Then he healed the man's ear. This was the last earthly act of healing that Jesus did, using his hand, and it was performed upon someone who had come as an enemy! (Jesus was putting into practice what he preached in Luke 6:27: 'Love your enemies.') In addition the Lord did not want to give the religious leaders any reason to say that he and his followers were causing an insurrection. That is why he said to those who had come for him, **'Am I leading a rebellion, that you have come with swords and clubs?'** (22:52).

The religious people could have arrested Jesus much earlier. As he said, **'Every day I was with you in the temple courts, and you did not lay a hand on me'** (22:53). The reason they did not arrest Jesus at that time was because, as we have seen, 'They were afraid of the people' (20:19). But here in the quiet of the garden, there was no one to raise any objection to his arrest — apart from the disciples. I wonder if they had brought all those armed men because they thought that Jesus might have made it difficult for them to arrest him, or because he might have run away. If so, they were wrong. He meekly allowed them to take him. **'This is your hour,'** he said. Perhaps they thought it was their hour of glory when, at last, they would be able to silence Jesus. But rather than their hour of glory, Jesus called it their hour **'when darkness reigns'** (22:53).

How awful it is for anyone to try to silence the Lord Jesus Christ, and how dreadful to have a part in his betrayal! All those engaged in such activities will surely, eventually, go to that place of darkness which the Lord called hell — unless they truly and sincerely repent in tears and supplication, as Peter was shortly going to do (see 22:62). But Judas was only filled with remorse. He later felt deeply sorry for what he had done, but he never repented; he did not forsake his sin and turn back to God. He said, 'I have sinned … for I have betrayed innocent blood,' but he never asked God's forgiveness and, as a consequence, he went away and hanged himself (Matt. 27:4-5).

Peter disowned Jesus

There seem to have been three Jewish trials of Jesus, followed by three Roman ones. Luke gives an abbreviated account of these. From verses 54-65 Jesus was examined by Annas (the former high priest) and then by Caiaphas (the official high priest — see John 18:24). Peter's denial that he knew Jesus took place in the central courtyard of the home of Caiaphas. Although all the disciples fled, Peter and another disciple (probably John) followed at a distance. Peter gained access to the high priest's house because the disciple who accompanied him was known to the high priest (John 18:15).

That night was a very long one, and Peter did not want to talk to anyone. He was very puzzled and depressed because the Lord had been arrested. He must have wondered why the Lord allowed himself to be taken (but he had learned the reason by the time he preached his sermon in Acts 2:23). In his bewilderment he sat down with the others by the fire which had been lit in the courtyard.

Then a servant girl noticed Peter in the flickering firelight and she said to the others, **'This man was with him'** (22:56). It was a very positive statement. She was not making a suggestion. She was sure that Peter had been in the group with Jesus. But, despite her firm assertion, he denied it. He was obviously taken off guard. He was not only feeling wretched but he was very frightened as well; and he quickly defended himself by spitting out, **'Woman, I don't know him'** (22:57).

This lie must have made Peter feel even more miserable, but the matter was allowed to rest for a while, and silence resumed as they all waited while Jesus was questioned in one of the rooms in the house — out of earshot.

'A little later someone else saw [Peter] and said, "You also are one of them." "Man, I am not!" Peter replied' (22:58). This time he appears to be even more uncomfortable, as he quickly denies the charge.

Then an hour or more elapsed. The people around the fire may have seen Jesus as he was led from room to room, or he may have been standing on a balcony. However, we know that Peter could see his face at the point when another person, a relative of the man whose ear Peter had cut off in the garden (John 18:26) declared, **'Certainly this fellow was with him, for he is a Galilean.'** People from Galilee spoke with a northern accent, and no one from that area of the country would have had any reason to have been in the high priest's house on that night.

Peter replied, **'Man, I don't know what you're talking about!'** It is illuminating that in Mark (Peter's own story) we are told that 'He began to call down curses on himself, and he swore to them, "I don't know this man you're talking about"' (Mark 14:71). As soon as Peter said these words of denial two things happened: **'The cock crowed,'** and **'The Lord turned and looked straight at Peter.'** These both caused a deep shock wave inside him. Luke tells us, **'Then Peter remembered the word the Lord had spoken to him: "Before the cock crows today, you will disown me three times"'** (22:61).

Jesus had looked at Peter, but Peter must also have been looking at the Lord. Campbell Morgan comments, 'So the watching eyes of Simon saw the love glance in the eyes of Jesus.'[6] Jesus did not look at Peter to condemn him, but rather to remind him. The Lord wanted Peter to remember that he had told him that he would deny him, but he also wanted Peter to remember that he had said, 'I have prayed for you, Simon, that your faith may not fail. And when you have turned back, strengthen your brothers' (22:32). Jesus looked at him in love, and Peter's faith did not fail, but his courage did. That is why **'He went outside and wept bitterly'** (22:62).

He shed tears of true repentance. He was not only sorry for himself. He was deeply sorry that he had sinned against the Lord. Moreover, he desperately longed to be forgiven. And he sought, and found, that forgiveness. Later on he was able to strengthen many believers as they too returned to the Lord in humility and penitence on account of their backsliding. This story about the denial by Peter is recorded in each of the four Gospels. It has been put there to tell us that even though we fail the Lord, he will forgive us when we repent.

The mockery by the soldiers

Prisoners were always handed over to soldiers. Their job was to see that the prisoners did not escape, but that did not mean that the soldiers could not have some fun at their expense. They may well not have known what the charges against Jesus were, but they saw this as an opportunity to mock their prisoner, and also to beat him — for no particular reason.

It seems that they had heard that he claimed to be a prophet. So they put a blindfold over his eyes, and then took turns to hit him in the face. They taunted him, **'"Prophesy! Who hit you?" And they said many other insulting things to him'** (22:64-65). All of this happened even before a verdict had been given and he had been pronounced guilty!

The trial before the Sanhedrin

It was contrary to Jewish law to hold a trial during the hours of darkness. It is obvious, therefore, that the Jewish authorities did not want to give any cause for someone to say that there had been any irregularities in the trial of Jesus. No doubt they would claim that the questioning of Jesus, which had been going on all night, was a mere preliminary to the official trial, but they were certainly in a hurry. We know that they wanted to have Jesus put to death before the Passover really got under way, and they wanted him dead and buried before the Sabbath day commenced. (That would have been some twelve to fourteen hours later, as soon as it got dark that evening.)

This is why Luke tells us that **'At daybreak the council of the elders of the people, both the chief priests and teachers of the law, met together, and Jesus was led before them'** (22:66). It was no longer night, but it must have still been very early in the morning. This made the hearing legal — just. What lengths people will go to, in order to give a semblance of respectability to their evil intentions!

We know from Matthew and Mark that the chief priests were looking for evidence so that they could put Jesus to death. 'But they did not find any. Many testified falsely against him, but their statements did not agree' (Mark 14:56). So they had to resort to direct questioning of the Lord, in the hope that he would say something by which he would convict himself. **"'If you are the Christ," they said, "tell us." Jesus answered, "If I tell you, you will not believe me."'** They certainly would not believe that Jesus was the Messiah; he did not measure up to their understanding of what the promised deliverer would be like. Next he said, **'And if I asked you, you would not answer.'**

The religious people were very prejudiced against Jesus. They had already made up their minds that he was guilty, and when he had asked them questions in the temple, they had refused to answer (see 20:3-7). There was certainly no reason to suspect that they would behave any differently now.

Then Jesus made a most profound statement. He said, **'But from now on, the Son of Man will be seated at the right hand of the mighty God'** (22:69). He was speaking about a turning-point. The religious people thought that they were sitting in judgement on Jesus, but they were wrong. 'From now on it is Jesus who will occupy the throne of judgement. By rejecting God's Christ, they forfeit their right to be leaders of God's people. In the act of judging him, they themselves are judged by him. From this point onwards the old Israel is replaced by the new, whose rightful ruler he shall be for evermore.'[7]

Without realizing the implications of what Jesus was saying, they saw in his words the opportunity to catch him out. **'Are you then the Son of God?'** they asked. They had been trying to get him to say that he was the Messiah, so they were pleased when he talked about being the Son of Man, but Jesus had now said something which, from their point of view, was far, far better than they could ever have dreamed possible. Jesus was saying that he will be seated at God's right hand. The Lord was, in fact, referring them to Psalm

110:1 (which he had previously spoken about in Luke 20:42-43). This is why they asked him, 'Are you then the Son of God?' And he replied by saying, **'You are right in saying I am.'**

They seized on this reply as just the evidence they needed to convict him, exclaiming, **'Why do we need any more testimony? We have heard it from his own lips'** (22:71). They never once considered that his claim might in fact be true. It never occurred to them that their ideas about the Messiah might be completely wrong. They were so bent on convicting him that they never considered the implications of what he said.

23.
The darkest day in history

Please read Luke 23

The trial of Pilate (23:1-25)

None of us likes to hear of injustice taking place. In most legal systems, justice is done, and it must be seen to be done. But when it came to the trial of Jesus, justice patently was not done: an innocent man was put to death. Even more amazingly, we learn that Jesus never said one word in his own defence. Isaiah had, long before, spoken of this when he wrote,

> 'He was oppressed and afflicted,
>   yet he did not open his mouth;
> he was led like a lamb to the slaughter,
>   and as a sheep before her shearers is silent,
> so he did not open his mouth'

(Isa. 53:7).

Jesus before Pilate

In Luke 22:70 we read that the Jewish council had found the Lord guilty of blasphemy (i.e. speaking against God). For this crime they required the death penalty, but, because they lived in an occupied country, they had no authority to order anyone's execution. The Jewish court could fine people, imprison them or order them to be beaten, but they had no power to put anyone to death. Only the Roman governor could sign a death warrant. Pilate normally lived on the coast at Cæsarea but he was in the city to make sure that no trouble arose during the Passover, especially as the crowds usually swelled the population of Jerusalem to about 500,000 people. This is why we read that **'The whole assembly rose and led [Jesus] off to Pilate'** (23:1).

The charges against Christ had to be altered for this hearing from those brought before the Jewish council. The religious leaders knew that it would be of no use to accuse Jesus of blasphemy. The Romans would not be prepared to take action on what they would have considered to be a petty religious quarrel (cf. Acts 18:12-15). In their own religious life there was room for many gods and goddesses. So they would not have understood the Jews' horror at the claim of Jesus that he was the Son of God. This is why the Jewish leaders had to take a different tack.

The first charge they brought against the Lord was one of subversion: **'We have found this man subverting our nation'** (23:2). They were trying to say that Jesus was attempting to bring down the government. What is more, they seemed to be identifying the Romans with themselves by saying that Jesus was subverting 'our nation'. Under normal circumstances the Jews would not have admitted that the Romans had any part in their nation.

Another charge they made to Pilate was that the Lord opposed payment of taxes to Cæsar (23:2). Again they were trying to make out that Jesus encouraged people to refuse to pay these, but this was not true; on the contrary, he had clearly stated, 'Give to Cæsar what is Cæsar's' (20:25).

How amazing it is that those who are determined to denigrate the name of the Lord Jesus Christ will go to any lengths to encourage people to think ill of him!

A third charge the Jews made was that Jesus claimed to be Christ, a king (23:2). This was true in one sense but, by making this charge, they were suggesting that Jesus was aiming to overthrow the existing rulers of the land. However, from John's Gospel we see that the Lord answered this when he explained to Pilate that his kingdom was a spiritual, not a physical one. He said, 'My kingdom is not of this world. If it were, my servants would fight to prevent my arrest by the Jews. But now my kingdom is from another place' (John 18:36). This is why we can see from verses 3 and 4 that Pilate was not unhappy when Jesus said that he was the King of the Jews.

After examining the charges against Jesus, **'Pilate announced** to the chief priests and the crowd, "I find no basis for a charge against this man"' (23:4). Having heard the evidence, the governor made this firm declaration: 'Jesus is not guilty.' That ought to have been enough for an acquittal, and probably in any other case those bringing the charges would have had to be satisfied with the verdict. But these Jewish leaders were not prepared to accept Pilate's findings. 'They insisted, "He stirs up the people all over Judea by his teaching. He started in Galilee and has come all the way here"' (23:5).

These men must have hated Jesus very much to have insisted that he was guilty. Mark 15:10 tells us that it was out of envy that they brought him to Pilate. In verse 18 Luke writes, 'With one voice they cried out' against Jesus, and in verse 23 Luke again refers to their insistence, saying 'With loud shouts they insistently demanded that he be crucified.'

Pilate hated the Jews. History records how he had done many things to offend their religious susceptibilities,[1] and Luke tells us about atrocities which had been committed at his orders (see 13:1). Yet he was not man enough to stand up to their religious leaders. Luke records three occasions when he declared that Jesus was innocent; and a careful reading of all four Gospels seems to suggest that Pilate said this at least five times. But, weak man that he was, he eventually allowed the Lord to be crucified.

With this dilemma in front of him he must have been delighted to discover that Jesus came from Galilee. This was territory ruled over by Herod Antipas, and Pilate would have known that Herod was also in Jerusalem at the Passover period. This is why Pilate gladly sent Jesus off to the king so that Herod could make the decision about what to do with him. The governor must have felt that he could now wash his hands of the whole problem.

Jesus before Herod

Herod was very pleased to met Jesus (23:8). 'For a long time he had been wanting to see him.' That sounds very commendable on the face of it, but Herod wanted to see Jesus for the wrong reason. He did not want to be made holy. He only wanted to meet Jesus so that he could be entertained. How sad it is that so many people are only seeking to be amused in this world, and in the church, today! They do not want to see the Lord so that they can deny themselves, take up their crosses and follow him. They only want to receive blessing for themselves. Their attitude towards Jesus is entirely selfish. They want to be made to feel good and be happy.

This was exactly the desire of Herod. In Luke 9:7-9 we saw that Herod was worried about the identity of the Lord. He was scared in case Jesus was John the Baptist come back from the dead to haunt him. He had arranged for the murder of John, and he had some kind of conscience about it. Then in chapter 13:31 Luke tells us that this same king had wanted to kill Jesus. But the Lord had sent him a message at the time: he had called him a fox and said that he was going to carry on with his work regardless of Herod's threats. Now at last King Herod and King Jesus came face to face.

Why did the king want to see Jesus? He hoped to see him perform miracles (23:8). He had no interest in the kingdom of God or the message of salvation. Indeed it was John's message of repentance that had caused Herod a great deal of heartache (3:19-20). All that this bored ruler of Galilee wanted was to be amused by some diversion. But Jesus made no move to perform any miracle. Indeed the Lord only ever performed miracles to help someone or to teach something.

When Jesus failed to respond to the request for miracles, Herod **'plied him with many questions, but Jesus gave him no answer'** (23:9). Herod is the only person that we read of with whom Jesus refused to speak. How far gone he must have been in his evil selfishness that the Lord refused to exchange even one word with him!

Then we read of further disgraceful scenes: **'The chief priests and the teachers of the law were standing there, vehemently accusing him. Then Herod and his soldiers ridiculed and mocked him. Dressing him in an elegant robe...'** (23:10-11). Although Jesus had never done anything wrong, he had to suffer all this humiliation. But that was only a foretaste of what was to follow. Jesus put up with it all without the merest protest.

How sad that so many treat Jesus in a similar way today! They may not jeer at him, but they ignore him altogether. Indeed anyone who refuses to follow the clear commands of Christ is behaving just like those religious people and Herod.

What are the commands which we are given by Christ? Jesus said, 'This is my command: Love each other' (John 15:17). Every time we fail to respect each other we are breaking that command.

When we put our own desires before the good of our fellow Christians, we are breaking that command. When we fail to make allowances for the weaknesses and the frailties of our fellow believers, we are breaking that command. When we speak and think unkindly about our fellow Christians, we are breaking that command. And when we are not prepared to forgive any of the Lord's people who have wronged us, we are breaking that command. How abominably God's own people sometimes treat the Lord Jesus Christ and his Word!

After this awful treatment of Jesus he was sent back to Pilate. One modern writer puts these words into the mouth of Herod:

Take him away —
He's got nothing to say!
Get out, you King of the Jews!
Get out of my life.[2]

How terrible for anyone to treat the Lord Jesus Christ like that!

Luke tells us, **'That day Herod and Pilate became friends — before this they had been enemies'** (23:12). We do not know what their quarrel had been about, but obviously Herod had been pleased that Pilate had recognized his authority over Galilee and, to prove it, had sent Jesus to him to be tried. However, he too felt unable to deal with the prisoner, so he returned him to the governor.

Jesus' second appearance before Pilate

Once again Pilate informed the accusers of Jesus that he had examined him in their presence (and, it seems also in private — see John 19:9), and had found no basis for their charges against him (23:14). Neither he nor Herod, he said, could find any fault with Jesus. They both came to the conclusion that **'He has done nothing to deserve death'** (23:15). Then, instead of releasing Jesus straight away Pilate said, **'I will punish him and then release him'** (23:17). We do not know what this punishment was for. It seems that it was solely to appease the religious leaders. But that was not sufficient for the crowds. **'With one voice they cried out, "Away with this man! Release Barabbas to us!"'** (23:18).

In the crowd there were people who had many different opinions, but the chief priests had gone among them and stirred them up against Christ (Matt. 27:20). So they were united in their condemnation of Jesus. They cried out for his blood with one voice.

How sad it is that we cannot have more people united in their desires for Jesus and his gospel! Matthew tells us that it was Pilate's custom 'at the Feast to release a prisoner chosen by the crowd' (Matt. 27:15). This is why they cried out for Barabbas to be set free. **'Barabbas had been thrown into prison for an insurrection in the city, and for murder'** (23:19). But these religious people would rather have had this murderer released than Jesus. We know very little about Barabbas, but Campbell Morgan suggests that he may have been one of the many false messiahs who had tried to get back the Jewish throne by using force.[3]

However, Pilate really wanted to release Jesus, presumably because he knew he was innocent. His wife had tried to convince him of this (Matt. 27:19) and his own conscience must have told him that it would be a great miscarriage of justice if he allowed Jesus to be crucified. Yet the crowds kept shouting, **'Crucify him! Crucify him!'** And John tells us that they were calling out, 'If you let this man go, you are no friend of Cæsar. Anyone who claims to be a king opposes Cæsar' (John 19:12). So, weak Pilate, looking after his own interests, **'decided to grant their demand. He released the man who had been thrown into prison for insurrection and murder, the one they asked for, and surrendered Jesus to their will'** (23:24-25). Yet it was not their will; it was, as Jesus prayed in Gethsemane, God's will (22:42).

What an injustice it was to let a criminal go free and allow an innocent man to be put to death in his place! However, that is what happened; and we can see in this tragic scene a picture of ourselves. We are all sinners. We have sinned in thought, word and deed against the Lord God Almighty — not just once but many, many times. And an innocent man, the holy Lamb of God, has been put to death in our place.

It may well have been that Barabbas actually saw Jesus on the cross at Calvary. If he did, then surely he must have thought, 'That should have been me, hanging and suffering there. I deserved to die; he is innocent.'

None of us deserves to be saved, yet we rejoice to contemplate the wonders of God's grace when he transferred our sin to the Lord Jesus Christ and clothed us with his precious robe of righteousness.

The crucifixion (23:26-43)

Ask anyone whether it was right that Jesus should die as a common criminal and they will probably say, 'No.' Ask them if they are sad that such a thing happened, and they might well say that they are not very concerned one way or the other. The Lord Jesus Christ is an irrelevance to most people. It is not that they are deliberately saying, 'We will not have this man to reign over us.' What they mean is, 'We don't even want to bother to stop and consider the question.'

Nevertheless the cross is central to the story of the Lord Jesus Christ. All the way through Luke's account he directs us to this greatest of all events in history. H. C. Turnbull said, 'Calvary shows how far men will go in sin, and how far God will go for man's salvation.'[4]

Jesus and Simon

Jesus had been cruelly treated. Although he was fully God, he was also fully man, so he would have experienced all the deep anguish of his trials. Consider his situation. He had had nothing to eat or drink since the evening before. That was at the Last Supper, which had taken place around six p.m. Later that evening Jesus had been arrested and marched away. This event in itself must have made his mouth go dry, and the long hours of standing in the halls of first Annas, then Caiaphas, followed by the interview with Pilate, must surely have exhausted him. But this was nothing compared to the cruel beating which he received from the Roman soldiers. That must have left him physically and mentally drained.

It is no wonder, then, that he could not carry his own cross. It was the custom for any victim to be forced to carry the cross-piece, on which he would soon be nailed. He would be marched in the centre of a hollow square of four soldiers and the procession would be preceded by a fifth solider who carried a placard detailing the reason why the man was being executed.[5]

John tells us that Jesus carried his own cross (John 19:17). Apparently it seems that he fell beneath the weight of it. If this happened, as it frequently did, then someone in the crowd would be commandeered to carry the cross instead of the prisoner. The man who was selected on this occasion was someone called Simon who came from Cyrene, in northern Africa (the country now called Libya).

Why was this man in the crowd? It seems that he had travelled some 800 miles from his homeland to attend the Passover, so we assume that he was a Jew. Acts 2:10 tells us that people came from Cyrene to Jerusalem for the great feast season. Simon may well have spent all his life saving up enough money for this momentous trip; and now he found himself being compelled to carry the cross of a criminal who was being led out to be crucified.

But why does Luke tell us his name? It must have some significance. Mark also tells us who he was, plus the fact that he had two sons called Alexander and Rufus. Mark probably wrote his Gospel, in the first instance, for Christians who were living at Rome. Might it not have been that this same Alexander and Rufus were members of the church at Rome, and that they were still alive at the time when Mark wrote? Certainly when Paul wrote his letter to the Romans he sent his greetings to someone called Rufus. He said that this man was chosen in the Lord (Rom. 16:13). The apostle also sent his greetings to the mother of Rufus, who may well have been the wife of this same Simon from Cyrene.

Whatever the reason we are told about Simon, he was the man who was forced to carry the cross and walk behind the Lord. He was the first one literally to 'take up his cross and follow Jesus'. We, too, are called upon to do the same thing, but we must do it in a spiritual sense. We are required to deny ourselves, take up our cross daily and follow Jesus (9:23).

If we have any knowledge of the Bible, we will know that no one who comes into contact with Jesus can fail to be challenged by meeting him. People like Pilate and Herod did not accept the challenge, and one of the thieves on the cross yelled insults at the Lord (23:39). We do not know what effect Jesus had on the women of Jerusalem (23:27-30), but we do know that the whole destiny of one of the dying thieves was dramatically changed when he spoke with the Lord Jesus Christ on that day. It may well be that Simon became a follower of Jesus too, through being compelled to carry the Saviour's cross that morning. God was even controlling the actions of the Roman soldier who selected Simon for that task on that first Good Friday morning.

Jesus and the women

Not everyone was rejoicing at the pending execution of Jesus. There were a large number of people following the solemn procession on that morning. Among them were women who wept and wailed because of him. To these Jesus turned. (Luke has been constantly telling us about the Lord turning to people.) He looked at them and made this rather long and sad speech: **'Daughters of Jerusalem, do not weep for me; weep for yourselves and for your children. For the time will come when you will say, "Blessed are the barren women, the wombs that never bore and breasts that never nursed!" Then "they will say to the mountains, 'Fall on us!' and to the hills 'Cover us!'"'**(23:28-31).

These were evidently women who lived in the capital. He called them 'Daughters of Jerusalem'. But in telling them not to weep for him, he was not spurning their sympathy. He was telling them that they should be weeping for themselves. This was the same thing that he had spoken about in the temple (21:5-24). A Jewish woman would normally weep for herself when it became obvious that she could have no children; some husbands regarded this as a sufficient reason to divorce their wives. It was a disgrace not to have children. Children were regarded as the special blessing of the Lord. The psalmist said,

> 'Sons are a heritage from the Lord,
>   children a reward from him...
> Blessed is the man
>   whose quiver is full of them'

(Ps. 127:3,5).

But here Jesus was saying, 'Blessed are the barren women, the wombs that never bore and the breasts that never nursed!' (23:29). One of the most terrible things for a mother to witness must be the killing of her own children. In times of war this has happened — and it is especially sad when helpless little babies are slaughtered.

Jesus quoted Hosea 10:8 when he spoke about people who were in such distress that they would call on the mountains and hills to cover them and destroy them. The destruction of Jerusalem by the Romans, some forty years later, was to bring terrible devastation upon the Jewish people. Many were wiped out by the onslaught of the Roman army at that time. John takes this same theme of destruction and likens it to the great Judgement Day at the end of the world (Rev. 6:15-17).

This judgement will surely fall upon all those who reject the Lord Jesus Christ, those who refuse to acknowledge his authority over their lives. Jerusalem, on that day, rejected Jesus and was sending him to his death. Jesus was the green tree (or wood) mentioned in verse 31. The dry wood was all of those who opposed Jesus. Dry wood is very suitable for starting fires; it is only when the fire is under way that green wood can be put on it. But Jerusalem, that day, was putting to death an innocent man. The Lord meant that if he, the innocent one, was made the object of such ill treatment and plunged into suffering, what will happen to those who are guilty?[6]

Jesus and the criminals

These two thieves remind us of the different responses which people can make to the Lord Jesus Christ. Both of these men had been found guilty and deserved to die. They were both being led out to be executed with Jesus. One of them was crucified on his right, and the other on his left; the Lord was in the centre. This is what, centuries beforehand, Isaiah had prophesied would happen when he wrote, 'He ... was numbered with the transgressors' (Isa. 53:12).

Soon they came to the place called 'the Skull'. None of the evangelists says that Jesus was crucified on a hill. Maybe this spot was called 'the Skull' because it was on a hill shaped like a skull (as is 'Gordon's Calvary' in Jerusalem), or perhaps it was called this because so many people had been put to death there (and the ground contained many of their skulls).

Luke simply says, **'There they crucified him.'** There are only four words in English (three in Greek) to describe this awful event. Luke does not tell us that those who were crucified died a thousand deaths. He does not dwell on the excruciating agony caused by the nails being driven through the nerve centres of the wrists (or maybe palms) and the ankles. He does not tell us that the crucified person sometimes took a week to die, hanging in the intense heat of the day and the extreme cold of the night. We read nothing about the physical agonies which the Lord underwent. He just says, 'There they crucified him' (23:33).

God wants us to consider the fact that Jesus bore in his body, at that time, the punishment of all those who had been, and all who would be God's children through faith in him. Jesus is the one who came to seek and to save what was lost (19:10). This is why he had to die upon the cruel cross that day. This is why he cried out, 'My God, my God, why have you forsaken me?' (Mark 15:34).

We can see his compassion when he prayed, **'Father, forgive them, for they do not know what they are doing'** (23:34). He is ever ready to forgive those who come to him in repentance. We can see what love there was, and is, in the heart of Jesus, that he could pray for his enemies at such a time. It makes us realize that if Jesus could pray for the forgiveness of those who nailed him to the cross, how much more should we be prepared to forgive those who have wronged us!

As Jesus hung on the cross, the soldiers **'divided up his clothes'** (23:34). Jesus would have only had peasant clothing consisting of a few simple items. But John tells us that his undergarment was 'seamless, woven in one piece from top to bottom' (John 19:23). Because they did not want to tear this garment, they drew lots for it.

Luke tells us of several different groups of people who watched these events. First he writes about the people who stood watching (23:35). We are not told anything about these people, but there must have been some there who had heard Jesus speak, and had been moved by his words.

Next we are told, **'The rulers even sneered at him'** (23:35). The words they shouted to one another showed that they still did not understand his mission. They said, **'He saved others'** (they acknowledged the validity of his miracles); **'let him save himself if he is the Christ of God, the Chosen One'** (23:35). By saying, 'If he is the Christ', they were casting doubts upon whether he was the Messiah.

Another group were the soldiers who **'also came up and mocked him'** (23:36). Why did they find it necessary to join in with the jeering? In their mocking, **'They offered him wine vinegar,'** and said, **'If you are the king of the Jews, save yourself'** (23:37). Again, this group says the word 'if'. They did not realize that if he came down from the cross he could not have saved his people from their sins (see Matt. 1:21). His purpose was not to save himself, but to save lost mankind.

Also as was customary, the notice which signified the charges against him was nailed above him: **'This is the King of the Jews'** (23:38). The chief priests had protested when Pilate wrote this. They wanted him to say, 'This man claimed to be king of the Jews.' But

Pilate said, 'What I have written, I have written' (John 19:21-22). Did Pilate refuse to change the sign because he had come to believe that the kingdom of which Jesus had spoken was a spiritual kingdom? (See John 18:33-37). Or was it that he was annoyed that the chief priests had forced him to order the crucifixion of Jesus, while he knew him to be innocent? Perhaps this was Pilate's way of getting his own back on the priests.

The fact that each Gospel gives slightly different wording for this inscription (but each one saying basically the same thing) may well be explained because the sign was written in Aramaic, Latin and Greek (John 19:20) and each Gospel may have translated the sign from a different language.

Finally, we have the record of a conversation between the two criminals. One hurled insults at Jesus, saying, **'"Aren't you the Christ? Save yourself and us!" But the other criminal rebuked him. "Don't you fear God," he said, "since you are under the same sentence? We are punished justly, for we are getting what our deeds deserve. But this man has done nothing wrong"'** (23:39-41).

'Then he said, "Jesus, remember me when you come into your kingdom"' (23:42). He spoke to the Lord in prayer. It was not a boastful prayer. He did not say, 'I have done nothing wrong.' Rather he had just said, 'We are punished justly' (23:41). He did not say, 'I deserve to be saved.' He said, 'We are getting what our deeds deserve.' Neither did he say, 'You must have done something wrong to be crucified like us.' Rather he said, 'This man has done nothing wrong.' He did not say, 'I deserve to go to heaven right now.' Instead he said, 'Remember me when you come in your kingdom.'

This man showed that he had repented of his sin. He confessed Christ. He had faith in the Lord's power and will to save him, and he showed a deep humility. He simply asked to be remembered — one day.

But Jesus replied, **'Today you will be with me in paradise'** (23:43). The man did not have to wait until the final coming in of Christ's glorious kingdom. He was promised that he would be with Christ that same day. Paradise means that place of eternal bliss and rest (2 Cor. 12:4; Rev. 2:7). Bishop Ryle sums up this event beautifully when he writes, 'The dying thief was never baptized, belonged to no visible Church, and never received the Lord's Supper. But he repented and believed, and therefore he was saved.'[7]

The death and burial of Jesus (23:44-56)

His death

Luke tells us, **'It was now about the sixth hour.'** By Jewish reckoning that meant that it was midday (the first hour being about 6 a.m., when it became light). For the Romans the first hour was midnight; so when John (who seems to have used this system) tells us that Jesus was handed over by Pilate at about the sixth hour he means dawn, or what the Jews called the first hour.

We read in Luke's Gospel about some remarkable things which happened at midday. These had a profound effect on everyone who saw, or heard about them. Firstly, **'Darkness came over the whole land'** (23:44). This lasted for three long hours. Everyone was conscious of it because it covered the whole area around (23:45). This was a miraculous act of God. It could not have been an eclipse of the sun because total eclipses do not last for three hours, neither can they happen when there is a full moon (as there always is at Passover time). The darkness was a sign given by God to show the blackness of the event which was then taking place. Erdman says that it was 'the blackest crime in all of man's dark history'.[8] This darkness was an earthly sign of the death of Jesus.

Another sign was a heavenly one: **'The curtain of the temple was torn in two'** (23:45). This must have been the curtain dividing the Holy Place from the Most Holy Place. Only the high priest could go into that area where God's special presence dwelt; and he could only enter it once a year— on the Day of Atonement (Heb. 9:7). But now that curtain, which had kept the presence of God away from mere men, had been opened up. Matthew, the evangelist who wrote especially for the Jews, tells us that the curtain was 'torn from top to bottom' (Matt. 27:51). By saying that the tear started from the top, it may be that he is telling us that God caused it to be torn (for certainly he did) and, in any case if the earthquake (recorded by Matthew in the same verse) had caused it, the curtain is more likely to have been torn from the bottom upwards — or rather it would have been left in tatters!

However, the writer to the Hebrews makes the meaning of this act perfectly clear. He tells us that the old system (the Jewish way) has been done away with by the death of Christ. 'A new and living way [has been] opened for us through the curtain, that is, [Christ's] body' (Heb. 10:20). Because of Christ's death on the cross, not only has the old order of Judaism been done away with, but also we can 'draw near to God with a sincere heart in full assurance of faith, having our hearts sprinkled to cleanse us from a guilty conscience' (Heb. 10:22). Also Paul tells us that through the cross Jews and Gentiles both have a direct approach to the Father (Eph. 2:16-18). We do not need to come to God through priests, sacrifices or ceremonies. Jesus is the only mediator who is necessary (1 Tim. 2:5).

Suddenly the Lord called out with a loud voice, **'Father, into your hands I commit my spirit.'** This was the last of the seven words from the cross. Jesus had taken the prayer that any little Jewish boy or girl would say just before he or she went to sleep. But the Lord prefixed it with the word, 'Father.' He had also addressed his prayer to his 'Father' in the first word from the cross (23:34). He was always one with the Father, and it is as though he anticipated waking up from death in the arms of his Father.

We, too, if we belong to him through faith in his name, can be assured that after we have died we shall wake up in the arms of our loving heavenly Father. Indeed we already often have the experience that 'The eternal God is [our] refuge, and underneath are the everlasting arms' (Deut. 33:27).

Then we read, **'When [Jesus] had said this, he breathed his last'** (23:46). These were amazing happenings. Luke only tells us about the darkness, the curtain in the temple and the loud cry of the Lord as he died. But the other evangelists record additional physical events.

Luke tells us that the death of Jesus had a great effect on one individual and on two groups of people. We read, **'The centurion, seeing what had happened, praised God and said, "Surely this was a righteous man"'** (23:47). The death of Jesus stirred this tough soldier to the depths of his being, and he was so moved that he had to declare that Jesus was righteous. This was equivalent to saying, as one of the other evangelists records, 'Surely he was the Son of God' (Matt. 27:54). This centurion could not understand what had happened, but he knew that he had never witnessed anything like this before. It was something for which he was compelled to praise God.

Next Luke tells us about the crowd in general: **'When all the people who had gathered to witness this sight saw what took place, they beat their breasts and went away'** (23:48). They had gathered to see a spectacle and, no doubt, to have some entertainment, but they had never seen anything like that before. It made them

beat their breasts. Surely they did this because they were convicted
of their sin against God. For a Jew to beat his breast was a sign of
anguish, grief or contrition.⁹ It was what the tax collector did when
he stood at a distance from Jesus and said, 'God, have mercy on me,
a sinner' (18:13).

It may be that many of the people in this crowd were still so
weighed down under the burden of their sin that, when some weeks
later, they gathered in the city and listened to the preaching of the
apostles, they cried out, 'Brothers, what shall we do?' Peter told
them, 'Repent and be baptized, every one of you, in the name of
Jesus Christ for the forgiveness of your sins' (Acts 2:37-38).

The third group of witnesses were **'all those who knew him,
including the women who had followed from Galilee'**. They
'stood at a distance, watching these things' (23:49). They had not
deserted him, but they were puzzled as to why these dreadful events
had taken place. None the less, they watched him die.

His burial

Normally the bodies of criminals were taken down from their
crosses (sometimes after a week of excruciating pain) and then
thrown into a pit. This was a kind of rubbish dump. There they were
left to be the prey of dogs and other wild animals. This was a most
degrading thing for a Jew, who regarded dead bodies as something
to respect. Even today the Jewish authorities will not allow certain
areas of Jerusalem to be excavated by archaeologists, for fear of
disturbing old bones.

However, the Lord's body did not suffer that kind of indignity.
Luke tells us, **'Now there was a man named Joseph, a member of
the Council, a good and upright man, who had not consented to
their decision and action'**, to have Jesus put to death (23:50),
Joseph must have been a secret disciple of Jesus — together with
Nicodemus (see John 3:1-21; 19:39). Both of them must have been
absent from the Jewish council when Jesus was condemned to death.
We know this because Mark specifically tells us that 'They all
condemned [Jesus] as worthy of death' (Mark 14:64). We do not
know whether Joseph and Nicodemus were not invited because of
their known views concerning Jesus, or whether they deliberately
stayed away. We only know that Joseph had not consented to their
decision to put Jesus to death.

Joseph came from Arimathea, which is thought to have been a

village about twenty miles north-west from Jerusalem. The other thing that Luke tells us about this wealthy man is that he **'was waiting for the kingdom of God'** (23:51). He was rather like Simeon in the temple. He was 'righteous and devout [and] waiting for the consolation of Israel' (2:25).

Even if Joseph had been a secret follower of Jesus before, he now came out into the open. He was courageous enough to go to Pilate and ask him for the body of Jesus (23:52). Pilate, the one who had signed the death warrant, was the only one who could have given permission for the release of the Lord's body. This permission he apparently gave without hesitation or problem.

Then Joseph, assisted by Nicodemus and presumably by their servants, took the body of the Lord down from the cross. It was not dealt with by uncouth workmen, who were paid a pittance to dispose of it. 'No hand but the hand of love ever touched the dead body of Jesus.'[10]

The body was wrapped in a linen cloth, into which were put seventy-five pounds of a mixture of myrrh and aloes. These had been purchased by Nicodemus (John 19:39). Even though they were in a great hurry (because the Sabbath was fast approaching, 23:54), they did everything very respectfully. They lovingly placed the Lord's body into **'a tomb cut in the rock, one in which no one had yet been laid'** (23:53).[11]

These cave-like tombs were designed to hold a number of bodies. Matthew tells us that this tomb belonged to Joseph (Matt. 27:60). Presumably he had bought it so that he could be buried in it one day.

Luke then tells us that **'The women who had come with Jesus from Galilee followed Joseph and saw the tomb and how his body was laid in it'** (23:55). They made a careful note of which tomb it was. They did this because they knew that more had to be done to the body before it could finally be laid to rest. They did not know that later on some, who wished to disprove the fact of Christ's bodily resurrection, would try to say that they had returned to the wrong tomb and, finding it empty, assumed that Jesus had risen back to life again!

They could not go back immediately to put these extra spices and perfume on the body because the Sabbath had begun. They knew that they must rest on the Sabbath day. This was a command from God (Exod. 20:8-11), because if God rested after the six days of creation, then so should man rest one day in seven.

24.
He has risen!

Please read Luke 24

The resurrection (24:1-12)

The story of the cross ended with women watching, chapter 23 closed with the women resting, and chapter 24 starts with these same women going to the tomb (24:1).

They started out very early in the morning. Mark tells us that their big worry was, 'Who will roll the stone away from the entrance of the tomb?' (Mark. 16:3). However, when they arrived, **'They found the stone rolled away from the tomb, but when they entered, they did not find the body of the Lord Jesus'** (24:2-3). The tomb was empty.

We have no account of the actual resurrection of Jesus, but we do not need details of how it happened. We only need to believe it; but that is what those first disciples did not do. If Luke and the other evangelists had invented a story that Jesus rose from the dead, would they really have portrayed these women, and the other disciples, as those who found it difficult to believe in the resurrection?

Luke tells us that the women wondered about it. Peter also wondered what had happened, as he went away from that empty tomb (24:12). On one hand, they were wondering in the sense that they were curious about what had happened. Yet there was also an atmosphere of awe and amazement as they thought about what had taken place that morning. We know that they had still not fully believed that Christ had risen from the dead. If they had done so they would not have gone to put spices on his dead body. Despite all their uneasiness they knew that something astounding had taken place.

Then we read, **'While they were wondering about this, suddenly two men in clothes that gleamed like lightning stood beside them'** (24:4). These beings were evidently angels.

Some sceptics try to cast doubt on these angels. They say, 'In other places we only read of one angel and Luke says there were two. Sometimes these beings are described as sitting and sometimes as standing.' They then conclude, 'There are too many discrepancies for us to believe this incident.'

The answer is, of course, that where there is only one angel *No* mentioned it is because only one spoke. That does not mean that there was not another angel present as well; and as for sitting and standing, is it not possible for angels to change their positions, and speak more than once if they want to?

When the women saw the angels, quite naturally, they were frightened, and **'bowed down with their faces to the ground'** (24:5). It was then that they received these words of rebuke: **'Why do you look for the living among the dead?'** (24:5). This was followed by the explanation: **'He is not here; he has risen! Remember how he told you, while he was still with you in Galilee: "The Son of Man must be delivered into the hands of sinful men, be crucified and on the third day be raised again"'** (24:6-7).

Jesus had said that these things would happen. We read about them in Luke 9:22. But they had not linked those words of Jesus to this particular event. Presumably they thought only of the general resurrection of the dead, as Martha did, when she said to Jesus, 'I know [Lazarus] will rise again in the resurrection of the last day' (John 11:24). It had never occurred to them that Jesus could come back to life on the third day after his crucifixion.

But then they remembered the words of Jesus (24:8). They not only recalled that he had said that he would come back to life again the third day, but they believed it. In fact, **'They told all these things to the Eleven and all the others'** (24:9).

The scene now returns to the place where all the disciples had gathered. We are given the names of some of the women who told the rest about these events. They were Mary Magdalene, Joanna,

Mary the mother of James, plus some others (24:10). John tells us that Mary Magdalene had stayed behind outside the tomb crying, and the Lord had appeared to her, and told her to go and tell the others that he was returning to his Father, and their Father, to his God and their God (John 20:17). So these women had the added testimony of Mary Magdalene, who said, 'I have seen the Lord' (John 20:18).

But, even though they had heard what Jesus had often said about his death and resurrection and had listened to the words of these women, the disciples still did not believe. It seemed **'like nonsense'** to them (24:11). Now, if they, who were right there on the spot, did not believe that Jesus had risen from the dead, it is not surprising that people today find it difficult to accept these things.

However, we have not reached the end of the story. Eventually they all, even Doubting Thomas, did come to believe. We, too, have to reach this place because (as Paul tells us), 'If Christ has not been raised, your faith is futile; you are still in your sins' (1 Cor. 15:17). However, Jesus has been raised, and through faith in him, we also shall be raised to life eternal.

At this point in the story Peter got up and ran to the tomb (24:12). Luke does not tell us that John went with him (John 20:3) because he only wants to relate what happened to Peter. Bending over (to get into the inner part of the tomb), Peter **'saw the strips of linen lying by themselves'** (24:12). So why did that sight make him **'[go] away, wondering to himself what had happened'**? (24:12). It was because it confirmed that the tomb was empty. It also indicated that no robber had stolen the body. A robber would not have stopped to take off the strips of linen and leave them behind. (Indeed John tells us that 'The cloth was folded up by itself, separate from the linen' — John 20:7).

These things were so mysterious that Peter could only marvel at them. We too, are left wondering at this scene. We do not query whether it happened, because we believe and know that it did. The gift of faith confirms that to us. We are left in 'wonder, love and praise' at the great things we have seen. Our response should be to have a greater love for Christ, and a stronger resolve to follow him more closely and want to please him in all we say, all we do and all we think.

The road to Emmaus (24:13-35)

Two sad people

These two were not members of the inner circle of the Lord's disciples. We know this because in verse 33 we are told that they returned to **'the Eleven'**. This is the designation given to the apostles at that time. They were only eleven because Judas had hanged himself by this time (Matt. 27:5). Even though Thomas was not with them on this occasion (John 20:24), they are still referred to as 'the Eleven'. It would seem that the place where they assembled was the same upper room where Jesus had instituted the Lord's Supper.

We only know the name of one of these disciples, Cleopas (24:18). The other one was certainly a follower of the Lord (24:13). Maybe it was Cleopas and his wife who were journeying home together. The point is that these two were not well-known disciples. However, it was to them that Jesus chose to reveal himself in his resurrection body. They were the entire congregation for what has been called 'the greatest Old Testament exposition in history'.[1]

Their destination was the village of Emmaus. We do not know where this village was, but it is thought to have been about seven miles north-west of Jerusalem.

What were they doing while they were walking homeward? **'They were talking with each other about everything that had happened'** (24:14) and they were sad because they could not understand why their Lord had allowed himself to be arrested and put to death. It was, to them, the greatest injustice in all of history.

This was especially so because they had hoped that he was the one who was going to redeem Israel (24:21). Everything that they had longed for had now been dashed to the ground. For them, Jesus was not just a great teacher who had been executed: he was the one on whom they had pinned all their hopes; he was a powerful prophet.

They had always known, from their Bibles (the Old Testament), that God had promised a great deliverer who would set his people free. And it seemed to them that Jesus was this one who would be so empowered by God that he would see that their Roman oppressors were driven from their land. They had been trusting that Jesus would be that coming King who would, once again, set up a glorious Jewish kingdom, such as had existed during the time of

King David. They really thought that Jesus was that promised one,
David's royal son.

Yet even though they were sad, that did not stop them talking
about the Lord. Bishop Ryle gives us some good advice here. He
says, 'If we believe we are journeying to a heaven where Christ will
be the central object of every mind, let us begin to learn the manners
of heaven, while we are yet upon earth. So doing we shall often have
one with us whom our eyes will not see, but one who will make our
hearts "burn within us" by blessing the conversation.'[2]

This means that, even though our understanding of the gospel
may be slight, we can still speak about Jesus. Malachi tells us that
'Those who feared the Lord talked with each other, and the Lord
listened and heard. A scroll of remembrance was written in his
presence concerning those who feared the Lord and honoured his
name' (Mal. 3:16).

A stranger

'Jesus himself came up and walked along with them' (24:15).
But **'They were kept from recognizing him.'** We do not know
whether they did not recognize him because they were so sad; or
whether it was because they knew he was dead, and therefore they
never expected to see him. Whatever the case, they did not realize
who he was until he chose to reveal himself to them.

As this stranger joined the two disciples he started to ask them
questions. We have often seen that the Lord did this before he was
crucified. He did not speak like this because he did not know why
they were sad. He did it in order to draw them out. He wanted them
to tell him what was in their hearts.

The other Gospel writers tell us about other post-resurrection
appearances of Jesus, but Luke does not mention them. But by
giving us a great amount of detail in this one story, it seems that he
wants to convey to his readers something of the bewilderment that
all of the disciples felt at that time. They were all cast down and
frightened because of the arrest, death and burial of the Lord Jesus
Christ — and the stories about his missing body.

Then the stranger asked them what they were talking about so
earnestly (24:17). This made them stop short in their tracks. The
looks on their faces showed how upset they were; it seems that they
could hardly bear to speak of those events which had so recently
completely shattered them.

Eventually Cleopas asked him, **'Are you only a visitor to Jerusalem and do not know the things that have happened there in these days?'** (24:18). It seems that the crucifixion of Jesus was such a great talking-point for everyone that they found it incredible that anyone journeying from Jerusalem had not heard what had happened to Jesus.

But the Lord asked another question. This was to draw them out further. **'What things?'** he asked (24:19). It was these two words which made them give a detailed account of all that had happened. Michael Wilcock calls their reply 'the Gospel According to Cleopas'. Indeed, it contains the whole of the gospel message. It speaks about Jesus being **'a prophet'**, who was **'powerful in word and deed before God and all the people'**. It goes on to tell of his death, engineered by **'the chief priests and our rulers'** (no mention of Pilate or Herod here). It tells the story of the women and the angels who said that he was alive, and it speaks of some of the others (i.e. Peter and John) going to the tomb and finding it just as the women had said, **'but [Jesus] they did not see'** (24:24). Yet despite their knowing all of the facts of the gospel message, they were still sad and downcast.

Why was that? Wilcock says, 'There is everything — everything except a personal word from the living Christ which would in turn make the facts live also.'³ Cleopas and his companion were like so many people who stand up in church Sunday by Sunday reciting, 'I believe in God the Father Almighty, maker of heaven and earth and in Jesus Christ his only Son our Lord ...' They know all the facts, but they have never experienced the Lord Jesus Christ personally.

How amazing it was that, at this particular time, Jesus himself drew near to them, and yet they did not recognize him!

The explanation

Jesus called these two people **'foolish'**. He meant that they were not very quick on the uptake! They only believed some of what the Old Testament prophets had said. The Lord reprimanded them for not believing the whole of the Bible's teaching. They had read about the Messiah in their Bibles but they had only concentrated upon those prophecies which told of the Messiah coming in all his glory to set up his kingdom. They had ignored the portions which spoke of his suffering.

So Jesus said to them, **'Did not the Christ have to suffer these**

things [i.e. the arrest, trial, crucifixion, death and burial] **and then enter his glory?'** (24:26). It seems that they had read passages like Isaiah 53 and said (as do modern Jews), 'This obviously refers to Israel.' They said this because the Jewish people have always suffered a great deal throughout their long history. They did not realize that it spoke so clearly about the Lord Jesus Christ himself.

Then Jesus preached his wonderful sermon to them. Luke tells us, **'Beginning with Moses and all the Prophets, he explained to them what was said in all the Scriptures concerning himself'** (24:27). What a privilege was theirs that evening! We can only guess at what the Lord said to them. It would have been wonderful to have eavesdropped on that scene. By saying, 'Moses and the Prophets', the Lord meant the books of Moses (the first five books in the Old Testament) and all of the rest of the Old Testament. What he drew out from the Scriptures was all the detail concerning himself, as their Lord and Saviour.

If we find it difficult to read the Old Testament, then it will help us if we look for the Lord Jesus Christ as we read. He is there in every section. Bishop Ryle says, 'Christ was the substance of every Old Testament sacrifice, ordained in the law of Moses. Christ was the true Deliverer and King, of whom all the judges and deliverers in Jewish history were types. Christ was the coming Prophet greater than Moses, whose glorious advent filled the pages of prophets. Christ was the true seed of the woman who was to bruise the serpent's head — the true seed in whom all nations were to be blessed, the true Shiloh to whom all the people were to be gathered, the true scapegoat — the true brazen serpent; the true Lamb to which every daily sacrifice pointed, the true High Priest of whom every descendant of Aaron was a figure.'[4]

We are not told of the reaction of these two disciples, but it must surely have been one of breathless amazement. Just then they began to enter the village of Emmaus.

Jesus reveals himself

Jesus acted as if he were going further (24:28) but they urged him strongly saying, **'Stay with us, for it is nearly evening; the day is almost over'** (24:29). It would soon be pitch dark, and therefore dangerous to travel. So they offered the Lord hospitality for the night. However, things turned out quite differently from what they had planned. Instead of their offering the Lord hospitality, it was he who became their host.

'**He went in to stay with them**' (24:29). They immediately started to prepare a meal. It would not have taken long because it would have consisted only of bread and wine — the basic staple diet of all ordinary people in those times.

But when they sat down to eat Jesus took the head of the table. They may well have been amazed at this but they did not protest as he started to serve the meal. '**He took bread, gave thanks, broke it and began to give to them**' (24:30). This sounds as though it was a service of Holy Communion, but it was not. Ordinary meals were like that too. The bread was broken by the host and, after a prayer of thanksgiving, it was passed around. (It could not have been a communion service because Jesus left before the wine was distributed!)

But by this action, '**Their eyes were opened and they recognized him.**' We do not know whether they saw the nail-prints in his hands, or whether it was because they had heard how he had broken the bread in the upper room — and also at the feeding of the five thousand. But, as soon as they realized who he was, '**he disappeared from their sight**' (24:31). No doubt they wanted to ask him many questions; however, they were not cast down by his disappearance; in fact, they were elated. '**They asked each other, "Were not our hearts burning within us while he talked with us on the road and opened the Scriptures to us?"**' (24:32).

Many centuries later John Wesley had the same kind of spiritual experience, when on 24 May 1738, he sat in a society meeting in London's Aldersgate Street and heard someone read from the preface to Luther's *Commentary to the Romans*. He said, 'I felt my heart strangely warmed.'[5]

Immediately the two disciples returned to Jerusalem (24:33). Even though it was too late for normal travelling, they were not put off. The fact that they had already walked the seven or eight miles from the city did not deter them; they immediately turned around and hurried back to Jerusalem. They did this because they had to tell the glorious news about '**how Jesus was recognized by them when he broke the bread**' (24:35).

However, when they arrived, before they could say anything at all, they were told with great excitement, '**It is true! The Lord has risen and has appeared to Simon**' (24:34). There was so much joy in that place that everyone was bursting to tell the good news. The apostles seemed to have been hesitant to accept the word of women, but the fact that Jesus had appeared to Simon Peter clinched it for them.

Even though Simon had denied that he knew Jesus, the Lord appeared to him; he was the first to see the risen Christ (cf. 1 Cor. 15:5). We have no scriptural account of this meeting — presumably it was too precious to record — but it does show that the Lord receives back those who are penitent and restores them to full usefulness. Peter himself tells us, 'In his great mercy [God] has given us new birth into a living hope through the resurrection of Jesus Christ from the dead' (1 Peter 1:3).

The appearance and disappearance of the Lord (24:36-53)

Jesus appeared to them all

Telling people what we know of the Lord Jesus Christ is a very effective form of evangelism. 'The Eleven' had heard several personal testimonies about the resurrection of Jesus in the past few hours, but still they were somewhat sad. They were glad for those who said that they had seen the Lord again. They were interested in what they said, but what they really wanted was to have a personal experience of the risen Lord Christ.

'**While they were still talking about this, Jesus himself stood among them and said to them, "Peace be with you"**' (24:36). The Lord chose to reveal himself to them all at that particular moment. They had longed to see Christ for themselves. It was what they had been hoping and praying for; so when he showed himself, were they excited? No. '**They were startled and frightened, thinking they saw a ghost**' (24:37). They were petrified because the Lord suddenly appeared in the room, even though the doors were locked and bolted. As no one had opened the door, it is not surprising that they thought he was a ghost. We cannot understand what kind of body the Lord had, but we know that it was one that could pass through solid doors or walls.

However, they recognized him and heard him say, 'Peace be with you' (24:36). Is that the kind of message a ghost would bring? Jesus gave them a normal greeting — one which is still used by Jews today. But it had a much richer meaning than 'Good evening'; Jesus had come to actually bring them peace. Here they were with their hearts and minds all churned up. They were frightened and anxious about the future because they did not know what would become of them. Yet Jesus spoke words of peace to them all. In that same upper room he had said similar words a few days previously. Then he said, 'Peace I leave with you; my peace I give you. I do not give to you as the world gives. Do not let your hearts be troubled and do not be afraid' (John 14:27).

The peace which Jesus gives to those who love him is a rich, deep and lasting peace. It is not just an absence of war and strife. It is something much more positive. It is his peace, 'the peace of God which transcends all understanding, [which guards our] hearts and … minds in Christ Jesus' (Phil. 4:7).

Those who are passing through great personal troubles and who are filled with fear and anxiety know what it means when the Lord whispers his peace into their souls. They experience such a calmness and inner contentment that the people of the world are amazed at their composure.

Jesus did not only give them his peace; he also proved to them that he was not a ghost. He said, **'Why are you troubled, and why do doubts rise in your minds? Look at my hands and my feet. It is I myself! Touch me and see; a ghost does not have flesh and bones, as you see I have'** (24:38-39). Not only did Jesus have a real, human body, but he still carried the nail-prints in his hands and feet. No ghost would have had wounds. These nail-prints were another confirmation of who he was. They were there for a purpose. Isaiah, writing some 700 years before this time said,

'He was pierced for our transgressions,
    he was crushed for our iniquities,
the punishment that brought us peace was upon him,
    and by his wounds we are healed'

(Isa. 53:5).

Not only did Jesus invite the disciples to touch him (as he would later invite Thomas to do — John 20:27), but **'He showed them his hands and his feet'** (24:40). This clinched the matter for them. They were overjoyed and overcome with amazement. Now they were convinced that the Lord had risen from the dead and was among them.

Then he gave them a further proof of his resurrection. He asked, **'Do you have anything here to eat?'** He did not need to eat. He had a new, heavenly body. In glory eating, drinking and sleeping are not necessary, but Jesus wanted to prove to them that he was not a ghost. So they gave him some broiled fish and he ate it in their presence.

The Lord taught his disciples

He had often given them teaching before his crucifixion but they did not fully understand what he had said to them then. They had misunderstood and said, 'Surely not, Lord', when he spoke of his death. But now he had risen from the dead they began to see things in a new light. He said, **'This is what I told you while I was still with you: Everything must be fulfilled that is written about me in the Law of Moses, the Prophets and the Psalms'** (24:44). These were the three divisions of the Old Testament and each one speaks about the Lord Jesus Christ. There is no part of the Bible which does not have a message about the Lord. We find him everywhere in pictures, types and shadows.

'**Then he opened their minds so they could understand the Scriptures'** (24:45). He had opened their eyes so that they could see that he had come back from the dead; now he opened up their minds. The word 'opened' is a very powerful one. It needs the power of the Holy Spirit to open anyone's mind so that he or she can understand the Scriptures. The key is the Lord Jesus Christ himself, and it is the Holy Spirit's task to testify of him.

Then he explained the gospel message which they had the responsibility of taking to the whole world. (He had done the same thing on the Emmaus road, 24:26-27.) He said that it concerned his own suffering, death and resurrection. When we preach the gospel, we must preach Christ. We must preach that he is God's Son and proclaim that he suffered and died for sinners. We must declare that he rose again for the justification of his people.

Then Jesus added something. He said that the gospel message concerns the repentance and forgiveness of sins preached in his name. When the gospel is truly preached in the power of the Spirit, people will repent of their sin. Men and women will see themselves as guilty, hell-bound sinners in the sight of God. They will realize that salvation is to be found in no one else but in Jesus Christ. They will know that 'There is no other name under heaven given to men by which we must be saved' (Acts. 4:12), and when the power of the Spirit comes upon them they will flee to Christ for forgiveness of their sins and they will be saved.

These eleven disciples, plus the other followers of the Lord, had the great responsibility of taking his wondrous message to the whole world. They were only a comparatively few frightened men and women, so how could they perform such a tremendous task? The Lord said they were to begin at Jerusalem. This is where they were at the time, and they were to take the message to all nations. The book of Acts tells us how they began that task. It says that Jesus told them to be his witnesses 'in Jerusalem, and in all Judea and Samaria, and to the ends of the earth' (Acts 1:8).

Where were they going to obtain the ability to do all of this? Jesus said, **'I am going to send you what my Father has promised; but stay in the city until you have been clothed with power from on high'** (24:49). In the upper room Jesus had previously taught them that when he went away another Counsellor would come to them (John 16:7). That Counsellor is the Holy Spirit. Luke records more fully, in his second book, the Acts, what Jesus told the disciples at this time. He said, 'Do not leave Jerusalem, but wait for the gift my Father promised, which you have heard me speak about. For John baptized with water, but in a few days you will be baptized with the Holy Spirit' (Acts 1:4-5). This happened to them on the Day of Pentecost. At the beginning of Acts 2 we read about how they were gloriously filled with the power of the Holy Spirit as they preached the gospel with great boldness.

Jesus finally left them

Luke also records this final incident at the beginning of the Acts of the Apostles. Jesus led his disciples out to the vicinity of Bethany. That was on the Mount of Olives. It was a favourite spot of the Lord's (see 21:37). Then he lifted up his hands and blessed them. **'While he was blessing them, he left them and was taken up into heaven'** (24:51), and 'A cloud hid him from their sight' (Acts 1:9). They were left gazing up into the sky — no doubt with open mouths. But 'Suddenly two men dressed in white stood beside them. "Men of Galilee", they said, "Why do you stand here looking into the sky?

This same Jesus, who has been taken from you into heaven, will come back in the same way you have seen him go into heaven'" (Acts 1:10-11).

That is why they were no longer sad. **'They worshipped him and returned to Jerusalem with great joy'** (24:52). They knew that they had work to do and that they would be given the power to do that work when the Holy Spirit came upon them. They also knew that their blessed Lord would one day come back to this earth.

'And they stayed continually at the temple, praising God.' At this point Luke ends his first volume. He ends it where he started, in the temple (cf. 1:8-20). By the time that Luke's second volume had been completed the temple had either already been destroyed, or it soon would be. The temple symbolized the presence of God in the midst of his people, but now that earthly building has been destroyed; it has lain in ruins for nearly 2,000 years. However, this is no cause for mourning among the people of God because God's people are the temple of God (1 Cor. 3:16) and Jesus is in the midst of them by his Spirit.

The story does not end with Luke 24:53. Nor did it finish with the last verse of the Acts of the Apostles. It still goes on, and it continues through God's people.

We today are still called upon to go and be witnesses of these things. Luke's second volume ends with Paul preaching the kingdom of God and teaching about the Lord Jesus Christ 'boldly and without hindrance' (Acts 28:31). That is what every believer should be doing everywhere he or she goes and on every possible occasion.

References

Chapter 1
1. June Osborne & Chris Sugden, *Luke*, Scripture Union, 1987, p.l6.
2. J. Norval Geldenhuys, *Commentary on the Gospel of Luke*, Marshall, Morgan & Scott, 1950, p.62.
3. William Hendriksen, *Luke*, Banner of Truth Trust, 1979, p.65.
4. Geldenhuys, *Commentary on Luke*, p.64.
5. J. C. Ryle, *Expository Thoughts on The Gospels, Luke*, vol. 1, Banner of Truth Trust ed. 1986 (originally published in 1858), p.17.
6. David Gooding, *According to Luke*, IVP, 1987, p.37.
7. Hendriksen, *Luke*, p.85.
8. As above, p.87.
9. G. Campbell Morgan, *The Gospel According to Luke*, Oliphants Ltd, 1954 reprint, p.23.
10. Hendriksen, *Luke*, p.129.
11. Campbell Morgan, *The Gospel According to Luke*, p.31.
12. Hendriksen, *Luke*, p.131.

Chapter 2
1. For a full explanation see Hendriksen, *Luke*, pp.135-141 and the special note, 'The Enrolment under Augustus' in Geldenhuys, *Commentary on Luke*, pp.104-6.
2. Michael Wilcock, *The Message of Luke*, IVP, 1979, p.43 footnote.
3. Hymn by John Newton.
4. *NIV Study Bible*, p.1508.
5. Gooding, *According to Luke*, p.56.
6. John Blanchard, *Look Through Luke*, Henry E. Walter Ltd, 1977, pp.15-16.

7. Hendriksen, *Luke*, p.185.
8. As above.
9. Geldenhuys, *Commentary on Luke*, p.129.

Chapter 3
1. Norman Bull, *Jesus the Nazarene*, Hulton Educational Publications, 1968, p.93.
2. Blanchard, *Look through Luke*, p.18.
3. Hendriksen, *Luke*, pp.207-8.
4. Ryle, *Expository Thoughts*, vol. 1, p.95.
5. As above, p.102.
6. Hendriksen, *Luke*, p.218.
7. Campbell Morgan, *Gospel According to Luke*, pp.52-3.
8. Blanchard, *Look through Luke*, p.19.
9. Ryle, *Expository Thoughts*, vol. 1, p.104.
10. Wilcock, *Message of Luke*, p.57.

Chapter 4
1. Quoted by John Blanchard, *More Gathered Gold*, Evangelical Press, 1986, p.317.
2. T. S. Eliot, from *Murder in the Cathedral* in *The Complete Poems and Plays of T. S. Eliot*, Faber and Faber, 1969, p.258.
3. Hendriksen, *Luke*, p.236.
4. Monica Parsons in her 'Church Notes' column in the *Bracknell Times* in July 1990.
5. Brian Edwards, *Revival!*, 1990, Evangelical Press, p.122.
6. Hendriksen, *Luke*, p.263.
7. Quoted in the May/June 1990 issue of *Wake Up* magazine.
8. Campbell Morgan, *Gospel According to Luke*, p.70.

Chapter 5
1. Geldenhuys, *Commentary on Luke*, p.181.
2. Campbell Morgan, *Gospel According to Luke*, p.76.
3. From the hymn, 'At even, ere the sun was set', *Hymns of Faith*, no.93 and in many other hymn-books.
4. Ryle, *Expository Thoughts*, vol. 1, p.144.
5. Gooding, *According to Luke*, p.109.
6. Barclay, *The Daily Study Bible; The Gospel of Luke*, The Saint Andrew Press, 1975, p.64.
7. Ryle, *Expository Thoughts*, vol. 1, pp.149-50.

8. Hendriksen, *Luke*, p.304.
9. Campbell Morgan, *Gospel According to Luke*, p.80.
10. Warren Wiersbe, *Be Compassionate*, Scripture Press, 1989, p.59 .
11. Campbell Morgan, *Gospel According to Luke*, p.82.

Chapter 6
1. Characters in the Victorian novel, *Barchester Towers*, by Anthony Trollope.
2. Ryle, *Expository Thoughts*, vol. 1, p.160.
3. *NIV Study Bible*, p.1467.
4. See Campbell Morgan, *Gospel According to Luke*, p.83.
5. Leon Morris, Luke, *Tyndale New Testament Commentaries*, IVP, 1968 ed., p.122.
6. Campbell Morgan, *Gospel According to Luke*, p.83.
7. Morris, *Luke*, p.123.
8. Geldenhuys, *Commentary on Luke*, p.203.
9. Gooding, *According to Luke*, p.116.
10. Quoted by John Blanchard, *Gathered Gold*, Evangelical Press, 1984, p.228.
11. Blanchard, *More Gathered Gold*, p.231.
12. Wiersbe, *Be Compassionate*, p.67.
13. Blanchard, *Look Through Luke*, p.33.
14. Iain H. Murray, *D. Martyn Lloyd-Jones: The Fight of Faith 1939-1981*, Banner of Truth, 1990, p.107.
15. Morris, *Luke*, p.129.
16. Hendriksen, *Luke*, p.350.
17. As above, p.351.
18. Morris, *Luke*, p.130.
19. Gooding, *According to Luke*, p.122.
20. Wiersbe, *Be Compassionate*, p.72.
21. *NIV Study Bible*, p.1519.
22. No. 1149 in *Gadsby's Hymn-book*, Gospel Standard Publications.

Chapter 7
1. Gooding, *According to Luke*, p.133.
2. Morris, *Luke*, p.140.
3. e.g. Barclay, *Daily Study Bible*, p.88.
4. Wiersbe, *Be Compassionate*, p.77.
5. As above, pp.78-9.
6. Morris, *Luke*, p.144.

7. *NIV Study Bible*, p.1521.
8. Campbell Morgan, *Gospel According to Luke*, p.102.
9. *NIV Study Bible*, p.1521.

Chapter 8
1. 'Jesus shall reign where'er the sun...' by Isaac Watts, found in many hymn-books, e.g. no.233 in *Hymns of Faith*.
2. Wiersbe, *Be Compassionate*, p.89.
3. Roy Irving (ed.) *Luke 1 - 12*, Scripture Press, 1984, p.85.
4. Gooding, *According to Luke*, p.142.
5. Wiersbe, *Be Compassionate*, p.91.
6. This is found in many hymn-books, e.g. *Hymns of Faith*, no.398.
7. See Campbell Morgan, *Gospel According to Luke*, p.112.
8. See Gooding, *According to Luke*, p.143.
9. Morris, *Luke*, p.158.
10. Campbell Morgan, *Gospel According to Luke*, pp.116-17.
11. Barclay, *Daily Study Bible*, p.113.
12. Morris, *Luke*, p.162.
13. Wiersbe, *Be Compassionate*, p.96.

Chapter 9
1. See Blanchard, *Look Through Luke*, p.51.
2. *NIV Study Bible*, p.1435.
3. Geldenhuys, *Commentary on Luke*, p.274.
4. Morris, *Luke*, p.169.
5. Wiersbe, *Be Compassionate*, p.105.
6. *Hymns of Faith*, no. 521.
7. Ryle, *Expository Thoughts*, vol. 1, p.315.
8. Gooding, *According to Luke*, p.170.
9. Wiersbe, *Be Compassionate*, p.108.
10. As above, p.109.
11. Hendriksen, *Luke*, p.519.
12. *Hymns of Faith*, no. 208 (also found in many other hymn-books).

Chapter 10
1. Hendriksen, *Luke*, pp.570-71, gives a lengthy discussion on the pros and cons of seventy or seventy-two disciples being sent out.
2. Morris, *Luke*, p.181.
3. Irving, *Luke 1-12*, p.107.
4. Osborne & Sugden, *Luke*, p.62.

5. From the hymn, 'O love divine, how sweet thou art!' *Hymns of Faith*, no. 423.

Chapter 11

1. Warren Wiersbe, *Windows on the Parables*, Victor Books, U.S.A., 1979, p.74.
2. Wiersbe, *Be Compassionate*, p.128.
3. Osborne & Sugden, *Luke*, p.66.
4. *Thought for the Day*, BBC Radio 4 on 23.4.91.
5. Osborne and Sugden, *Luke*, p.68.
6. Barclay, *Daily Study Bible*, p.158.
7. Ryle, *Expository Thoughts*, vol. 2, p.53.

Chapter 12

1. See Albert Barnes, *Notes on The New Testament, vol. 2, Luke-John*, Blackie and Son, p.81.
2. Campbell Morgan, *Gospel According to Luke*, p.153.
3. Hendriksen, *Luke*, p.656.
4. Wiersbe, *Be Compassionate*, p.192.
5. Barclay, *Daily Study Bible*, p.170.
6. Gooding, *According to Luke*, p.248.
7. Morris, *Luke*, p.220.

Chapter 13

1. See Kenneth E. Bailey, *Through Peasant Eyes*, Eerdmans, 1980, p.82.
2. As above, p.83
3. Hymn by Ryland in *Gadsby's Hymn-book*, no.64.

Chapter 14

1. Warren Wiersbe, *Be Courageous*, p.14.
2. Bailey, *Through Peasant Eyes*, pp.90,100.
3. Blanchard, *Look Through Luke*, p.80.
4. Craig L. Blomberg, *Interpreting the Parables*, Apollos, 1990, p.281.
5. Warren Wiersbe, *Be Courageous*, p.24.

Chapter 15

1. Wilcock, *Message of Luke*, p.150.
2. Bailey, *Poet and Peasant*, p.162.
3. This is the phrase used by Charles Swindoll when describing those who keep doctrine without any love.

4. Henry Moorhouse *et al.*, *The Prodigal*, Moody Press, 1898, p.21.
5. Helmut Thielicke, *The Waiting Father*, James Clarke and Co. Ltd, 1960, p.26.
6. Stuart Briscoe, *Pattern for Power*, Regal Books, U.S.A., 1978, p.134.

Chapter 16
1. Wiersbe, *Be Courageous*, p.44.
2. Ryle, *Expository Thoughts*, vol. 2, p.205.
3. *NIV Study Bible*. p.1540.
4. But see also what Paul says in 1 Corinthians 7:15.
5. Quoted in Blanchard, *Gathered Gold*, p.61.
6. Barnes, *Notes on the New Testament*, p.118.

Chapter 17
1. Morris, *Luke*, p.256.
2. Wiersbe, *Be Courageous*, p.56.
3. *NIV Study Bible*, p.1542.

Chapter 18
1. *NIV Study Bible* p.1543.
2. As above, p.1483.
3. From the hymn, 'Oh, for a closer walk with God', *Hymns of Faith*, no. 322.
4. Hendriksen, *Luke*, p.839.

Chapter 19
1. See G. Campbell Morgan, *The Great Physician*, Marshall, Morgan and Scott, 1937, p.255.
2. *NIV Study Bible*, p.1544.
3. Hendriksen, *Luke*, p.874.
4. Wilcock, *Message of Luke*, p.180.
5. Wiersbe, *Be Courageous*, p.85.
6. Gooding, *According to Luke*, p.314.
7. Barclay, *Daily Study Bible*, p.240.
8. Michael Bentley, *Building for God's Glory*, Evangelical Press, 1989, p.174.

Chapter 20
1. Blanchard, *Look Through Luke*, p.102.
2. Morris, *Luke*, p.286.

3. Quoted in Morris, *Luke*, p.286.
4. Hendriksen, *Luke*, p.896.
5. Geldenhuys, *Commentary on Luke*, p.498.
6. Hendriksen, *Luke*, p.902
7. See, for example, Michael Bentley, *Living for Christ in a Pagan World*, Evangelical Press, 1990, pp.88-94.
8. Roy Irving, *Luke 13-24*, Scripture Press, p.86.
9. See comments in chapter 11 on Luke 11:43.

Chapter 21
1. From the hymn, 'Take my life and let it be consecrated Lord to thee', *Hymns of Faith*, no. 476.
2. This information is from Geldenhuys, *Commentary on Luke*, p.531.
3. See my comments on this in *Building for God's Glory*, p.27.
4. *NIV Study Bible*, p.1549.

Chapter 22
1. R. C. Lucas, in a lecture on 1 Corinthians 11 in St Helen's Church, Bishopsgate, London, on 21.11.91.
2. *NIV Study Bible*, p.1551.
3. Hendriksen, *Luke*, p.965.
4. Campbell Morgan, *Gospel According to Luke*, p.247.
5. Barnes, *Notes on the New Testament*, p.156.
6. Campbell Morgan, *Gospel According to Luke*, p.254.
7. Wilcock, *Message of Luke*, p.194.

Chapter 23
1. See e.g. Hendriksen, *Luke*, pp.1007,1008.
2. Tim Rice in *Jesus Christ Superstar*, Pan Books. This musical portrays the Lord in a very wrong, unscriptural and misleading way but, in my opinion, its description of King Herod is similar to that found in the Bible.
3. Campbell Morgan, *Gospel According to Luke*, p.264.
4. Quoted in Blanchard, *Gathered Gold*, p.58.
5. Barclay, *Daily Study Bible*, p.282.
6. Greijdanus, quoted in Hendriksen, *Luke*, p.1026.
7. Ryle, *Expository Thoughts*, vol.2, p.473.
8. Irving, *Luke 13-24*, p.117.
9. *NIV Study Bible*, p.1555.

10. Campbell Morgan, *Gospel According to Luke*, p.274.
11. See my comments on Luke 19:30.

Chapter 24
1. Blanchard, *Look through Luke*, p.122.
2. Ryle, *Expository Thoughts*, vol. 2, p.499.
3. M. Wilcock, *Message of Luke*, pp.208-9.
4. Ryle, *Expository Thoughts*, vol. 2, p.501. Hendriksen gives us a list of possible Old Testament scriptures which Jesus may have interpreted (*Luke*, p.1065); and Campbell Morgan gives us a summary of descriptions of Christ in many of the prophets from Isaiah to Malachi (*Gospel According to Luke*, pp.276-9). Also A.M. Hodgekin's, *Christ in all the Scriptures*, Pickering and Inglis, 1907, deals entirely with this subject.
5. Quoted from A. Skevington Wood, *The Inextinguishable Blaze*, Paternoster Press, 1960, p.110. This can also be found in many other sources.